W9-APL-912

History of Libraries in the Western World

Compact Textbook Edition

by
Michael H. Harris

The Scarecrow Press, Inc.
Metuchen, N.J., and London
1984

Library of Congress Cataloging in Publication Data

Harris, Michael H.
History of libraries in the western world.

Rev. ed. of: History of libraries in the western world / Elmer D. Johnson. 3rd ed. 1976.
Bibliography: p.
Includes index.
1. Libraries--History. I. Johnson, Elmer D. History of libraries in the western world. II. Title.
Z721.H227 1984 027 83-20133
ISBN 0-8108-1666-0

Manufactured in the United States of America

CONTENTS

PREFACE

The work before you represents a new edition of a book first published in 1965, incorporating significant changes. First, in the light of the recent publication of dozens of books and hundreds of articles on various special aspects of the history of libraries in the West, I have heeded reviewers who called for the deletion of certain detailed portions of the text that slowed the reader interested in a general overview of the subject. Substantial cuts have been made on this basis since the reader who wishes to pursue any specific aspect of the subject in detail may now do so with considerable ease by consulting the specialized literature.

Second, bibliographies for each chapter have been shortened and updated. A considerable body of new work in library history, especially American and English, has been completed since the publication of the last edition. I have attempted to cite that new work wherever appropriate. At the same time the end-of-chapter bibliographies have been shortened considerably due to the recent appearance of a number of comprehensive bibliographic guides to the literature of library history. The ready availability of these bibliographic tools, cited in the relevant chapters, made unnecessary the extensive bibliographies found in earlier editions of the _History of Libraries in the Western World_.

Third, the last chapter of the third edition has been dropped entirely. Since that chapter, entitled "The Library in History," recapitulated themes already covered in other parts of the text, it was not considered essential.

Fourth, it will be noted that Dr. Elmer Johnson's name no longer appears on the title page of this work. Dr. Johnson's retirement and other interests persuaded him to withdraw from involvement with this project. This change should not, however, obscure the fact that he was the author of the pioneering first edition of this book. That the _History_ has been a mainstay of library history courses for some twenty years attests to his wide knowledge of the subject and the value of his accomplishment in undertaking the formidable task of writing the first comprehensive history of libraries in the West.

A number of other people helped in the preparation of this edition, including reviewers of the third edition who made pertinent and useful suggestions. My colleagues Dr. Wayne Wiegand and Dr. Robert Cazden furthered my knowledge of this and kindred subjects through many discussions. That we often disagreed about specific interpretations proved of considerable value, leading me to examine more critically my own positions on various aspects of the subject. Finally, I am pleased to acknowledge the help of Albert Daub of the Scarecrow Press.

Michael H. Harris
April 1983

PART I

LIBRARIES IN THE ANCIENT WORLD

Chapter 1

THE ORIGIN OF LIBRARIES

The origin of libraries, like the origins of speech and of writing, is not known. Unlike speech and writing, however, the beginning of libraries came after the end of the prehistoric era, since the preservation of written records is considered to have begun the historic age. Conceivably, it should be possible to decide just when and where the first library existed, but all we know is that at certain times and in certain locations early libraries existed. Before that, there were undoubtedly collections of graphic materials approaching the form of libraries, but specific details are more difficult to pin down. One of the purposes for the development of writing was to preserve human communication--to extend its duration beyond the sound of the human voice and beyond the memory of mortal man, and it is probable that written communications were kept almost from the beginning of writing. Early written forms were often considered sacred, which was another reason for their careful preservation. If these early records were kept in an orderly manner, suitable for future use when needed, then they had all the earmarks of a proto-library or archive.

In order to discuss the history of libraries, it is necessary to have a working definition for the term *library*. What is a library? What distinguishes it from a collection of graphic materials or from an archive? For the purposes of this work it is assumed that a library is a collection of graphic materials arranged for relatively easy use, cared for by an individual or individuals familiar with that arrangement, and available for use by at least a limited number of persons. This definition includes early religious and governmental archives. The distinction between a library and an archive is relatively modern, and for historical purposes the two can be considered together, although where they diverge distinctively, only the library proper will be considered.

Before we discuss the kinds of libraries to be found in the ancient world, it would seem appropriate to pause for a moment to consider the societal conditions which contribute to the rise of libraries. Library historians, from the publication of Justus Lipsius' _Brief Outline of the History of Libraries_ in the late 16th century to the work of contemporary scholars, have dedicated themselves to discovering not only the ways in which libraries influence their coeval society, but also the ways in which society inhibits, encourages, or directs library growth. The conditions which, most historians agree, are important prerequisites for library growth may be conveniently grouped under the following headings:

Social Conditions: Under this heading might be cited such positive influences as the rise of urban centers, which in their myriad activities produce innumerable records and require sophisticated information systems. These needs naturally encouraged library, or archival, development. Another social factor of significance is education; a formal system of education requires not only records and record keeping but also library facilities that will support the instructional system. And, of course, the extent and nature of literacy will have an obvious impact on library growth. Finally, social conditions such as the stability of home life, the availability of leisure time, the size of families, and the size of the population at large are all factors of significance to libraries.

Economic Conditions: Economic conditions are significant in many ways. First, it is nearly axiomatic that large-scale library growth is directly related to the economic health or prosperity of a country. Generally speaking, surplus wealth has had to be available in large amounts before the resources necessary for widespread library development become available. Equally important is the fact that a well-developed and prosperous economy rests upon a sophisticated record-keeping system. Libraries become essential "instrumentalities" of the economy; both as repositories for the records of business and as the research facilities from which future technological and commercial developments will be mined.

Many historians have also noted that an economic factor of real importance is the availability and cost of materials upon which written or printed records can be preserved. The availability of an inexpensive and readily obtainable raw material is an essential prerequisite for large-scale library growth. Finally, libraries will develop most rapidly when books are widely available and inexpensive; that is, when the book trade is well established.

Political Conditions: Libraries and their contents are in serious hazard in times of strife and turmoil. In contrast, conditions of political and social tranquility are conducive to widespread library growth. At the same time, libraries are far more likely to develop rapidly and strongly when the governing establishment encourages their growth. And finally, effective government generally requires access to great amounts of domestic and foreign information, which from the earliest of times has been gathered together and organized in libraries.

In summary then, libraries will flourish generally in those societies where economic prosperity reigns, where the population is literate and stable, where the government encourages library growth, where large urban areas exist, and where the book trade is well established. However, it should be noted that there are numerous cases in history, some to be discussed later, where these "favorable conditions" appeared to be inoperative. In such cases one must look more carefully into the historical record in order to discover the motives of those who, for instance, encouraged library growth in times of financial depression or who inhibited library growth when conditions appeared to support widespread library development.

Although early libraries were often associated with religious edifices, it cannot be assumed that the temple library was the only, or even the most important, early form of library. In fact, there seem to have been at least three, if not four, types of graphic collections that contributed to the general development of the early library form. The first of these was the temple collection; the second the governmental archive; the third, organized business records; and the possible fourth, the collection of family or genealogical papers. Where religious and temporal rule were in the same hands the first two types of collections sometimes merged; the second two were also close when family and business records came together. In either case, the written records contained facts or information that were meant to be preserved for future use, and for such use a logical order of arrangement was necessary wherever the number of items amounted to more than a dozen or two.

The temple collection will be considered first, since this is the usual example of the proto-library. A temple or any other religious edifice of an advanced type presupposes a formalized method of worship, a priesthood, and a hierarchy of deities to be worshiped. Usually there is a story of creation and a genealogy of the gods to be remembered. For generations, possibly for centuries, such a religious literature could be handed down orally from parents to children, or from priest to neophyte, but eventually it would become necessary to regularize this story and to provide for an established, orthodox form of religious worship. This need might have been brought about through political change, migration, the threat posed by other cults, or simply by the growing complexity of the religious literature itself. Perhaps the development of writing made such a religious stabilization possible, or perhaps the need for such a stabilization of religious practices helped to bring about the development of writing. In either case, the temple collection began with copies of the sacred laws, rituals, songs, creation stories, biographies of the gods and, later, the commentaries of religious authorities on all of these. The basic scripture might be carved on stone, inscribed on leather, copper or brass, or embossed on clay to be baked into imperishable bricks. Less important religious writings might be on the common writing materials of a given time and place, such as papyrus or parchment.

The theological collection was kept in a sacred place and presided over by a priest. Only the most important of the temple officials might have access to this library, and probably only a few of them could read. In most early societies, the scribe or the trained individual who could read and write was a most important person, and often only a few of the temple personnel belonged to this select group. The temple library may have been of the few, and by the few, and for the few, but it preserved the most important literature of a given religion, which was a basic cultural heritage for that particular group. In Egypt, Palestine, Babylon, Greece, and Rome, the temple collection certainly was among the earliest and most important forms of the proto-library.

Next in importance were the government record collections, or archives. To support the government, taxes or tributes were necessary, and to make these sources of income reasonably accurate and honest, property ownership had to be guaranteed and tax records compiled and kept. Deeds and property transactions had to be recorded and a graphic representation of their legality filed in some government office. Laws and decrees had to be published and preserved. On a wider scale, agreements, treaties, and understandings between rulers had to be put down in some permanent form. Partnerships between kings and vassals were made and broken, tribute was exacted from defeated powers, satellite governors made their reports and pleas for aid in times of stress. Some of the earliest known records are such quasi-diplomatic bits of correspondence between chief rulers and their subordinates. These were all official government records, and when they were preserved and arranged for future use, they became government archives. However, when codifications of laws, accounts of military campaigns, genealogies of rulers, and histories of reigns were added to these archival collections, the latter took on the aspect of a library, and examples of such collections are known. Since records of military conquests and biographies of kings often included as much fiction as fact, they added an element of literature to an otherwise staid collection. Governmental archives are prominent among the early library forms. They existed as clay tables, as papyrus or parchment rolls, even as copper strips or bronze plates, but whatever their format they preserved an account of the major activities of governments and formed a basis for future histories.

The civilization that had progressed enough to have government and temple libraries was also more than likely to have a rather advanced state of business and commerce. Centers of government or of religious worship were usually in relatively densely populated areas. Such urban or semi-urban areas developed along rivers, on harbors, or at junctures of overland trade routes. Advanced civilizations required something beyond barter and simple exchange of goods, and hence some form of money became a necessity. As business went beyond the barter stage, records had to be kept. Records of property, inventories, purchases and sales, taxes and tributes had to be preserved and arranged for ready use. Reports from and instructions to employees or agents in distant towns had to be recorded and kept. Such records, of course, formed a business archive, but eventually the nature of the information included might be broadened. Accounts of ocean voyages or land explorations in search of trade, military and political events affecting trade, natural disasters, manufacturing methods, or formulas for products--all these might well enter into the business archive which then took on more of the nature of a library. Whether archive or library, such collections were familiar in the great trading houses of Egypt, Phoenicia, and Babylonia, and later in Alexandria, Athens, and Rome. The business archive as an ancestor of the modern library is not so obvious, unless we think of it as an industrial or "special" library.

The relationship between the family manuscript collection and the development of libraries may also be tenuous, but it had a direct connection with the development of private libraries and is part of library history. Some of the earliest known examples of written records relate to private matters. Property ownership and inheritance are important factors in any organized society, and wills, deeds, sales forms, inventories of cattle or of slaves form some of the earliest surviving family records. Genealogies indicating family lineages and relationships were often kept for generations. If the family were of an upper class, religious scriptures and rituals or works of astrology and divination might be added to the collection. Lists of omens seem to have been a favorite family item in Babylonia. Perhaps a king-list, a historical chronology, or even the works of a local poet or storyteller might be added. Finally, the family collection might become a genuine private library with the addition of religious commentaries, traditional epics and tales, and other writings of historical or literary content. The family archive is thus the ancestor of the private library, and by the time of the Greeks and Romans, if not earlier, the well-stocked private library was not unusual.

One other factor in the early development of libraries was the official or "copyright" collection of manuscripts. As literary works were produced and widely copied, assurance of the accuracy, or purity, of the copied text was required. Historical texts might vary slightly from copy to copy, and so long as the actual facts were unchanged, little damage was done. But when poems and plays came to be written, the author's original words were all-important to its literary value. For this reason, in ancient Athens in the days of Sophocles and Euripides, official copies of plays were placed in a public collection to guarantee that any person might have access to the correct texts. Because plays and other literary works could be pirated with ease, corrupted texts often circulated as readily as the original wording of the author. When correct texts were always available in an official library, all other copies could be checked against the official one at any time, and any question as to accuracy or authenticity could always be answered. Egypt had a similar practice in connection with religious scriptures. The official, or orthodox, scriptures would be kept under guard as a guarantee of the authenticity or authority of their contents. The Ark of the Covenant of the early Hebrews is also an example of this. Where such collections were large enough, arranged and available for use, they became early forms of public libraries.

Central to the rise of libraries was the form of the graphic materials utilized to store information, since historians have clearly shown that the use and arrangement of libraries will vary as the form of their contents vary. In the course of history people experimented with almost every known material in search of the most suitable writing instrument and the most satisfactory writing surface. In the process they tried wood, stone, various metals, many types of hides and leather, leaves, bark, cloth, clay, and paper as writing surfaces, and succeeded fairly well with all of them. For writing instruments they applied chisels, brushes, sticks, wooden and metal styluses, bird feathers, and quills--in fact, almost any kind of pointed object that could be used with paints or inks.

Generally, however, three forms of writing surfaces were most widely used in the ancient world, and most of the surviving records are on one of these three. The first of these, and probably the most widely used in time and geographic area, was papyrus, which grew along the lower Nile and throughout the Mediterranean area. To prepare a writing surface from the papyrus reed, the outer bark was removed and the inner, soft pith was sliced into thin, narrow strips. When these strips were placed in two layers, the top layer perpendicular to the lower one, and pressed or pounded lightly while moist, a sheet of rough paper-like material was produced. This sheet was then dried and polished with pumice stone to form a good writing surface that would readily take ink and still withstand ordinary handling. Papyrus of various weights and grades was produced, with the grade depending upon the quality of the reed, the care with which it was made, and the size of the sheets. Once the sheets were finished, they could be used singly for letters, short poems, or documents; and for longer works, they could be glued side to side to form a long strip. The writing was usually done in lines parallel to the length of the strip, forming columns or pages perpendicular to the length. A completed strip could form a roll from ten to thirty feet in length, and from six to ten inches wide. Some rolls were wider and longer, apparently for special purposes. The Harris Papyrus, for example, is 133 feet long by 17 inches wide. The end of a completed manuscript was glued to a cylindrical stick of wood, metal or ivory, and the strip wound around the central core. The complete roll might be encased in a cylinder of pottery, metal, ivory, or leather. A note on the contents of the roll and perhaps the seal of the owner could be attached to the roll on a tab of wood, metal, or ivory. Such rolls could be ornate or plain, but the roll in this form constituted the "book" of the Greek, Egyptian, and Roman libraries. Small collections or rolls might be kept in pottery jars, but larger numbers were usually kept in niches or "pigeon-holes" on the library walls.

Very different in substance and appearance, but similar in form, was the parchment roll. Parchment, or vellum, its close relative, was the cured hide of the young sheep or goat. The hide was scraped clean of hair and fat and then cured or tanned until it was thin and of almost translucent whiteness. The completed parchment was trimmed to page size and also glued into long rolls. Parchment was developed after centuries of using hides and leather in cruder forms, but leather continued to be used for writing for special purposes, especially religious works and ceremonial scrolls. Both leather and parchment were more durable than papyrus in ordinary usage, and parchment had the advantage of being suitable for writing on both sides. Papyrus, on the other hand, was more porous, allowing the ink to show through, and restricting the writing to one surface. Parchment came into general use in the second century B.C., and it and papyrus were equally popular for several centuries.

The third popular and widely used writing material in ancient times was the clay tablet, used in the cuneiform writing of the Mesopotamian Valley and neighboring areas. It was used from Persia to the Mediterranean from the fourth millennium B.C. on into several centuries of the Christian era. Essentially the clay tablet was just that--a tablet of soft, pliable clay of a firm consistency--suitable for taking impressions from a stylus of wood, bone, reed, or metal. The clay was kept soft until used, then kneaded into the required size and shape. If the writing took more than a short period of time, or if additional writing was to be added at a later date, the clay had to be kept moist, and this was usually done by wrapping it in a dampened cloth. The usual clay tablet was pillow-shaped, about two or three inches wide by three or four inches long, and about one inch think. Some tablets were larger, reaching eight by twelve inches, and not all were rectangular; some were circular, triangular, cylindrical or cone-shaped. The writing instrument, a stylus with a square or triangular tip, was held at an angle to the writing surface, and was used to make an impression rather than a continuous stroke. This gave the writing the appearance of wedge-shaped dents with long tails; hence the name cuneiform or wedge-shaped, for this style of writing. After the writing on the tablet was completed, it was left to dry; if it was to be kept permanently, it was baked in an oven. Sometimes an outer sheath of clay was placed around the baked or inscribed tablet, and for legal documents the text might be repeated on the outside tablet. If the outer envelope of clay was unbroken, the inner text could be considered intact and correct, thus giving a sort of carbon copy to prevent tampering with texts.

The earliest writing on clay tablets was in vertical columns, beginning at the top of the right-hand side of the tablet and ending at the bottom of the left-hand side. Many centuries later the method of writing changed; it was done in horizontal lines beginning at the top left-hand side and ending at the bottom right-hand side, as in the modern style. Works of some length might require several, even dozens of tablets. A favorite method of keeping series of tablets together was in baskets, although sometimes they were merely kept together on shelves. Each tablet was numbered separately, and a key word or text was prominently inscribed on the end of the tablet. In some cases a lengthy text was simply inscribed on a larger tablet. One of the larger ones, containing the Annals of Sennacharib, was six-sided, about one foot high and five inches thick. It was found at Nineveh in 1830 and is now in the British Museum.

Since it is known that clay tablets were widely used in Egypt along with the papyrus roll, it is likely that papyrus and parchment were also used in Babylonia, particularly in the later centuries before Christ. Because the climate in Babylonia was humid, any papyrus or parchment would have decayed long ago, but clay seals that were apparently originally attached to inscribed rolls have been found there. Moreover, there are also illustrations to be seen on the walls of excavated Babylonian palaces depicting scribes reading from a roll. There are also illustrations showing writers using what was apparently a waxed wooden tablet for keeping temporary records.

In the classical ages of Greece and Rome, the roll, either of papyrus or parchment, remained the dominant form for preserving written records, and it continued to be used in Europe, especially for legal documents, into the modern era. By the 4th century A.D., however, another book-form, the codex, was becoming widely used. Basically the same as our modern book, the codex took its name from the Latin caudex, or trunk of a tree. The earliest form of the codex was the diptych, which was two wooden or ivory leaves hinged together on one side. The inner faces of these leaves, coated with wax, could be inscribed with a sharp stylus. The wax could be easily smoothed to make an erasure, and the surface was ready for another writing. These wax diptychs developed from the single wax tablet; hinges were simply added on the side. The diptych could be used for sending letters, computing accounts, preparing lessons, or for other writing that did not need to be preserved. Eventually, more than two leaves of metal, wood, or ivory were hinged together, and thus the modern book-form was approached. When parchment, which folded easily, came into wide use as a writing material, one large sheet folded like a diptych formed a folio of two leaves or four pages. When additional sheets of parchment were folded, inserted and stitched along the fold, a codex in the form of a small pamphlet or single signature resulted. Several of these signatures sewn, glued, and bound together with leather or wooden covers became the form the codex was to keep for hundreds of years.

The codex has generally been considered a product of the Christian era, since the early Christians used this form for their scriptures, but hinged, waxed tablets were used by the Assyrians as early as the 8th century B.C. In the ruins of Nimrud, sixteen ivory tablets and several walnut tablets were found in 1953, each with evidence that it had at one time been hinged. One set of fifteen thin ivory leaves with heavier covers and gold hinges was found, indicating that this wax-tablet "book" had at least thirty pages. It may have been used as a student's workbook, or perhaps as an easier method of keeping current accounts. One palace wall-illustration shows a scribe using a similar tablet to record the number of dead after a battle.

In summary, what began as a collection of records--government, temple, business, or private--gradually grew into a library as other materials of historical, literary, or informative nature were added to it, and as its use grew beyond that of the individual who formed it. Organized archives existed in both Egypt and Babylonia before 3000 B.C., and before 2000 B.C. there were institutions in both countries that were libraries in the true sense of the word. Libraries developed as civilizations reached their peak and declined or were destroyed in periods of stress or conquest. But whereas individual libraries could be, and were, destroyed, the idea of the library, once established, was indestructible, and since the beginning of recorded history it has served a vital purpose as a main communicative link in both time and space. A written record, on reasonably durable material, can immortalize the ideas or actions of a given generation, but only if those records are organized and preserved in libraries will they seriously affect the development of generations to come.

Additional Readings

Archeologists have been responsible for generating most of the information that we now have on the origins of libraries. The interested student can learn much from a thorough and laborious search through what has become a massive literature. However, several recent texts stand out as relevant and comprehensive treatments of the topic and each of the following contain extensive bibliographies: Ernst Posner's Archives in the Ancient World (Cambridge: Harvard University Press, 1972) and Felix Reichmann's The Sources of Western Literacy: The Middle Eastern Civilizations (Westport, Conn.: Greenwood Press, 1980). In addition there are a number of general histories of libraries in the western world which cover in more or less detail the origins of libraries. The reader should note that the works cited here are relevant to the other chapters of this book as well.

Hessel, Alfred. A History of Libraries. Translated by Reuben Peiss. (New Brunswick, N.J.: Scarecrow Press, 1955).

Jackson, Sidney. Libraries and Librarianship in the West: A Brief History (New York: McGraw-Hill, 1974).

Thompson, James Westfall. Ancient Libraries (Berkeley: University of California Press, 1940).

Vleeschauwer, H. J. de. "History of the Western Library," Mousaion nos. 70-74 (1963-64); "Survey of Library History," ibid. nos. 63-66 (1963).

Chapter 2

BABYLONIAN AND ASSYRIAN LIBRARIES

It is difficult to say whether the first library in the western world was located in Egypt or in Mesopotamia, but it is certain that in the civilizations emerging in those two areas in the fourth and third millennia B.C., writing produced "books" and these were preserved in sufficient numbers to form libraries. In the Mesopotamian Valley, inhabited successively by Sumerians, Babylonians, and Assyrians, the process that gave rise to libraries was certainly under way during those periods. Writing in pictographs had developed there possibly as early as 4000 B.C., and by 3600 B.C. the Sumerians in the lower valley were developing a cuneiform script from the pictographs. By about 3000 B.C. a cuneiform "alphabet" of about 400 signs or characters was commonly used by scribes in government, temples, and businesses. In the next few centuries, libraries, or at least well-arranged collections of records, were fairly widely established throughout the valley. Thanks to the durable qualities of baked clay, we know of these libraries. More than 200,000 clay tablets have been unearthed in the ruins of Mesopotamian towns, and since the cuneiform script has been deciphered, we can not only read the tablets, but we can also tell quite a bit about how they were originally collected and arranged into libraries.

The Sumerians in the lower valley were a non-Semitic people, but the upper reaches of the Tigris and Euphrates Rivers were inhabited about 2500 B.C. by a Semitic people known as Akkadians. About 2250 B.C., a Semitic leader, Argon I, united the whole valley into the old Babylonian Empire and built a powerful state that extended from the Persian Gulf to the Mediterranean. Culturally, however, the Babylonians built upon the Sumerian foundations, and the resulting civilization lasted some 2,000 years. Under the rule of Hammurabi (ca. 1700 B.C.) a high point was reached with the publication of the famous Code of Laws and the compilation of historical chronicles and king-lists. A thousand years later, while the Mesopotamian Valley was ruled by the Assyrians, a series of progressive kings brought literature and libraries to an even higher degree of development, but, after 625 B.C., conquest of the valley by Chaldeans, Persians, and Greeks in turn put an end to an era of history that was to be unknown for the next 2,000 years. Not until the archeologist's spade exposed the myriads of clay tablets would the western world again know the glories of the Sumerian-Babylonian-Assyrian era.

However, while this civilization existed, the Mesopotamian Valley was one of the most enlightened and progressive areas in the world. As the many ancient townsites of the valley have been excavated and studied, the clay tablet collections have unfolded a long and virtually continuous story of library development. One of the earliest finds in clay tablets comes from the Red Temple at Erech. This town was in the lower valley of the Euphrates, and the tablets, dating from about 3000 B.C., are in a pictographic script. At Jemdet Nasr, near the site of the later Babylon, another more advanced script has been found, dating from about 2700 B.C. From Tello, near Lagash, a collection of almost 30,000 tablets, all in cuneiform, have been dated at about 2350 B.C., while thousands more have been found at Nippur, south of modern Baghdad, dating from around 2000 B.C. More than a score of other collections of clay tablets, apparently the remains of temple or palace libraries, have been found in the valley, along with many smaller collections that appear to have been private or business libraries or archives.

Although these surviving tablets are the sources of much of our known history of Babylonia, there is remarkably little history as such to be found among them. About the time of Hammurabi, an attempt was made to bring together a complete history of the Mesopotamian Valley. Chronologies of the reigns of kings were compiled and the history of all wars and international disputes was written down. A religious history was also composed, giving the story of the various gods, their temples and priests, half mythological and half historical. Unfortunately neither of these histories survived, but remnants of the political history, in the form of lists of kings, were copied by the later

Assyrians, along with the story of how the histories were compiled. These king-lists, purporting to cover all the rulers of the valley from before the Flood to Hammurabi, are questioned by modern historians, but they still form a basis for the study of early Mesopotamian history. Hammurabi's reign is also noted for the codification of laws known by his name. It was not the first Babylonian code of laws, but it is the best known, and it must have been compiled from a well-arranged collection of works of law. In fact, it presupposes an excellent legal archive or law library. From the viewpoint of library history, the important thing is that in order to compile such histories or codes of laws the writers must have had thousands of clay tablets to draw on, and those tablets must have been well arranged and organized for use.

There is undoubtedly a question as to how well organized the tablet collections of the Babylonians and Sumerians were. By the time of the Assyrians, however, we are on firmer ground since we are able to recognize the remains of true libraries, arranged by subject matter, and available through a primitive form of catalog. Not only were the Assyrian libraries large and well organized, but they were apparently open to the reading public and well used. Particularly under Sargon II, who died about 705 B.C., the Assyrians developed a palace library at Khorsabad that was a notable beginning. Ruins of this library have been excavated; in it, among hundreds of other tablets, was a king-list dating from about 2000 B.C. to Sargon himself. Sargon's immediate successors increased the size of the palace library, but it was his great-grandson, Assurbanipal (ca. 668-627 B.C.), who developed the library into one of the greatest of the ancient world. Assurbanipal moved the royal capital to Nineveh and there in his palace accumulated a library of over 30,000 tablets. Under his personal direction, agents were sent to all parts of the Assyrian kingdom, which then extended from the Persian Gulf to the Mediterranean, and even to foreign lands to collect written records of all kinds and on all subjects. Assurbanipal had his scribes taught to read early Sumerian and Babylonian texts in order to translate the ancient records into Assyrian. He was particularly interested in religious texts, incantations, and verbal charms, but his agents were instructed to bring back everything in writing. He is reported to have asked Nabu, the Assyrian god of writing, to bless his library and to grant him the grace to erect it. Like the Alexandrian Library a few centuries later, the library of Assurbanipal was open to scholars, both official and unofficial. In fact, many scribes and scholars were employed by the king to revise, compile, and edit the thousands of texts brought together in his library.

Assurbanipal's library was kept in many rooms in his palace, and apparently there was some subject arrangement by rooms. One room, for example, was filled with tablets relating to history and government, including agreements with subordinate rulers, biographies of officials, and the king-lists. In this same room there were tablets of information on neighboring countries, copies of letters to and from the royal ambassadors in other lands, and of orders to military officials. Another division of the library was given over to geography, with descriptions of towns and countries, rivers and mountains, along with lists of commercial products available from each area. One division concerned laws and legal decisions, while still another contained commercial records, including contracts, deeds, bills of sale and the like. Tax lists together with accounts of tribute due from the nobility made up another division. One important room was given over to clay tablets containing legends and mythology, the basis of the religion of Assyria. Included were the accounts of the Flood, lists of the gods, their various attributes and accomplishments, and the hymns of praise dedicated to them. Rituals, prayers, and incantations made up an important subdivision of the group. Still other divisions of Assurbanipal's library were made up of works in the sciences and pseudosciences--astronomy and astrology, biology, mathematics, medicine and natural history. In all, the library must have contained about 10,000 different works on about 30,000 tablets, and it should be pointed out that much of its contents consisted of copies and translations of non-Assyrian works, drawn from their predecessors in the valley and from their neighbors on all sides.

The clay tablets inside the rooms of Assurbanipal's library were kept in earthen jars, and the jars in turn were kept in orderly rows on shelves. Each tablet bore an identification tag, indicating the jar, shelf, and room of its location. On the walls of each room, beside the door, was a list of the works to be found in that room. This would correspond to a rough shelf list of the room's contents. Moreover, something like a subject catalog, or a descriptive bibliography, has been found on tablets that were apparently kept near the door in each room. These tablets include entries giving titles of works, the number of tablets for each work, the number of lines, opening words, important subdivisions, and a location or classification symbol. The worn condition of some of these "catalog" tablets indicates that they were well used.

Assurbanipal took pride in his library and in having collected it from all parts of the then-known world. His official seal is an example of this pride. On it, after invoking the aid of his favorite god, Nabu, he says: "I have collected these tablets, I have had them copied, I have marked them with my name, and I have deposited them in my palace." That he meant them for the instruction of his subjects is also indicated, but from another source we learn that he also controlled or censored the contents of the collection. One of his scribe-librarians is reported to have said: "I shall place in it whatever is agreeable to the king; what is not agreeable to the king, I shall remove from it." Censored or not, it is well for history that Assurbanipal's library was compiled, for in it have been found many unique sources for the earlier history of Mesopotamia. The Epic of Gilgamesh, for example, was preserved on twelve tablets in Assurbanipal's library, as was a Babylonian tale of creation on seven tablets, and many other legends, epics, and hero-tales. The remarkable thing is that the library survived as nearly intact as it did, and the reason for its survival is, oddly enough, probably due to a disaster. When Nineveh was destroyed in 612 B.C., the invading Chaldeans and Medes apparently cared little for the clay tablets and simply destroyed the palace containing them by pushing in the walls with battering rams. The collapsing walls buried the tablet libraries beneath them and helped preserve them until their discovery by archeologists in the nineteenth and twentieth centuries.

Although Assurbanipal's library is the best known of those in ancient Mesopotamia and may well have been the most spectacular in size and contents, it was far from being the only major one. In fact, from the many excavations in the area, evidence of many more palace and temple libraries has been found, with their approximate dating ranging from 2000 to 500 B.C. Evidence is available that wealthy private families also had libraries, and collections of business archives have been found. However, it is in the ruins of palaces, temples and government buildings that the most useful collections of clay tablets have been found.

Temple libraries were quite different in nature and use from the government libraries. In content they included histories of the gods, texts of formal rituals, hymns, incantations, invocations, and prayers, as well as the sacred epics and scriptures. In addition, since Babylonian religion was closely connected with science, or pseudoscience, the temple libraries also contained works on agriculture, biology, mathematics, astronomy, and medicine. Near the above-mentioned palace at Nimrud, there was also a temple library with tablets containing hymns, incantations, omens, and medical texts. Assurbanipal also had a temple library apart from his main library, and this, too, was entirely religious and pseudoscientific in nature. As the temple was not only the intellectual center of the community but also an economic factor in its large land-holdings and business enterprises, it employed scores of nonreligious workers and kept collections of business records in addition to its theological writings.

One of the more important functions of the temple was its school for scribes. The writing of cuneiform was a difficult process, and long years of study were necessary before one could become proficient in the art. Students were trained not only as priests and scribes but also in other professions such as astronomy, mathematics, medicine, and accounting. Tablets of practice work have been found, indicating how the pupil progressed from the simpler cuneiform symbols to the more complex ones and then on to the writing of complete tablets. In the "school library" there were textbook tablets to show the student how to write, dictionaries, grammars, and examples of business forms and letters. There were lists of place names, similar to a gazetteer, and also lists of plants, animals, minerals, and commercial products. Dictionaries of foreign language words translated into Babylonian were available for the scribe or student who was working with current or ancient languages. There were even interlinear translations of important works in other languages. There was a school for scribes in the temple at Nippur, and from its surviving tablets comes a series of dialogues or debates between schoolboys on the art of learning.

Physically, the Babylonian and Assyrian libraries were quite different from anything resembling a modern library, but this difference was largely due to the nature of the "books"--the clay tablets. Most of the tablet collections have been discovered scattered among ruins and it is difficult to tell how they were originally arranged. In a few cases, as in Assurbanipal's library, it is possible to tell at least what rooms or areas they were originally in, but sometimes even this is difficult. However, a few generalizations can be made from the numerous collections that have been found. It is apparent that, whether in temple or palace, the tablets were kept in a designated area, properly arranged, and supervised by experienced personnel. In some cases a few tablets have been found in other offices, as if they were being consulted by an official in his working quarters, or as if they constituted an individual's own private library. Inside the regular library rooms, the tablets have been found, at different times and places, to be housed in various ways. Some were on narrow shelves, some in shallow bins, some in a pigeonhole arrangement, some in baskets or clay jars. Writing materials other than clay tablets, such as papyrus, animal hides, waxed tablets, or even smooth wooden boards, were sometimes used, but these have not survived. We know of them through surviving illustrations and their being mentioned on the tablets. There are also great variations in the size and shape of the surviving tablets, although the usual tablet seems to have been about three by six inches in pillow form.

Since the average clay tablet could contain the equivalent of only two to three modern pages, it was necessary to use several tablets for most works. In these longer works, the tablets were numbered consecutively and kept together by means of a running "title" made up of the first word or words of the text. For example, the account of the creation found in Assurbanipal's library begins with the words "Formerly that which is above ..."; so the several tablets containing the story are labelled "Formerly that which is above, No. 1," "Formerly that which is above, No. 2," and so on for seven tablets. In some collections there was a sort of colophon on the first tablet, identifying the owner, the scribe, the first line or running title, and the number of tablets in the series. Sometimes the complete series of tablets would be tied together with strings, or kept in separate baskets or jars. Shelving was apparently by a location symbol, although related works in larger collections were kept together. As in Assurbanipal's library, finding-lists or "catalogs" were often inscribed in the wall near the door, or on clay tablets kept easily available. Multiple copies were noted on the list, with as many as six copies of favorite works being found in some libraries. One "catalog" of a collection at Agene, which mainly consisted of works on astronomy and astrology, advised the would-be reader to write down the number of the tablet he needed and present it to the librarian who would find it for him.

The librarian, or "keeper of the books," was of

necessity a well-trained person. First of all, he had to be a graduate of the school for scribes, and then he had to be thoroughly trained in the literature or type of records that he was to keep. After this, he served an apprenticeship for a number of years, learning the trade of librarian and several languages at the same time. That the librarians must have been polylingual is indicated by the numerous cases of works in several languages being found in the same collection. In addition to serving as librarian, he was often called on to edit, transcribe, and translate works needed by higher government or religious officials. He was variously titled "Man of the Written Tablets," "Keeper of the Tablets," or "Master of the Books." One of the earliest Babylonian librarians known by name was Amit Anu, who was "Tablet Keeper" in the royal library at Ur nearly 2000 years B.C. In the temple libraries the librarian-scribe was a priest, often a high-ranking one, while in the palace libraries he was often an important official. In either case, he was usually of the upper classes, often the younger son of a noble family.

Whatever their other contributions to western civilization--and they were many--the chief claim of the Sumerian-Babylonian-Assyrian peoples to permanent fame lies in their contributions to communications. They developed a method of writing; an economical, readily available, and relatively permanent writing material; and a system of arranging and using this recorded information in archives and libraries. Whatever the immediate purposes of the collection--commercial, legal, political, educational--the ultimate result was the preservation of the records of civilization's progress in this particular part of the world. This, in the long run, probably contributed more to western civilization than Hammurabi's code of laws or the Assyrian war chariot. With the exception of Hellenic Alexandria in the last three centuries B.C., and Rome in the first three centuries A.D., no region in the ancient world had such well-developed libraries as those of Babylonia and Assyria. It can well be argued that the continuity of Sumerian-Babylonian-Assyrian civilization for 3,000 years, despite many wars and conquests, can be largely attributed to its method of writing and its means of preserving records. Thanks to these records, each civilization was able to build upon the past. Moreover, it is quite obvious that without the remains of those libraries and archives we would know virtually nothing today of that 3,000 years of history in the Mesopotamian Valley. Few periods in the history of Western man so well demonstrate the cultural role of the graphic arts of communication and the practical value of well-organized archives and libraries.

Additional Readings

All of the works cited in Chapter 1 are relevant to this chapter as well. Felix Reichmann's _The Sources of Western Literacy_ is particularly useful. Also of special interest is M. Weitemeyer's "Archive and Library Technique in Ancient Mesopotamia," _Libri_ 6 (1956): 217-38.

Chapter 3

EGYPTIAN LIBRARIES

The earliest known libraries in Egypt, as in Babylonia, were connected with palaces and temples. Recorded history in Egypt is thought to go back at least to 3200 B.C., or roughly about the same time that writing and records began in Babylonia. The earliest form of writing by the Egyptians was pictographic, and many surviving examples of this writing have been found on inscribed monuments. Since this early pictographic writing was carved on stones, it is known by the Greek term hieroglyphic, which means sacred stone-writing. This form of writing had attained a classic form early in the third millennium B.C., and as it came to be written widely on papyrus, leather, and other materials, it was modified into a cursive script known as hieratic. Both forms were used for more than 2,000 years, and a third form was added by 700 B.C. This relatively late arrival was the demotic script, a kind of shorthand developed from the hieratic, and widely used in business and commerce. In time, the stylized hieratic characters developed to the point where they could be used as a syllabary or even for separate sounds and letters, but they were used in this manner only in reproducing foreign names and words; the writing of Egyptian continued with each word represented by one character, with or without a determinative. Thus the Egyptians came close to producing a phonetic syllabary and even an alphabet, but they conservatively adhered to their ancient forms instead.

With the advent of writing, records began to be kept. In both temples and palaces, special rooms were designated for the preservation of official manuscripts. Undoubtedly the archive preceded the library, and records of government, church, or business were kept in orderly arrangement long before the addition of history, literature, or theological works brought the first real library into existence. As in Babylonia, the early archives and libraries were under the direction of specially trained scribes, and as early as the Fifth Dynasty (ca. 2400 B.C.) there are references to a "House of Writings" which was apparently a public archive. Such titles as "Scribe of the Archives," "Scribe of the Sacred Writings," and "Keeper of the King's Records" can be found on the tombs of men who were highly honored officials. Apparently, until about 2000 B.C. only a few people could read and write, and the art practiced by the scribe was considered to be an almost mystical or sacred rite. The fact that one early Pharaoh could read and write was considered significant enough to record on his tomb-biography. After about 2000 B.C. literacy became more common, and evidence is found of business records and of private libraries in the homes of wealthy merchants and noblemen.

Although we have reliable evidence that libraries did exist in ancient Egypt, the archeological evidence for specific collections is much scarcer than in Babylonia. Instead of the thousands of tablets found in the Mesopotamian ruins, we have only fragments of texts, tomb illustrations, and inscriptions from walls and monuments to rely on for the history of Egyptian libraries. There is, for example, evidence that Khufu (Cheops), a monarch of the Fourth Dynasty (ca. 2600 B.C.), had a "House of Writings," and this practice continued under his successors. That more than one such collection was kept can be gathered from the different titles assigned to them, such as "Archives of the Ancestors," "Hall of the Writings of Egypt," and "House of Scared Writings." King Rameses II (ca. 1300 B.C.), also known as Ozymandias, was reported to have a library of some 20,000 rolls in his palace at Thebes. This room was designated "The Healing Place of the Soul," so it was apparently a religious or philosophical library rather than merely a government archive. At least one of Rameses' librarians is known by name. Amen-em-haut, whose bibliographic profession was noted on his elaborate tomb. As the government headquarters of Egypt existed at different places at different times, evidence of various "royal libraries" have been found at Memphis, Thebes, Heliopolis, and other places.

The palace library about which most is known was that at Tell-el-Amarna (Akhetaton), a capital built by Amenhotep IV about 1350 B.C. Here the remains of a library have been found in a room designated as the "Place of the Records of the Palace of the King." This library consisted of clay tablets--or at least all that has survived are the clay tablets--written in Babylonian cuneiform characters. As already noted, cuneiform was something of an international diplomatic language at various times in the ancient world, and the collection of tablets at Tell-el-Amarna consisted mainly of correspondence between King Amenhotep III (ca. 1400 B.C.) and various Egyptian vassal states and foreign rulers in Asia Minor. Although these letters were mainly diplomatic, much history can be obtained from them for this period of the Eighteenth Dynasty, and much social and economic information as well. They disclose, for example, that Egyptian doctors were much in demand at the royal courts of Asia Minor. It is quite probable that other records in this library were kept on leather or papyrus and have failed to survive.

Evidences of Egyptian temple libraries are somewhat more plentiful than for the palace collections, although it should be pointed out that for the first few dynasties the temple and palace were often the same building, since the king was also a god. The temple library apparently began as a collection of sacred scriptures. The _Book of Thoth_, attributed to the Egyptian god of learning, was possibly the nucleus around which such a collection began. Books about other Egyptian gods were added, along with writings of exposition and comment about them. In addition there were books of ritual with instructions on how certain religious rites were to be performed, together with hymns and incantations. There were even sacred dramas, such as the _Drama of Osiris_, a kind of passion play dating from about 1800 B.C., of which only a fraction has been discovered. Gradually the temple libraries came to include much secular literature, especially science, since, as in Babylonia, medicine and astronomy were closely connected with Egyptian religion. Thus, the Egyptian temple library was much more than an archive of the church; it came to be a library in the fullest sense of the word.

Some temples, such as that at Abu Simbel on the upper Nile, were communities in themselves. In addition to the fairly large staff of priests, the temple community included farmers, tradesmen, skilled craftsmen, and a host of minor officials and clerks, all engaged in the maintenance of the temple and its lands and properties. To keep up with all this communal activity, a number of scribes kept records, taught school, and served as "keepers of the books" in libraries that contained not only theological works but also technical writings, literature, historical annals, and practical texts in many fields. In some of the temples there were apparently two libraries, one a general library for the use of all who could read, and another inner library of theological works for the exclusive use of a select circle of high priests. In one temple, called the "House of Life," there was a special group of priests and scholars whose duties were to preserve temples, and record important discoveries and technical advances. This group had its own library, a kind of copyright collection of authentic religious texts kept separately to guarantee their validity and authenticity.

As in Babylonia, the temple was the scene of schools for the training of scribes. In fact, most education, or at least most formal education in writing and the literary arts, was carried on in the temples, and these schools for scribes had libraries of reference works and texts. To become a scribe, the Egyptian boy began serious study at an early age and then served many years of apprenticeship. He had to learn as many as 700 different hieroglyphic characters in order to write proficiently, and many of those characters had two or more meanings, while many words could be written in two or more ways. In addition to texts and grammars, dictionaries and business forms, these "school libraries" also contained works on history and literature as well as books on ethics and moral living for the students.

Some of the Egyptian temples were particularly known as centers of healing, and their library rooms contained collections that might easily be considered early medical libraries. In the "Hall of Rolls" at Heliopolis, long works with lists of diseases and their cures were found. In the temple of Ptah, at Memphis, remnants of books of medical prescriptions were discovered, and in the temple of Horus at Edfu, there were tracts on "the turning aside of the cause of disease." Keepers of these medical books were given such titles as "Scribe of the Double House of Life" and "Learned Men of the Magic Library." One of the largest papyrus rolls ever found is on medicine. This is the Ebers Papyrus, consisting of 110 pages of medical information and prescriptions, thought to have been written about 1550 B.C. Another example, the Edwin Smith Papyrus (Egyptian papyri are often called by the names of their discoverers or early owners), was on both surgery and internal medicine, covering both diagnosis and treatment of diseases. One of the largest medical collections of papyri discovered was that of the Temple of Thoth at Hermopolis where six intact works were found along with fragments of others. The scribe-priest who was "Keeper of the Sacred Books" at this temple had an assistant, a woman librarian with the title of "Lady of Letters, Mistress of the House of Books." There was also a medical school connected with this temple.

In addition to temple and palace libraries, the several thousand years of Egyptian culture also saw the growth of private book collections ranging from a few rolls to fairly large libraries in the homes of wealthy merchants or noblemen. The private library, as indicated by fragments that have survived and a few cases where remains of a whole collection have been found, varied to suit the taste of the collector. It might consist almost entirely of family history and genealogy, or business records, or the popular literature of the period, including fiction and travel tales. Again, it might be a fairly general collection, representative of wide interests and tastes. The wealthier collector might have a scribe to copy books for him, or he might purchase them from public scribes and copyists. His library might be housed in a separate small room or closet equipped with special cupboards pigenholed for rolls of papyrus. In other, less wealthy homes, the rolls might be kept in a few jars, and the jars themselves kept on shelves or the rolls might be kept in leather cases. Both cases and jars were often highly ornamented. The site of El-Lahun, excavated by Flanders Petrie, revealed many private homes of a higher class and remains of papyrus rolls were found in nearly every one of them, indicating a high degree of literacy and literary interests in this social group. Not only were personal business files, family correspondence, legal papers, and wills found in some quantity, but there were also many examples of literature, history, theology, and even medical and veterinary works. Fate often played strange tricks on the archeologists, however, since one fine example of a papyrus roll, almost complete and in good condition, turned out upon translation to be the equivalent of a grocery list for a large household for a period of twelve days!

Although it is generally assumed that only the upper classes could read and write with ease, it is interesting to note the results of the excavation of a "workers' town" from the period of Rameses II (1299-1232 B.C.), when the village of Der El-Medina was constructed for workers who were building a large project, probably a monument to the king.

The homes of these workmen and their families revealed large numbers of papyrus scraps and even more ostraka, that is, scraps of limestone and broken pottery used for miscellaneous and less important writings On these odd bits of written records were found bills, records of trades, payment of wages, contracts, law suits, work reports, letters, memoranda of all kinds, and many bits of literature and religious writings. Although such miscellaneous collections of scraps could not be considered evidence of private libraries, they indicate literacy among working people and also provide a wonderful picture of the economic and social life of this period. If not evidence of libraries, they represent the sources from which history is compiled and libraries are eventually formed.

Closely related to Egyptian libraries were those of the neighboring area of Palestine. In an area from which the Bible came, one would naturally expect a long history of preserved information that preceded and formed the foundation for such a lengthy scriptural text. For long periods of time much of that combination of history, literature, and mythology was preserved through memory and repeated orally from generation to generation. However, there is evidence in the Bible itself for the existence of collections of holy writings, similar to the Egyptian temple writings, going back at least to the days of Solomon. In the Hebrew Temple in Jerusalem, the Books of the Law, the writings of Moses, and those of the Prophets were preserved in a most secret place which was open to only a few priests. The Book of Joshua was added to this collection in due time, and still later the sermons and exhortations of the Prophets were included. All of this was preserved in and for the use of the Temple; it was also preserved for posterity. Much, if not all, of this first collection of sacred Hebrew writings was destroyed during the period of the Babylonian captivity. After the Hebrews returned from Babylon, Nehemiah reassembled the Books of Moses and those of the Kings and the Prophets to re-form the sacred library. He was aided in this task by Esdras, who some believe first edited the Pentateuch. This library was probably burned when Antiochus captured Jerusalem in the 2nd century B.C., and may have been reestablished a third time by Judas Maccabeus. There are various references in the Old Testament to this sacred collection of Hebrew writings. For example, Jeremiah speaks of the "book of the records of the fathers" that was kept in the Temple, and Ezra speaks of rolls being kept in a "scribe's chamber." In Second Kings, there is a note on a scribe being sent for the "Book of the Law" which was kept in the House of the Lord. In later pre-Christian years, there were probably small collections of scriptures in all synagogues, and libraries were maintained for the use of the students in the schools for priests in the larger ones. By tradition, the Hebrew scriptures were usually preserved on leather rolls. Internal evidence in the Old Testament indicates that much of it was compiled from older written sources as well as from oral tradition and this indicates that organized collections of these sources were probably available to the scholars.

The physical nature of the Egyptian libraries is a subject about which comparatively little is known. For example, it is apparent from excavations and from illustrations found in tombs and on walls that the papyrus rolls were kept in rooms on shelves or in pigeonholes but the method of arrangement of the rolls is not known. Individual rolls were kept in cloth or leather covers, and one or more of them might be kept in a clay jar-like container with a cover. More valuable ones were sometimes kept in metal containers, often inlaid with jewels. Where there were large numbers of rolls, it seems fairly certain there was a system of arrangement because the "keeper of the books" was supposed to be able to supply any requested book on demand. In some cases, as found in excavations, a list of the books in a library room was written or inscribed on the wall, and the contents of the multi-roll containers were also listed on the outside.

Although papyrus was widely used over a long period of time, other materials were also used for writing in ancient Egypt. Clay tablets have already been mentioned, but leather and other forms of animal hides were used before papyrus was developed and they continued to be used for important writings. Wax tablets, or simple wooden leaves with a coating of wax, were used for temporary writings such as lessons, letters, and accounts. Incised inscriptions on stone monuments and walls were among the most durable Egyptian writings, but walls were also widely used for writings in ink and colors. In fact, virtually anything that would take ink--flat stones, broken pieces of pottery (*ostraka*), and even uncoated wood--was used for ordinary writing purposes.

The librarian of ancient Egypt was an important and highly educated person if we can assume that title for the many "keepers of the books" and "masters of the rolls" whose names have been found. He was often of high political position or trained in other professions besides that of scribe. We know of some of these scribes from the "funeral literature," the laudatory biographies that were frequently buried with the Egyptian dead. The various titles of the deceased and the accounts of his activities indicate that the scribe-librarian was also an editor, if not an author. He corrected, translated, amended, and criticized the material that passed through his hands--and probably censored it, too. Among the titles given to scribes in Egyptian funeral literature are such designations as "Scribe and Judge," "Scribe and Priest," "Inspector of Scribes," "Keeper of the King's Document Case," and simply "Royal Scribe" or "King's Scribe." Of course, not all of the scribes could be considered librarians by any stretch of the imagination, but enough of them could be so designated. Whatever his title, the Egyptian librarian was a credit to his profession if he was even half as important as his funerary biography reported him to be.

For more than 2,000 years the civilization of Egypt remained relatively constant, using much the same tools, social forms, and political and religious systems. Particularly, they used the same writing forms and materials, and this consistency in the communicative arts undoubtedly aided in the performance and relative lack of change in society. Internal disorders and even defeat by more primitive peoples, such as the Hyksos (17th century B.C.), did not bring permanent change to the well-established social and political systems, but the final defeat and end of ancient Egypt came with military conquest by more advanced and warlike rivals, the Assyrians, Persians, and Greeks. First came the Assyrians who sacked Thebes about 661 B.C. and ruled Egypt for a century; then Egypt was dominated by the Persians for another century. Finally, under Alexander the Great in 332 B.C., Egypt was conquered by the Greeks, and its subsequent culture was to be more Hellenic than Egyptian for several hundred years. The result of these invasions was the near obliteration of ancient Egypt. Palaces, temples, even tombs were sacked and razed. The hieroglyphic, hieratic, and demotic forms of writing were forgotten, to be replaced in turn, for the few who could read and write, by Greek, Latin, and finally Arabic. Only the deeply entombed or virtually indestructible material survived, but from the written fragments a fairly reliable history of ancient Egypt can be written and if we know little of the libraries of that magnificent epoch of history, we know at least that they played a significant role in producing, prolonging, and preserving the culture of what has been called "the cradle of western civilization."

Additional Readings

The most detailed treatment of literacy and libraries in ancient Egypt is now Felix Reichmann's *The Sources of Western Literacy: The Middle Eastern Civilizations* (Westport, Conn.: Greenwood Press, 1980). This work also includes an extensive bibliography. In addition to the general surveys listed in Chapter 1 on the origins of libraries, the following works are of special significance:

Possner, Ernst. *Archives in the Ancient World* (Cambridge, Mass.: Harvard University Press, 1972).

Sperry, J. A. "Egyptian Libraries: A Survey of the Evidence," *Libri* 7 (1957): 145-155.

Wright, H. Curtis. *The Oral Antecedents of Greek Librarianship* (Provo, Utah: Brigham Young University Press, 1977).

Chapter 4

GREEK LIBRARIES

In considering the history of libraries in Greece, it is usual to begin with those of the classical era, from the 6th century B.C. onward. However, it is now known that there was a literate civilization in Greece and the Aegean Islands almost a thousand years earlier, and that there were archives or collections of writings at Pylos and Mycenae on the mainland and at Knossos on Crete. This knowledge has come largely from the 20th-century excavations at those points and in the decipherment since 1950 of some of the inscriptions and tablets found there.

Since the late 19th century, clay tablets and inscriptions on stone and pottery have been collected in the vicinity of Knossos on the island of Crete. Some of the earliest of these inscriptions were pictographic, but from a later era, approximately 1400 to 1100 B.C., there were two types of linear inscriptions, using some pictographic signs but other apparently phonetic characters. These tablets were associated with the Minoan period of the island's history, when it was inhabited by a non-Hellenic people, and the period of its conquest by the Mycenaens, an early Greek people. Later, examples of these two scripts, designated as "Linear A" and "Linear B" were found on the Greek mainland in the area from which the Mycenaeans came. Although the Linear A script remains very difficult to translate, Linear B was finally deciphered in the early 1950s by Michael Ventris and others, who discovered it to be an early form of Greek.

With this development, the Linear B texts took on new meaning, and hundreds of them have been studied. This form of writing seems to have been used almost exclusively for business purposes, or at least all of the surviving texts are on business and military subjects. Tablets have been discovered concerning land tenure, rations and equipment for soldiers, inventories of agriculture products and stock, lists of employees, and the like, but much social and economic history can also be gathered from them. The absence of literature, or even of much in the way of historical writing, is notable. Several possible explanations have been advanced for this absence. The first is that there was simply no literature at that period, or that all literature was then oral. Another explanation suggests that the literary and historical materials might have been kept in other places, either completely destroyed or yet to be discovered. Probably the most logical reason is that any literary compositions of the Minoans and Mycenaeans may have been written on materials other than clay tablets (papyrus for example) that have decayed with time, whereas the cheaper materials used for business records have survived.

Both at Mycenae and at Pylos, special rooms have been found in the palaces with large numbers of clay tablets in them, some in jars neatly arranged in rows on shelves. This indicates a well-preserved archive with trained attendants. At Knossos many tablets were found, but they were so scattered that it was difficult to ascertain in what room or rooms they were originally kept. Clay tablets here were apparently only dried, rather than baked, and hence they are found usually in fragments. Elsewhere, the Linear B collections contained similar business and governmental information, ranging from the purely archival to the more usable "ready-reference" type of information in the form of commodity prices, sources of various goods, and even information on ship sailings and cargoes.

On a smaller scale, similar collections of tablets have been found in the ruins of private homes, particularly at Pylos. Here, in what were apparently the homes of wealthy merchants, many scattered clay tablets have been found, indicating a highly literate business society. One of the homes seems to have been that of an oil merchant, and the tablets found there dealt with accounts and inventories of trade in oil and other goods, along with some business contracts and official papers.

By the 12th century B.C., the Minoan-Mycenaean civilization had been overrun by the less-civilized Dorians from the north, and their literary culture disappeared. Several centuries followed in which the peoples of Greece and the nearby islands seem to have had little or no written language. This period includes the era of Homer, when the Iliad and the Odyssey were composed and transmitted as oral epics for many generations before they were finally written down. By the 7th century B.C., however, a literate society again emerged, and once more the appearance of a written literature was accompanied by the rise of archives and libraries.

Actually the libraries of classical Greece, which we might date from the 6th century B.C. through the 3rd century A.D., have left us few physical remains. Instead, we must rely upon references in ancient Greek and Roman literature for information concerning them. The survival of that literature is in itself fair proof that Greek libraries existed, but references to specific libraries are few and scattered. Moreover, these references are sometimes contradictory. For example, there are at least two accounts of the ultimate fate of Aristotle's library.

Some time prior to the 7th century B.C., and probably as early as the 9th, the Greeks obtained the alphabet from the Phoenicians and adapted it to their own language. The first known Greek writers of note, with the exception of the semi-legendary Homer, lived in the 6th century B.C., and some of their writings have come down to us. Poetry, philosophy, and science, as represented by Sappho, Thales, and Anaximander, existed in this era.

If we are to believe the writer Aulus Gellius (2nd century A.D.), Athens had a public library after 560 B.C. Gellius says that the tyrant Pisistratus (605-527 B.C.) collected a large library and later gave it to the city of Athens, where it was opened to the public. The people of the city added to the collection and took care of it for many years, until the Persian conqueror Xerxes confiscated it when he captured Athens in 480 B.C. Continuing with Gellius' account, we learn that long after Xerxes had carried the library to Persia, that country was conquered in turn by King Seleucus, who returned the books to Athens. This makes an engaging story, but one for which there is little corroboration elsewhere and which is generally doubted. However, the story may, like many ancient tales, contain a thread of truth in its web of fiction. From other sources we know that Pisistratus was a builder of temples, a lover of music and art, and that he caused a critical edition of the works of Homer to be compiled during his period as ruler of Athens.

That he could and did compile a small library is not difficult to believe, but verification is difficult, and it is very doubtful that he ever instituted a "public library" in anything like the present sense of the term. Similar dubious evidence refers to a 6th-century B.C. library at the court of the tyrant Polycrates of Samos, and an early 5th-century B.C. collection in the palace of Hieros at Syracuse.

For the 5th century B.C., the library history of Greece is still vague but on somewhat firmer ground. This is the era of the development of prose writing, particularly history and philosophy, and there is strong evidence suggesting that Greek authors and scholars had access to substantial library resources.

Moreover, there were now schools in the Greek cities, and although the method of instruction was strictly lecture, the teachers must have had some collection of written sources to aid their excellent memories. Plato (427-348 B.C.), the great philosopher and teacher of Aristotle, must have had a private library of considerable size, although we have little direct evidence to prove it. Plato was widely traveled and well-read, and he must have had access to many volumes for his education, writings, and lectures. One source mentions his purchase of books from one Philolaus of Tarentum, and another has him buying books from the Greek colony of Syracuse in Sicily. What happened to these books after Plato's death is unknown, although one writer notes that Aristotle purchased some of them from his nephew, Speusippus. Aristotle went on to collect one of the largest private libraries of ancient times. The two Greek historians, Thucydides and Herodotus, must have had many written sources from which to compile their works, and the latter particularly mentions written records as one of the legitimate tools of the historian.

Aristotle (384-321 B.C.) founded a school of philosophy or lyceum known as the Peripatetic school. He taught his followers, or pupils, while walking about in the grove of the hero Lycus. His library of several hundred volumes was acquired by purchase and gifts from his many followers, and was apparently available for use to his pupils and friends. Upon his death, this library was inherited by Aristotle's teaching successor, Theophrastus of Lesbos. Theophrastus formalized the lyceum and built it into a school or university that was to survive for several centuries. With lecture rooms, quarters for teachers, and a colonnade for walking lectures, Theophrastus' school was a model for others to come throughout the Mediterranean world. Theophrastus in turn enlarged the library and later bequeathed it to his nephew Neleus. Neleus was not a successful teacher, and in his later years withdrew from the school, taking his library with him to Scepsis in Asia Minor. His descendants, apparently unlettered but aware of the value of the books, saved them by burying them, according to the geographer Strabo, to keep them out of the hands of the Attalid kings of Pergamum who were building up their famous library. Finally, about 100 B.C., the mildewed and worm-eaten remnants of Aristotle's library were sold to Apellicon of Teos, a minor Athenian military leader and book collector. Apellicon tried to restore the damaged volumes but only succeeded in damaging them further when he made incorrect "corrections" for missing fragments of pages and otherwise edited the works. After his death, Athens was captured by the Roman general Sulla, who carried the library off to Rome, where it eventually became a part of Tyrannion's library. Another account relates that Ptolemy II (285-246 B.C.) acquired Aristotle's library directly from Neleus and brought it to Egypt to become a part of the great Alexandrian library. It is possible that both stories are partially correct, and it is quite probable that copies at least of Aristotle's library reached Alexandria eventually. In any event, Aristotle's library goes down in history not only as one of the greatest ancient private libraries but also as an example of an early academic library. Its complex wanderings, many trials, and eventual preservation, provide us with some insight into the remarkable ways in which books were transmitted from one generation to another.

The actual size and content of Aristotle's library are unknown. It is reasonable to suppose that it contained many of the sources he used in his own writings, and they alone would make up a sizable collection. Also, it contained most if not all of his own writings, estimated to have been at least 400 rolls. Since it is known that Aristotle's friends and followers often sent him botanical and geological specimens from their travels outside Greece, it is likely that they sent him manuscripts as well, either copies of their own writings or writings of others in which they knew he would be interested. His library, in short, was large for its time and as well-rounded in subject fields as his own multifaceted writings.

A library founded at Heraclea in Bithynia about 364

B.C. was reported to have been opened to the public by the ruler Clearchus. The Aegean islands, including Cos, Rhodes, and Cnidos, were known for their "public" libraries. Excavations on Cos revealed an inscription on the wall of a library enumerating donors of money and books. Frequent mentions of "100 drachmas and 100 books" indicate fairly wealthy donors. Apparently, "drives" for donations were in practice even in the classical era. Portions of a similar inscription have been found on the island of Rhodes, indicating a similar practice there. Still another inscription from Rhodes, and possibly from the same library, seems to be a catalog of a small library or a list of books in a gift collection. Other pre-Alexandrian libraries are mentioned as having existed at Corinth, Delphi, and Patrae in Greece, at Ephesus, Smyrna, Soli, Mylasa, and Halicarnassus in Asia Minor, and at Syracuse in Sicily.

An interesting story is told of the formation of a second "public" library in Athens in the 4th century B.C. This collection came about because of the popularity of the plays of Aeschylus, Sophocles, and Euripides. When some groups of players began performing the plays of these authors with additions and corrections to the accepted texts, other playgoers objected. In order to make sure that only authentic versions of the plays were produced, official copies were deposited in a public collection. These could not be removed, but anyone could read and copy them. Thus we witness a faint glimmer of modern public library service; that is, the desire to provide people with ready access to the day's intelligence so that they can develop informed opinions on matters of public interest.

The most famous Greek library of all, indeed the most famous of all antiquity, was not in Greece, but in Egypt. When Alexander the Great had conquered most of the known world during his brief reign (336-323 B.C.), the glory of Greece was spread far from the borders of that land itself. Alexander's empire broke up after his death, but his various lieutenants and successors imposed Hellenism, or classical Greek culture, on much of the Mediterranean world. In lower Egypt, after 305 B.C., a series of rulers known as the Ptolemies created a nation that was strongly Greek in population and culture. Ptolemy I (Soter), a tough-minded soldier-king, characterized by an unusual sympathy for the life of the mind, attracted scholars and scientists from all over the Greek world with his interest in learning.

One of the scholars who was attracted to Alexandria was Demetrius of Phalerum, who was driven from Athens in 307 B.C., and turned up about 297 at the court of Ptolemy, where he soon became a court favorite. Being familiar with the school of Aristotle, then headed by Theophrastus in Athens, Demetrius may have suggested to Ptolemy the establishment of a school or "museum" with a well-stocked library to add to the glory of his regime and make his name remembered for generations to come. The term "museum" was used to indicate a "house of the muses," or of the arts and sciences. Demetrius became the guiding hand of the Museum established in the Brucheion or palace arena of Alexandria, which in time became something of a loosely organized "college" of scholars and students. In the group of buildings making up the Museum were lecture halls, study rooms, dining rooms, cloisters, gardens, and an astronomical observatory, all connected by covered walks or porticoes, and in the midst of the palace grounds were statuary and pools. The whole was dedicated to the gods of learning, and the director was technically a priest but usually a scholar as well. The paid scholars who made up the staff of the Museum included mathematicians, astronomers, geographers, and physicians, as well as historians, poets, writers, and editors.

One of the major functions of the scholars seems to have been that of revising, collating and editing the works of earlier writers, beginning with Homer. In fact, the division of Homer's works into individual "books" is thought to have taken place here, with each "book" being an appropriate length to fill one roll. Most of the scholars were Greeks, but some were natives of other countries, particularly those who could translate from their languages into Greek. Manethos, an Egyptian, was employed to translate Egyptian works and to compile a chronology of Egyptian history. Also, according to tradition, seventy Hebrew scholars were engaged to translate the Old Testament into Greek (the Septuagint) at the Alexandrian Library. Research, editing, and experimentation rather than teaching seem to have been the functions of most of the scholars, but the presence of lecture halls and students indicates an atmosphere of learning.

Demetrius apparently directed the organization of the Museum Library and supervised its early acquisitions. Upon the accession of Ptolemy II (Philadelphus), however, he lost favor and was sent into exile. Philadelphus was interested in the Library also, and other scholars took up where Demetrius had left off, with Zenodotus of Ephesus serving as librarian during a period of particularly rapid growth. Philadelphus founded a second library at the Serapeum or Temple of Serapis in the Egyptian section of Alexandria. This smaller collection, sometimes called the Daughter library, never became as large as the Brucheion library, but it was apparently more of a public collection, used by ordinary students and citizens.

To enlarge the Museum Library, copies of all known books in the city of Alexandria were added to the collection, and since Alexandria was then the largest city in the world, this must have been a large number. In addition, agents were sent to all parts of the known world in an effort to acquire other texts. Ships arriving in the harbor of Alexandria were forced to lend any books they might have aboard to be copied. Sometimes deposits were left for borrowed books until they could be copied and returned, but according to some stories the deposits were sometimes forefeited and the originals never returned.

An important feature of the history of the Alexandrian Library is the list of outstanding figures who served it as librarians, or who were at least connected with it as scholars. There is some uncertainty as to which of the scholars known to have been associated with the Library were actually librarians, but the following names are worth considering, along with their estimated dates of activities with the Library:

Demetrius of Phalerum	290-282 B.C.
Zenodotus of Ephesus	282-260 B.C.
Callimachus of Cyrene	260-240 B.C.
Apollonius of Rhodes	240-230 B.C.
Eratosthenes of Cyrene	230-196 B.C.
Aristophanes of Byzantium	196-185 B.C.
Apollonius the Eidograph	180-160 B.C.
Aristarchus of Samothrace	160-146 B.C.
Onesander of Cyprus	100- 89 B.C.
Chaeremon of Alexandria	50- 70 A.D.
Dionysius, son of Glaucus	100-120 A.D.
Caius Julius Vasinus	120-130 A.D.

It is not known if all these men were "head librarians," but their names are associated with the Library during the periods indicated. Callimachus, in particular, was quite possibly only a scholar connected with the Library, or perhaps an assistant librarian. Whatever their capacity, surely few libraries in western history could boast such a distinguished list of scholars in residence. Callimachus and Apollonius of Rhodes were poets, and Zenodotus, Aristophanes, and Aristarchus were critics, editors, and Homeric authorities. Eratosthenes was a geographer and astronomer who taught that the earth was a sphere and computed its circumference.

Callimachus was possibly the most important, at least from the point of view of library history, since he compiled a catalog of the famous Library. At any rate, to him is ascribed a work, of which only a few fragments remain, entitled "Tablets of those who were outstanding in every phase of culture, and their writings." This work itself is thought to have been made up of 120 rolls, but whether it was a catalog of the library or merely an extended bio-bibliography is uncertain. Certainly it was something more than a mere bibliography, since the extant fragments give something of each author's life, his works, and even the number of lines of text in each work. Callimachus' catalog is usually called the Pinakes, from the word meaning tablets. Callimachus is also credited with devising the system of dividing longer words into "books" or parts in order to make the rolls more even in size and more easily handled and stored. That he was a classifier as well as a cataloger can be inferred from his division of his Pinakes into eight major subject categories: Oratory, History, Laws, Philosophy, Medicine, Lyric Poetry, Tragedy, and Miscellany. Callimachus was unable to complete the gigantic task which he had begun, and his bibliographical work was carried on by succeeding librarians, particularly Zenodotus and Eratosthenes. Recent scholarship demonstrates that Callimachus was involved in a number of significant bibliographical projects in addition to his famous Pinakes, and that he now seems to merit fully the title of "father of bibliography."

The Alexandrian Library flourished for several hundred years, and for at least 200 years it was of tremendous importance in the cultural development of the Hellenic world. It drew scholars from great distances and from almost all fields of knowledge. Thousands upon thousands of rolls were bought, copied, stolen, and compiled for its shelves until it contained, according to some estimates, over 700,000 rolls. It must be pointed out that this figure may well be an exaggerated estimate, that many works were present in several editions or copies, and that one roll was probably only about one-tenth of an average modern book. With all these factors considered, the Alexandrian Library was still a tremendous collection and it must have contained most, if not all, of the extant literature of the period. In addition to the volumes in the larger Museum Library, the smaller collection in the Serapeum was reported to contain over 40,000 rolls.

Some authorities think that the Alexandrian Library may have had a stultifying effect on Hellenic literature, that the desire of the scholar-librarians to collect and preserve the record of Greek civilization consumed their energies to such an extent that nothing remained to sustain creative scholarship and writing. Once the literature had been gathered, then scholarship took the form of editing, compiling, and criticizing, rather than originating or composing new literature. Indeed, many compilations came out of the Library. A philologist named Didymus is supposed to have compiled 3,500 rolls of commentaries on famous works of literature in the Library. Athenaeus, in the 2nd century A.D., said he studied 1,500 volumes in the Library at Alexandria in order to compile his <u>Deipnosophistae</u> in fifteen volumes.

Unfortunately, the flowering of Alexandria as a cultural center was not to last forever. After several Ptolemies who were friends to literature and learning--as well as good businessmen who provided funds for the Museum--Ptolemy VIII (Cacergetes) came to the throne. Having been forced to leave Alexandria by his enemies, he returned in the course of a civil war (88-89 B.C.) and burned much of the city. The students and fellows of the Museum were at least temporarily scattered, and Athenaeus reports that "great numbers of grammarians, philosophers, geographers, and physicians [were roaming] the entire world, forced to earn their living by teaching." Though never reaching their former greatness, the Museum and its library were reconstituted and survived for several hundred years longer.

After this period, the history of the Alexandrian libraries becomes even more uncertain. Wars and civil strife continued to plague Egypt, and conquerors came from all directions. To bring the story of the Library to its conclusion, it is necessary to go beyond the Hellenic era and several centuries into Roman domination. In 47 B.C., when Julius Caesar was conquering Egypt, the Library is thought to have been at least partially destroyed. This story is based on the translation of a passage from the historian Dio Cassius concerning a fire that spread from burning ships to nearby wharves. Possibly some stored volumes in warehouses were burned, but it is doubtful that the fire extended into the Museum area. However, the story claims that Mark

Antony gave Cleopatra some 200,000 rolls taken from the library at Pergamum to replace those burned by Caesar. The Library undoubtedly became less influential after the beginning of the Christian era, and at least some volumes were taken to Rome to replenish libraries there. As mentioned above, Athenaeus used the Library in the 2nd century A.D., and the Emperor Hadrian visited it during his reign (117-138 A.D.). In 273 A.D., the Roman Emperor Aurelian, conquering Egypt once again, burned much of Alexandria, including the Brucheion area, but it is possible that a library and museum may have been rebuilt on a smaller scale. The Serapeum is thought to have survived until 391 A.D., when it was destroyed by the Christian Bishop Theophilus because of its presence in the pagan Temple of Serapis. Finally, anything left of a major library is supposed to have been destroyed by the Moslem conqueror Omar or his armies in 645 A.D. According to one account the papyrus and vellum rolls were used as fuel to provide hot water for the soldiers' baths. If a library was burned at this time, it was more probably a Christian library established in a church or monastery on the original site of the Serapeum.

Turning from Egypt to other areas under Greek influence during the post-Alexandrian epoch, there are several other libraries of note. In fact, as Alexander marched east to India, he made use of the libraries and archives of the countries he conquered, by ordering the administrators he left there to study the laws and records for the best means of governing the new satellites. Antiochus the Great, the Seleucid king, established a library at Antioch on Orontes about 200 B.C., and opened it to scholars. Antigonus Gonatus, king of Macedonia, founded a library at Pella about 250 B.C. Among all the libraries established by Alexander's successors, however, that at Pergamum was second only to Alexandria. Attalus I, King of Pergamum, is probably responsible for the beginning of a library in his city, but it was his son, Eumenes II (197-159 B.C.), who brought it to its highest point. Eumenes strove to match the library at Alexandria and was even accused of trying to tempt one of its librarians, Aristophanes of Byzantium, to come to Pergamum from Egypt. This library was also something of a school, or group of scholars, similar to that at Alexandria, and the grammarian, Crates of Malus, headed it for a while under Eumenes II. He was probably responsible for the early growth of the library, but Athenodorus of Tarsus was also its head for a while, and he was invited by the Roman Cato the Elder to visit Rome and advise on the construction of libraries there.

Related to the library at Pergamum is the story of the origin of parchment. The Egyptians are supposed to have cut off the supply of papyrus being sent to Pergamum, to prevent its library from growing as large as that in Alexandria. The librarians at Pergamum then developed a new writing material, parchment (from the Latin Pergamene), as a substitute for papyrus. This is probably an exaggerated tradition, since tanned and cured skins were used for writing in Egypt and Palestine for hundreds of years before Pergamum existed. It is probable, however, that Pergamum made greater use of parchment or even developed a finer, whiter type of parchment that became famous throughout the Mediterranean world and inspired the story. It is also most probable that the great majority of the rolls in the library at Pergamum were of papyrus.

Attalus II (159-138 B.C.) continued to develop the library at Pergamum, which flourished for some time, but after his death it declined and in 133 B.C. Pergamum fell to the Romans. The library suffered some loss to the captors, but it must have remained of considerable size if we are to believe the story of Antony seizing 200,000 rolls from it in 43 B.C. as a gift for Cleopatra. The Emperor Augustus may have returned part or all of the gift to Pergamum, for a library survived there for several hundred years. According to a Russian tradition, Moslem conquerors carried some of the Pergamum manuscripts to Bursa in Asia Minor, where Tamerlane found them in 1402. He in turn carried these remnants of a classical library to Samarkand in Central Asia where they remained until at least as late as the 17th century, but all records of them are lost after that.

The ruins of the Temple of Athena in Pergamum have been excavated, and from them we have our best example of a Hellenic library. The plan of the library may have been adopted from that of Aristotle's in Athens, with the library rooms located off a colonnade, in this case the north colonnade of the Temple. The largest library room, some forty-five by fifty-five feet in area, had a narrow platform about three feet high around three sides. Behind the platform the walls had holes that could have held shelf brackets, or served to anchor book cases. Assuming pigeonholes for rolls located on three walls, this room couldn't have held much more than 17,000 rolls, indicating that other rooms must have been used for library purposes at the time of its largest size. A bench kept the readers away from the rolls, and may have provided a place where they could be unrolled for examination. In the middle of one end of this room was the statue of the Greek goddess, Athena, to whom this temple was dedicated. Crates probably compiled a catalog of the Pergamum library, and he also may have carried its plans to Rome where libraries along similar lines were later established. Crates was in Rome as a member of the Senate about 160 B.C., and the Porticus Metelli, built about that time, was used as a model for temple libraries constructed under the Emperor Augustus.

In Greece proper, as distinguished from the Hellenic world resulting from Alexander's conquests, by the end of the 3rd century B.C. libraries were common in all parts of the peninsula. After Alexander, Greece tended to become a quiet political area as his successors built empires elsewhere, and the Romans gradually conquered the Mediterranean world. Instead of the center of an empire, Athens became and remained for several hundred years an educational center, famed for its scholars and schools. Public libraries became common not only in the larger towns and cities, but also in the smaller ones and in the inland areas. Apparently there was more than one in Athens, in addition to academic and private libraries. Polybius says that there were so many libraries in Athens that one scholar, Timaeus of Sicily, spent fifty years doing historical research in them. Polybius also reported that research could be carried on by any citizen in any one of Greece's major cities. Among academic libraries were those of the secondary schools, the general colleges or universities, and the special schools of philosophy and medicine. There are records of one secondary school, the Ptolemaion in Athens, where the students presented one hundred books annually to the school library as a graduation gift. On the university level, the institution sometimes termed the University of Athens was in operation about 300 B.C. and continued until after 500 A.D. Little is known of its library, but because of the scholars associated with it one can assume a notable collection. Such academic libraries must have been fairly common in all the cities of the Hellenic world, since fragments of textbooks and lesson sheets have been found in Egypt, on the island of Rhodes, and elsewhere.

Private libraries also became common among the wealthier Greeks. Vitruvius, a 1st-century Roman writer on architecture, says it was always considered correct to have the library rooms of a mansion on the east side in order to have the best light for reading. Book collectors, of whom Appellicon of Teos has already been mentioned, became common and books themselves were plentiful. More than a thousand authors are known to have written during the classical period of Greek literature and the collection of Greek writers alone would have been a major occupation for a wealthy bibliophile. In addition to scholars and wealthy collectors, many political leaders amassed fair-sized collections of books, as evidenced by the Macedonian King Perseus whose library was captured by the Romans in 187 B.C. and carried to Rome as spoils of war.

In addition to public and private libraries there were many specialized collections in ancient Greece. The city of Athens had its official archives, kept in the Metroon, or Temple of the Mother of the Gods, and other cities quite probably had similar collections. Near Epidaurus was one of the great medical schools, the Asklepieion, which flourished from about 500 B.C. to later than 100 A.D. It was a combined school and temple, with many buildings, accommodations for teachers, students, officials and visitors, ceremonial halls, baths, and a library. The library was dedicated to Apollo Maleates, and to Asklepios, the God of healing. Other medical schools are known to have existed at Cos, Cnidos, Pergamum, Rhodes, Cyrene, and Alexandria, and each would have required a considerable medical library. According to one tradition, the library on Cnidos was burned at the order of Hippocrates because its students refused to follow his teachings. Special schools of philosophy, such as the Sophists, the Stoics, and the Epicureans, each had collections of their favorite writers. The works of Epicurus alone consisted of approximately 400 rolls. As late as 150 A.D. there were still four major schools of philosophy in Athens.

Physically, the typical library in classical Greece was usually associated with a school or temple, with special rooms off colonnaded approaches to the temple itself. Inside the library rooms, the rolls were kept in pigeonholes or on shelves on the walls. Individual rolls, especially the more valuable ones, were wrapped in cloth or some other protective covering, and an identifying tag was attached. The writing material was largely papyrus, although parchment was coming into wider use after 200 B.C. Librarians during this period were usually scholars, often outstanding ones, but it is possible that some of the names associated with great libraries were administrators or advisers rather than librarians. Be that as it may, the librarian and the library were important in Hellenic society, playing a major part in creating and preserving the culture of that era.

In studying the history of libraries it is worthwhile to ask at this point: Why do we know so little about Greek libraries when such a relatively large amount of classic Greek literature has been preserved? It is estimated that perhaps ten percent of the major Greek classical writings have survived. If libraries were common, why did so few of the writers, historians, and compilers mention them? Why do we have only fragmentary, incidental references to libraries in all the surviving pages of Greek literature? There are two possible answers. First, much that was written about libraries may have been lost. Particularly, local history and religious history, two fields in which libraries might have been mentioned, are subjects on which very little has been preserved. But the more probable answer is that libraries were considered so necessary to a well-ordered society that writers did not consider it of importance to mention them. They could well have thought that libraries had always existed and would always exist. Athenaeus, for example, writing about the great library at Alexandria, said: "And concerning the number of books, the establishment of libraries, and the collection in the Hall of Muses, why need I even speak, since they are in all men's memories?"

If our facts about Greek library history are few, the results in the preservation of Greek literature speak for themselves. For the heritage of ancient Greece, with the exception of sculpture and architecture, has come down to us in the form of books preserved in Greek libraries. If western library history began with the Egyptians and Babylonians, it reached its first "golden age" in classical Greece.

Additional Readings

A large literature exists relating to Greek culture, much of which treats libraries at least in passing. One book of special use is H. Curtis Wright's The Oral Antecedents of Greek Librarianship (Provo, Utah: Brigham Young University Press, 1978). Wright's difficult and controversial book contains a detailed bibliography and an appendix and discusses in detail the Alexandrian Library and the recent literature on that pivotal institution. Other works of interest are:

Harvey, F. D. "Literacy in the Athenian Democracy," Revue des Etudes Grècques 79 (1966): 585-635.

Johnson, Elmer D. "Ancient Libraries as Seen in the Greek and Roman Classics," Radford Review 23 (1969): 73-92.

Parsons, Edward Alexander. The Alexandrian Library: Glory of the Hellenic World (Amsterdam: The Elsevier Press, 1952).

Pfeiffer, Rudolf. History of Classical Scholarship from the Beginnings to the End of the Hellenistic Age (Oxford: Clarendon Press, 1968).

Reynolds, L. D. and N. G. Wilson. Scribes and Scholars: A Guide to the Transmission of Greek and Latin Literature (Oxford: Oxford University Press, 1968).

Turner, E. G. Greek Papyri: An Introduction (Princeton, N.J.: Princeton University Press, 1968).

Witty, F. J. "Reference Books of Antiquity," Journal of Library History 9 (1974): 101-19.

Chapter 5

ROMAN LIBRARIES

The libraries of ancient Rome were directly inherited from those of Greece, in types, organization, and contents. In fact, many of the actual manuscripts from the Greek libraries found their way into Roman collections. This cultural inheritance was a part of the general succession of the Roman world over that of classical Greece. From about 200 B.C., the Roman Republic gradually spread its military and political influence eastward and southward across the Mediterranean and westward and northward into Europe until by the beginning of the Roman Empire, about 30 B.C., the Roman world extended from Asia Minor to England. The conquering Roman legions greatly affected the cultures they overran, but they in turn were influenced by the material effects and cultures of those they conquered. Sculptures and manuscripts, architectural plans, and educated slaves were carried back to Rome, along with more immediately valuable gold and jewels. Thus it was that Rome's first major libraries were acquired as spoils of war from Greece and Asia Minor.

The earliest "libraries" of Rome were collections of historical records and laws, such as the *Annales Pontificum* that appear to have been brought together in eighty volumes about 120 B.C. These were strictly annals, brief accounts of major happenings in the Republic, and were kept in the official residence of the *Pontifex Maximus*, or chief priest. Even earlier than this, according to legend, the Twelve Tablets of Roman law were engraved on bronze and exhibited to the public about 450 B.C. Another early collection of public records was the *Libri Magistratum*, or Books of the Magistrates, recording their names and official actions over a long period of time. Some of these were recorded on linen, known as the *libri lintei*, and were preserved in the Temple of Moneta, the goddess of memory, on Capitol Hill. Just as in Egypt and Babylonia, the early Roman temples had their schools for priests and probably had collections of books as well as copies of the formal religious works kept in the temple sanctuary. There were also a few private libraries in the 2nd century B.C., but there is little precise information about them.

The first notable Roman library of which we have recorded information was that of Paulus Aemilius. This Roman general, who was also a scholar, defeated King Perseus of Macedonia in 168 B.C. While his victorious soldiers ransacked the palace for everything of value, Aemilius himself claimed only the library, saying that he preferred it to gold for the benefit of his sons. A few years later, Crates of Mallos, then librarian at Pergamum, came to Rome as an envoy to the Roman Senate. His public lectures and private discussions with citizens of Rome greatly stimulated their interest in Greek literature and civilization, and the Hellenization of Rome is frequently dated from his appearance in that city.

After Aemilius, it became common for the Roman conquerors to bring home books as spoils of war. One particularly notable collection was that acquired by Cornelius Sulla, the Roman general who took Athens in 86 B.C. and seized the library of Apellicon of Teos. This is the private collection that contained at least part of Aristotle's library. Tyrannion served as librarian for Sulla's collection after he carried it to Rome, and Andronicus of Rhodes is supposed to have studied Aristotle's works there. Apparently Sulla opened the library to his scholarly friends and became something of a literary lion in his later years. He passed the books on to his son, Faustus, in whose home Cicero saw the library in 55 B.C., but its later history is unknown. Lucius Lucullus, who had earlier fought under Sulla, became a conqueror in turn and carried the Roman banner deep into Armenia. He returned from his conquests with great quantities of books, including the library of the King of Pontus, and set them up in his private library in Rome. After losing political favor, Lucullus became a dilettante, opening his library and gardens to visiting friends and scholars. Scipio Aemilianus, conquering Carthage in 146 B.C., also found libraries to be taken, but since they were largely in unknown languages, he took only a few books on agriculture and allowed the remainder to be destroyed.

By 50 B.C. private libraries were becoming common among the wealthy families in Rome, but the only public collections were the temple and government archives. Julius Caesar planned to establish a public library to equal or surpass the one at Alexandria, and to this end he appointed Terentius Varro (116-27 B.C.), a noted scholar and book collector, to gather together copies of the best-known literature for a Roman public library. Unfortunately, Caesar was assassinated (44 B.C.) before his library plans could be accomplished. Instead the first public library in Rome, like so many of the private collections, came into being as the result of spoils of war. G. Asinius Pollio, who had amassed a fortune in his conquest of Dalmatia, used his wealth to consolidate several collections already in Rome possibly including those of Varro and Sulla, to form a library in the Temple of Liberty (Atrium Libertatis) on the Aventine Hill. Public archives had already been housed there, but Pollio reorganized the collection, added the libraries he had acquired, and opened the whole to the public about 37 B.C., making it the first-known public library in Rome.

Beginning with Augustus, the Roman emperors took over the task of building libraries in Rome. Actually, Augustus was responsible for two public libraries. The first, in the Temple of Apollo, was begun in 36 B.C., and dedicated in 28 B.C. It was divided into two separate collections, one Greek and one Latin. Pompeius Macer was the first librarian, and Julius Hyginus, a noted grammarian, also served in that capacity. Later enlarged by the Emperors Tiberius and Caligula, this library on the Palatine Hill was one of the two major libraries in Rome for several hundred years. It was damaged at least twice by fires but survived well into the 4th century. The second Augustan library was in the Porticus Octaviae, a magnificent structure built in honor of Octavia, the Emperor's sister. Although the building was constructed by orders of Augustus, it is thought that the library was founded by Octavia in memory of her son, Marcellus, who died in 23 B.C. Caius Melissus was the first librarian for this collection, housed in chambers over a promenade. Although damaged by fire in the reign of Titus about 80 A.D., the Octavian Library probably survived into the 2nd century.

The successors of Augustus maintained the tradition of founding libraries. Tiberius established one in his palace on the Palatine Hill about 20 A.D., and his collection remained in existence into the 3rd century. Tiberius is also credited with establishing a library in the Temple of Augustus, which was dedicated in 36 A.D. Since this temple also had a statue of Apollo, there may be some confusion with the Temple of Apollo established by Augustus, or with Tiberius' own palace library. The Emperor Vespasian established another public library about 75 A.D., decorating it with spoils captured in Jerusalem. Josephus, the Jewish historian, says that copies of the Books of Moses were deposited there. This library was damaged by fire about 190 A.D., later restored, and survived into the 4th century. The Emperor Domitian (81-96 A.D.) restored the libraries and other public buildings damaged in the fires of Nero's reign, and he is credited with establishing a public library on the Capitoline Hill, for which Hadrian is also given credit; little else is known about it.

Probably the greatest of the Roman libraries was the Ulpian Library, founded by the Emperor Trajan in 114 A.D. in his Forum. This collection may have been based on the 30,000-volume private library of Epaphrodites of Cheronea and, like other Roman libraries, it was divided into Greek and Latin sections. Early in the 4th century, this library was moved to the Baths of Diocletian. There was a theater and lecture room along with the Baths, so it was more of a gentlemen's club than a public bath. This move was apparently only temporary, possibly while the Forum was being repaired, since the library is reported to have been returned at a later date. Trajan's library was still in existence in 455 A.D. when a bust of Sidonius Apollinarius was placed there by the Emperor Avitus. The custom of founding public libraries continued while Rome's power waxed and waned, and there were reported to be no fewer than twenty-eight or twenty-nine located in the city before the 4th century. If so, we know little or nothing of twenty or more of them. Some may have been in other public baths; one may have been in the Temple of Esculapius or in a school of medicine associated with it; others may have been Christian collections begun as private libraries and opened to congregations in the 4th century, or large private collections charitably opened to the public.

The Emperor Hadrian (76-138 A.D.) is also noted for his library interests. At his palatial residence outside Rome at Tibur (Tivoli), he maintained a private library of great size and value modeled on a Greek library with covered walls or colonnades leading off from the library rooms. Hadrian also constructed a magnificent library in Athens, the remains of which have been excavated. It was a square enclosed by a colonnade of 120 columns, with spacious rooms of alabaster and gold, filled with paintings and statuary. About its book contents we know little, but we do know that in addition to the library there were rooms for reading and for lectures and there was a central area from which books may have been delivered to readers in a proper "circulation desk" atmosphere. Hadrian is also credited with having revived or established libraries at Ephesus and Pergamum, and with founding an Athenaeum in Rome which probably included a library.

The public libraries were by no means the only sources of literature available to the wealthier Romans, since private libraries were common for several hundred years at the height of the Roman era. That most of the Roman writers had access to well-stocked libraries is apparent from their writings, but it is often verified by references in their correspondence and elsewhere. Also, there is evidence that other Romans, including physicians and lawyers, collected books and built up sizable libraries.

The writings of Cicero frequently mention his library and those of his friends. About 56 B.C. he wrote to his friend Atticus:

> Mind you don't promise your library to anybody, however keen a collector you may find for it, for I am hoarding up all my little savings to get it as a resource for my old age. If I succeed I shall be richer than Crassus and look down on any man's manors and meadows.

Cicero called his library "the soul" of his house. At one time he employed Tyrannion as librarian, praising him highly for the work done in arranging the books and in attaching title slips to them.

Titus Pomponius Atticus was a book collector in his own right, as well as a prominent book dealer who counted Cicero and other noted Roman literary figures among his customers. Atticus was also something of a book publisher in that his servants made numerous copies of the works of popular authors and presented them for sale. Atticus' own library was reputed to contain some 20,000 rolls, but was dwarfed, some two centuries later, by that of the writer Q. Sammonicus Serenius, who amassed over 60,000 volumes.

The library of Sammonicus went eventually to the Emperor Gordian, who may have opened it as a public library.

Other private libraries must have been common, since Seneca (d. 65 A.D.) wrote that they had become as necessary in the homes of the wealthy as baths with hot and cold water. He deplored the buying of books by those who were not scholars, and asked:

> What is the use of having countless books and libraries, whose titles their owners can scarcely read through in a whole lifetime? ... It is better to surrender yourself to a few authors than to wander through many.

A later author, Lucian, wrote an essay on "The Ignorant Book Collector," and asked:

> For what expectation do you base upon your books that you are always unrolling them and rolling them up, gluing them, trimming them, smearing them with saffron and oil of cedar, putting slip covers on them, and fitting them with knobs, just as if you were going to derive some profit from them?

Even Petronius in one of his satires introduces a character, Trimalchio, who boasts of his Greek and Latin library but displays ignorance of its contents. While the Roman villa libraries were frequently the subjects of scorn in their own time, modern scholars credit them with being the repositories of much of the classic Roman literature which survived the fall of the Empire.

Rome was by no means the only city in the Empire to be graced with one or more libraries. In fact, while early Rome benefited enormously from the book-collecting ways of her conquering generals, Rome in the Imperial and Christian eras developed a substantial publishing and book trade of her own, becoming the locus of a national book distribution system. Moreover, philanthropists from Rome provided the means to establish libraries in many cities and towns. Augustus, having set the example by founding libraries in Rome, encouraged wealthy citizens to endow temples, libraries, and schools throughout the provinces.

The later era of the Roman Empire saw a decline of the great libraries of the ancient world, but it also saw the beginnings of Christian libraries. The early Christians felt the need to preserve and disseminate their scriptural literature and hence made good use of books and libraries. The sayings of Jesus, the letters of Paul, and the early gospels were kept by each congregation and guarded zealously at or near the altar of each church. Paul himself refers, in 2 Timothy 4:13, to his own private library and requests that books from it be brought to him. Bishop Alexander founded a Christian library in Jerusalem before 250 A.D., and about the same time Origen (ca. 182-251 A.D.) was establishing his theological school and library at Caesarea. At Alexandria in Egypt there was a Christian library as early as 175 A.D. That city was the capital of Christian scholarship in the 3rd century, and Clement of Alexandria, who died about 215, quoted from 348 authors in his works, indicating access to a fairly sizable library. Origen had been a pupil of Clement, and he in turn passed on his books to a pupil, Pamphilus, who studied and taught at Caesarea for many years. In 303 the Emperor Diocletian made a concerted effort to destroy all Christian libraries, and many perished, but the one at Caesarea survived. Eusebius, writing in 330, says that he used this library in writing his history of the Christian Church. Jerome used it in the 4th century also, and Euthalius in the 5th; in fact, it may well have survived until the Persians captured Palestine in 614, when all Christian records were destroyed.

With the recognition of Christianity by the Roman Emperor Constantine (ca. 288-337), the situation in the Christian churches improved considerably, and the remainder of the 4th century saw the rapid spread of Christian churches and the establishment of many Christian libraries. Eusebius (265-340 A.D.), the church historian, studied and worked in Pamphilus' library at Caesarea and after the latter's death built it into a learned collection of over 20,000 volumes. Jerome, born in Dalmatia, studied in Rome and became a secretary to Pope Damasus. He edited the Latin Vulgate Bible, and wrote many commentaries on the scriptures, becoming one of the greatest Christian scholars of all times. In his later years he retired to head a monastery in Bethlehem and carried with him a large personal library. In a letter written in 397, Jerome described his library and noted that it contained much history and philosophy as well as theology. George, Bishop of Alexandria, built up a library that was also both secular and religious. When he was murdered in 361 by an anti-Christian mob, the Emperor Julian secured his library and placed it in a temple in Antioch. Unfortunately it was burned a few years later, according to tradition, on the orders of Emperor Jovian to please a whim of his wife.

In the early Christian churches, the small collection of scriptures and related books was kept to the left. The early Christians were among the first to use the parchment codex instead of the papyrus roll as a book form. This was probably because the parchment was more durable and the codex form more suitable for frequent consultation than the more cumbrous roll. For instance, when the papyrus rolls that made up the library of Pamphilus in Caesarea became worn in the early 4th century, they were recopied onto parchment codices. This was accomplished over a number of years by two dedicated priests, Acacius and Euzoius.

Turning from consideration of specific libraries and types of libraries, it will be worthwhile to look briefly at the physical nature of the Roman library, both public and private. As we have seen, most of the publicly owned libraries were connected with temples even though they contained public archives and general literature as well as religious works. The temple libraries, in whatever part of the Empire, usually followed the same general plan, being adjacent to or over a colonnade leading to the main structure of the temple. There were often two divisions of the library, Greek and Latin, with sometimes a third division for archives. There were rooms for the storage of books and also rooms for reading, although the colonnades lent themselves to reading or discussing books while walking. Some of the libraries were associated with meeting rooms where public readings of an author's works could be given. Quite often there was a statue connected with the library, as for example that of a bronze Apollo, some fifty feet high, in the Temple of Apollo in Rome. On the walls above the books were paintings, semi-reliefs, or sculptures of famous writers. The organization, format, and handling of the rolls were similar to that in the Greek libraries, but the Romans added the armarium or chest for keeping more valuable rolls. Then, as the codex replaced the roll, the shelf replaced the pigeon-hole, but the armarium continued to be generally used for storing books well down into the Middle Ages.

Although books in the Roman public libraries did not circulate outside the building as a general rule, it is apparent from several classical references that influential people could on occasion borrow them for home use. Marcus Aurelius, for example, writing to his friend Fronto about 145

A.D., tells him that there is no need for him to send to the libraries of Apollo for certain volumes since he, Aurelius, already has them out. Instead he suggests that Fronto try Tiberius' library, although he may have to bribe the librarian there in order to be permitted to take them. Owners of private libraries were also known to lend their volumes to their friends, and there are references to such loans in the letters of both Cicero and Pliny. That the circulation of books was a problem can be seen from the rules of an Athenian library of about 100 A.D., found on an excavated wall:

> No book shall be taken out, since we have sworn an oath to that effect. It will be open from the first hour until the sixth.

Libraries in private homes varied in physical accommodations according to the wealth of the owner and the size of the collection. A few rolls might be kept in a container of wood or lead, similar to a modern hatbox. A larger collection would be kept in its own armarium. As the collection became even larger, it would be kept in a special room or apartment with armaria, desks, and works of art. A typical library in a rich private home would have been about fifteen by twenty-three feet with several armaria in it. The single armarium would have been about three feet high by five feet wide, and a medallion above it would indicate the author whose works it contained, or perhaps a favorite author of the owner. Such a library room has been unearthed in Herculaneum.

The average Roman papyrus roll was about twenty to thirty feet long, and about nine to eleven inches high. The roll was usually wrapped in a linen cloth, particularly if it was treasured, and tied with a string. More valuable rolls might be kept in envelopes or jackets made of parchment or leather, sometimes dyed in bright colors. Considering the size of the roll and the dimensions of excavated Roman libraries, the average temple collection must have been about 20,000 to 40,000 rolls, unless others were stored elsewhere. The armaria themselves were divided into nests (*nida*) by both horizontal and vertical shelves for rolls, or by horizontal shelves only for codices. Sometimes the armaria were built into the walls, but usually they were separate, movable pieces of furniture. Pliny notes that he had an armarium built into the walls of his bedroom.

The early Roman librarian was often a highly educated

slave or prisoner of war from Greece or Asia Minor, like many early teachers and scholars. Later on in Roman history, the librarian was a native scholar, often an author as well. Still later, however, the position became more that of a civil servant. Titus Atticus (109-32 B.C.), scholar and friend of Cicero, noted that all his librarians were slaves. Tyrannion, librarian for Cicero, was captured by Lucullus on the Island of Rhodes about 72 B.C. and brought to Rome. He soon obtained his freedom and set himself up as a teacher of Greek. Later he became wealthy as a book publisher and seller, friend and confidant of both scholars and statesmen. He advised Cicero and Sulla on the building up of their collections and helped catalog Cicero's library. Terentius Varro served as librarian, or at least as book collector, for Julius Caesar. He was a man of great learning, a writer of history, satire, and poems. Andronicus of Rhodes, an Aristotelian scholar, is supposed to have cataloged the library of Sulla.

Under the Emperors, the several libraries in Rome seem to have been administered by a central library chief known as the _procurator bibliothecarum_. About 100 A.D. this post was held by Dionysius of Alexandria, a noted grammarian, who also served as secretary to the Emperor. Under Hadrian it was held by C. Julius Vesinus, a former tutor who later became administrator of the Museum in Alexandria. About 250 A.D. the position was held by Q. Vetturius Callistratus, according to an inscription discovered in Rome. Under this director of libraries, each library had its own librarian (_bibliothecarius_ or _magister_). Library staff members were numerous, many of them slaves and some of them women. Lesser library positions carried the titles of _librarius_, _vilicus_, and _antiquarius_, with probably other titles at different times and places. The _librarius_ seems to have been a worker of various duties, from cataloger to copyist, and from translator to clerical worker. The _vilicus_ was a general attendant, somewhere between custodial and clerical. The _antiquarius_ was the scholar-librarian, historian and paleographer. Generally speaking, the librarians of Rome did not equal in importance those of Alexandria or Pergamum in their more prosperous days. Instead, the administrative positions became political appointments or civil-service jobs, while the actual library work was done by well-educated but less important assistants. The work in the larger libraries became highly specialized with many types of work and varying degrees or ranks of service. Closely allied with the librarians were the booksellers, who often doubled as publishers in their production of multiple copies of popular texts. Many of them aided in the selection and acquisition of desired works for the libraries, particularly the private ones. Often the public libraries produced their own texts by copying others.

That the books within the Roman libraries were arranged according to general subjects is known, but just what those subject classifications were is uncertain. Certainly they were divided into Greek and Latin, and apparently all the works of a single author were kept together under his major subject. The works in the various schools of philosophy were separated, as were those of different religious groups. Catalogs of two types were known, and sometimes both were used. The first type was a sort of classified catalog, or shelf list, arranged just as the rolls themselves were stored. The other was a bibliographical catalog, arranged by author but giving titles or first lines, lengths of works, and sometimes biographical information about the author.

While the Romans did not invent censorship, it is obvious that they did control vigorously the kinds of reading material made available to the people. The Emperor Augustus was a builder of libraries, but he also controlled their contents. He ordered the works of Julius Caesar removed from the public libraries and did the same for the works of the poet Ovid. The latter was not only subjected to censorship but also banished to the Black Sea area for the later years of his life. The writings of the Christians were suppressed by most of the emperors before Constantine, and later, when Christian bishops came into power in certain areas, they in turn sometimes suppressed non-Christian writings. In doing so, they destroyed many works of classical authors now known to us only through excerpts or bibliographical notes in later writings. For example, while the Emperor Diocletian attempted to suppress all Christian libraries in 303, the Emperor Theodosius I in 391 tried to destroy all "heathen" libraries. Under his direction, the Temple of Serapis in Alexandria was reported to have been destroyed along with most if not all of its library. A Christian church replaced it with a small collection of Christian works. The Emperor Julian also tried to destroy Christian texts, but he founded libraries of classical works at Antioch and Constantinople. Justinian in 529 preserved Roman law and Christian theology but ordered classical works at the Academy in Athens confiscated, and forbade the teaching of Greek philosophy there. In the same century, Pope Gregory I is reported to have suppressed the works of Cicero and Livy, not because of their contents, but because young men were reading them when they should have been reading the Bible. Gregory is also accused of having ordered the burning of the Palatine Library in Rome, but this is generally discredited. Between the activities of the Christians and non-Christians in burning books, and the later censorship by the Moslems after the 7th century, many works of classical authors that might have otherwise survived, were lost forever.

The great libraries of the classical world were, one and all, destined to be destroyed. Some of them met their end in accidental fires or natural disasters, such as those of Rome and Herculaneum. Many more were destroyed in wars, internal conflicts, and barbarian raids. The northern hordes who swept down on Rome and Greece in the 5th and 6th centuries had little or no respect for learning, and books were just so much papyrus or parchment to them. Athens' last great library, that of the Academy, was destroyed in 529. Just when the last classical library in Rome disappeared is uncertain, but it is doubtful that more than one or two of them survived the 5th century, and none came through the sixth. Finally, it should be noted that a large number of Roman libraries simply decayed and disappeared as a result of neglect and disuse. Political disturbances, rulers uninterested in books and learning, economic disasters--all contributed to an atmosphere in which libraries were closed and books deteriorated.

Ammianus Marcellinus, writing about 378, reported that the libraries of Rome were even then like tombs, closed forever. This was possibly a premature judgment, for some of them are known to have been open after that, but in general he was right. The days when Rome's great libraries were popular were over. The great period of Roman literature and learning had passed; the classical era was gone, and the Dark Ages had begun. But in many corners of the western world the sparks of learning were still alive in the 6th century. The Eastern Empire was still alert and libraries were growing there, with many books flowing eastward from Rome. Also, on the western fringes, in Spain, France, and even England, private libraries were still being collected and used, and in Italy itself the monastic system that was to preserve learning throughout the Middle Ages was already beginning.

Additional Readings

In addition to the works cited in Chapter 4, the paper by Lorne D. Bruce, "A Reappraisal of Roman Libraries in the Scriptores Historiae Augustae," Journal of Library History 16 (1981): 551-73, is a current survey with a critical examination of the earlier literature on the subject. Other items of special note are:

Cramer, F. H. "Bookburning and Censorship in Ancient Rome," Journal of the History of Ideas 6 (1945): 147-96.

Davis, Donald G., Jr. "Christianity and Pagan Libraries in the Later Roman Empire," Library History 2 (1970): 1-10.

Reichmann, Felix. "The Book Trade at the Time of the Roman Empire," Library Quarterly 7 (1938): 40-76.

PART II

MEDIEVAL LIBRARIES

Chapter 6

BYZANTINE AND MOSLEM LIBRARIES

Of all the libraries of antiquity, those in Constantinople came nearest to surviving intact through the Middle Ages. In particular, the Imperial Library, founded by Constantine the Great in the 4th century, varied in size and importance with the fortunes of the Byzantine Empire, but in one form or another it survived until the capture of the city in 1453 by the Ottoman Turks.

The background of Byzantine history is both Greek and Roman. The site of the city of Constantinople on the European side of the Straits of the Bosporus between the Mediterranean and the Black Sea was known to the Greeks as Byzantium. After the Emperor Constantine had won control over both the Eastern and Western Roman Empires about 325, he established his capital at this spot and renamed it Constantinople. In the course of time, the Western Empire declined and was overrun by barbarians from the north, but the Eastern or Byzantine Empire continued to exist, at times powerful and at other times weak, but always culturally effective for more than a thousand years. Essentially, the Byzantine culture was more Greek than Roman, more eastern than western. Its role in western civilization is due to its effect on the Balkans and Russia and to its preservation of many of the Greek and Latin classics. In general, more Greek writings than Latin were preserved in Constantinople, as Greek was the dominant language in the eastern area. A thousand years after Constantine, in the 14th and 15th centuries, copies of these manuscripts found their way to Italy and western Europe, heralding the dawn of the Renaissance. In founding Constantinople and in adopting Christianity as a state religion, Constantine made his name one of the most remembered of all the Roman emperors.

An imperial library in the Eastern Empire had been established by the Emperor Diocletian at Nicomedia, his capital, before 300, but little is known about it. Constantine founded an imperial library at Constantinople sometime after 330 and before 336. His agents searched throughout the Empire for Christian books for his library. He also collected the writings of the Greek and Latin secular writers for his library, but it apparently grew quite slowly since there were reported to be only about 7,000 books in the library at Constantine's death in 337. A generation later, the Emperor Julian tried to overthrow Christianity and he may have ordered the destruction of some Christian works in the library, but he also established a library of classical literature in Antioch and gave his own book collection to the Imperial Library in 362. Theodosius II (401-450) is credited with enlarging the library to about 100,000 volumes, but it declined again under Leo I. His successor Zeno (474-491) saw the library partially destroyed in a fire and rebuilt it with copies of works gathered from other libraries. The library at this time probably contained over 100,000 volumes, with more codices than rolls.

In the 5th century, the library of the Academy, a university or school of philosophy, was founded under Theodosius II (408-450) in Constantinople. This school flourished for several centuries, particularly under the Emperor Justinian (527-565). Under Leo the Isaurian (717-741), both university and imperial libraries suffered in the Emperor's fight against the worshipers of idols or icons. Books containing religious pictures were sometimes destroyed by the "iconoclasts," who regarded them as heathen. The Academy ceased to exist in the late 8th century, and the Imperial Library declined to some 35,000 volumes, but in the 9th century a university was reestablished. This institution was staffed with a noted group of scholars headed by Leo the Mathematician, and its library played a large role in the Byzantine "renaissance" that was to come in the 11th century.

The Emperor Justinian is noted in library history for two reasons. First, it was he who closed the last surviving classical school, then at Athens, in 529, because he felt that the curriculum there was contrary to the teachings of the Christian Church. A more positive accomplishment under Justinian was the codification of Roman law. This work, done by a commission of scholars appointed by the Emperor, involved the study and condensation of some 2,000 volumes of legal works, going back nearly a thousand years in Roman history. The Justinian Code, with its Digests and supplementary works, forms the Corpus Juris Civilis, the basis of all civil law in western Europe through the Middle Ages and into the modern era. Around this work there grew up in Constantinople a school of law which was formalized into a legal university in the 11th century. To compile Justinian's Code, a well-organized law library must have been available, and undoubtedly a library was provided for the law students throughout the history of the school of law. In 1045, the Emperor Constantine VII is recorded as having ordered that the law library contain "all the books useful and necessary for the teaching of law," and that it be administered by a "devout" librarian. The value of the legal work of Justinian's era, and its effect on the legal and juristic history of the western world, can scarcely be overemphasized.

Besides the libraries of the Emperor and the university, there was usually a third major library in Constantinople, the library of the Patriarch, the head of the Eastern Church, and it, too, fluctuated in size and importance throughout the long history of Byzantium. Constantine the Great is reported to have also started this library with a gift of fifty volumes, elegantly inscribed on parchment. In time, a school or college grew up under the direction of the Patriarch, distinct from the Imperial University. This school, although taught by religious scholars, usually educated the administrators and higher civil servants of the Empire, while religious leaders themselves were educated in the monasteries. Whether this school made use of the library of the Patriarch or had its own library is uncertain, but it is known that some of the Patriarchs had private libraries of their own.

Monastic life flourished in the Eastern Empire even earlier than it did in the West and many monasteries were founded in Asia Minor and Greece before 500. For several centuries these monasteries followed the laws of monastic life laid down by St. Pachomius of Egypt (d. 346) which encouraged study but did not insist on the formation of libraries. About 825 at Studium, a monastery near Constantinople, the Abbot Theodore produced a new set of monastic regulations that emphasized the scriptorium and the library and outlined the duties of the librarian. After this, each monastery was encouraged to form a library of its own. The monastic libraries on the Greek peninsula of Mt. Athos are particularly notable for their longevity, some of them surviving down to the modern era. Religious works were the texts usually preserved in the monasteries, but some secular works were also found there. Since some monastic orders provided hospitals and even taught physicians, their libraries also contained medical and scientific works. An example of one of the most important texts to survive in a Byzantine monastery is the Codex Sinaiticus, one of the earliest extant manuscripts of the Bible, now in the British Museum, but originally found at the monastery of St. Catherine on Mt. Sinai.

The period from 850 to 1100 saw a renaissance in Byzantine learning and literature. This rebirth of interest in knowledge and learning stimulated a revival of the university and encouraged the work of a number of significant authors, although their works for the most part consisted of compendia or anthologies rather than original productions. In the 9th century, the scholar and patriarch Photius compiled his Bibliotheca (or Myrobiblion), which was a summary or digest of some 280 earlier works, many of them now lost. Whether or not he had in his own library all of the works mentioned, he must have had access to an excellent collection. Included in the works discussed were many theological titles, as well as much Greek history and literature with some works in the arts and sciences. Arethas of Caesarea, a 10th-century follower of Photius, had a private library of which something is known from his surviving letters. He owned copies of Euclid, Lucian, Aristides, Aristotle, and Plato, and he wrote commentaries on some of the classic authors. One volume of his library has survived and is now in the Bodleian Library at Oxford.

Suidas, a 10th-century encyclopedist, also culled from many sources in compiling his Lexikon, a dictionary-encyclopedia of general knowledge. Among the few examples of literature as such, John Geometres' 10th-century poems are as filled with references to classical authors as the works of his prose-writing contemporaries. An 11th-century poet, John Mauropous, expressed his feeling for his library in a couplet:

> Living among my books like a bee among flowers
> Nourished on words like a grasshopper on dew.

Outside of Constantinople, most of the major cities of the Byzantine Empire contained, at different times, one or more libraries in monasteries, schools, and churches. Since the Empire itself expanded and contracted several times during its 1,000-year history, so the fortunes of its various provincial cities also fluctuated considerably.

Libraries under Byzantine control are mentioned at Caesarea, Berytus (Beirut), Thessalonika, and Athens, among others. Eustatius, Archbishop of Thessalonika in the 12th century, quoted from more than 400 authors in his writings, indicating access to a good library. On the other hand, when Michael Acominatus became Archbishop of Athens in 1175, he noted that the city had no libraries at all, and that his two chests of books constituted the largest collection of literature in the city. When the Norman Crusaders overran much of Greece in the late 12th century, they took books from both private and public collections as spoils of war, possibly initiating the flow of manuscripts from East to West.

At various times during its long history, Byzantine influence extended from Ceylon to Paris and from Spain to Moscow. Charlemagne, for example, obtained copies of books from the Imperial Library at Constantinople for his palace library at Aachen. Monasteries in Armenia borrowed books from Constantinople, and copies of them are still preserved in the Miansikian State Public Library in Erevan. The Moslems, close neighbors and frequent enemies of Constantinople for 800 years before its fall, borrowed not only literature but art, education, political science, and philosophy from the Byzantines. Their influence was strong in Sicily and southern Italy, where an 11th-century monastery library contained Greek classical authors that were virtually unknown in the rest of western Europe. The Serbian Empress Elizabeth in the 13th century obtained a Greek library from Constantinople. Basil Lapu, Prince of Moldavia in the next century, also had a library containing classical Greek authors. Thus it can be seen that the great writings of the classical era, particularly those of Greece, were never completely lost to the western world. They were always available to the Byzantines, and to those western peoples in cultural and diplomatic contact with the Eastern Empire. However, during most of the Middle Ages these contacts were few and tenuous, and, for all practical purposes, scarcely significant.

Unfortunately, the glory of Byzantium, that had for many centuries withstood wars both external and internal, gradually came to an end after 1200. Norman invasions of the Greek peninsula in the late 12th century presaged that end, and when Constantinople itself was captured in 1204, the city was almost completely destroyed. Some of the invaders realized that the books in the public and private libraries were valuable, and so began a trade in manuscripts with eager Italian buyers. Many more were probably destroyed than sold, and it is not unreasonable to assume that greater damage was done in the destruction of Constantinople by the Christians in 1204 than by the Turks in 1453.

After the fall of Constantinople, the capital of Byzantium was removed to Nicaea, where Emperor John III (1222-54) reestablished the imperial library. In the 13th century, Nicaea became a center of culture, with schools, churches, monasteries, and hospitals the equal of any in the western world. From Nicaea, the Byzantines began a return to power, recapturing Thesalonika from the Normans in 1246 and returning to Constantinople in 1261. There, Emperor Michael Paleologus reinstated the imperial library in a wing of the palace. The last two centuries of Byzantine history are an anticlimax because the once great empire was gradually reduced until it was little more than the city of Constantinople by 1450. Pressed on all sides by enemies, including Italians, Serbs, Bulgars, and Turks, and troubled with dissension and lack of leadership, the Eastern Empire finally fell to the Ottoman Turks in 1453 and a great era in Eurasian history was ended.

Oddly enough, while Constantinople was weakening politically between 1260 and 1450, it was experiencing a revival in literature and learning. In schools, libraries, monasteries, and hospitals, Constantinople was far ahead of either the declining Moslem world or pre-Renaissance Europe. This, of course, came to an end when Mohammed II led his conquering forces into the city. Churches and monasteries, homes and palaces alike were sacked, and everything of value was taken. Many books were undoubtedly destroyed, but some of the Turkish soldiers realized that they were potentially valuable and hundreds were saved and sold. At first it was reported that volumes of Aristotle and Plato sold for a penny each, but soon after the conquest their value rose as the Italian traders resumed their traffic in manuscripts and other treasures. It is impossible to say just how many libraries and how many volumes were in existence in Constantinople in 1453, but it is known that despite the large number of books destroyed, traffic in Greek manuscripts remained a profitable business for more than a hundred years afterward.

The significance of Constantinople in western civilization is great, not because of its own art and literature--although that was prodigious if not original--but because it preserved so much of classical literature through the Middle

Ages when it was virtually lost in the West. Of the Greek classics known today, at least seventy-five percent are known through Byzantine copies. The flow of manuscripts from East to West had begun even before 1200, but it reached its high point in the 14th and 15th centuries. For some traders, manuscripts were the most valuable single item of trade, and the effect of this literary trade on the West was the re-birth of interest in classical literature, history, and philosophy which we call the Renaissance. In this sense, it was the decline of Byzantium that provided the impetus to the end of the Middle Ages in Europe and the birth of the modern era.

Constantinople was not the only center of culture in the eastern Mediterranean during the Middle Ages. Close neighbors and long-time enemies of the Christian Byzantines, the Moslems sprang into prominence in the 7th century. In a few decades after 622, when the Moslem era began, the religion of Islam swept the Arabic world and its fringes from Persia to Morocco. The Moslems came close to Constantinople on several occasions, but were unable to capture the city until 1453. Under the inspiration of the Islamac religion, the Arabs developed both a military power and a literary culture that was to flourish for several hundred years.

Before the coming of the Prophet Mohammed, however, there was little literature or literacy among the Arabic peoples. Instead, an oral literature of tales and poetry was handed down from generation to generation, much as in Homeric Greece. The first major item of written literature among the Moslems was the Koran itself. This collection of sayings of the Prophet came to represent both the "Bible" and the philosophical base of Mohammedanism. To know the Koran and its teaching became the duty of all Moslems, and hence literacy became all-important and schools began to be organized. To teach the Koran, scholars and priests were necessary and higher institutions of education were started, many of them connected with the churches or mosques. The result of all this was a stabilized Arabic language that was suitable for a secular as well as a religious literature. Another fortunate development aided the expansion of Arabic literature and learning. This was the use of paper as a writing material, much cheaper and more available than parchment or papyrus. An economical writing material meant that more copies of literary works could be produced and that reading material of all kinds could reach a wider audience. The technique of manufacturing paper came to the eastern Moslems from China by way of central Asia about 800, and the knowledge of the process spread gradually through the Moslem world, reaching Spain about 950. Paper could be made from a variety of fibrous materials, but the best varieties were produced from linen or cotton rags.

Although Mohammedanism spread largely through the strength of its military power, and some Moslem leaders were known to have held that no book was necessary except the Koran, the world of Islam in general was a book-loving society. Seldom in the history of the world have books been held in such high esteem, at least among the upper classes. Along with studying the Koran, the devout Moslem was encouraged to copy it and make it available to others, so the craft of the scribe became popular in the Arab world, and thousands of copies of the Koran were produced, many of them in beautiful scripts and bindings.

The first center of the Moslem world was Damascus, where the Umayyid dynasty ruled from 661 to 750. These rulers promoted learning and established a royal library that also included the archives of the church and state. About 690, the archives were separated from the literary and religious works, the latter forming a palace library, and the former being relegated to a House of Archives. For the palace library, which was open to use by serious students and scholars, copies of books from all parts of the known world were obtained. Works of alchemy, medicine, and astrology were included as well as literature, history, and philosophy, and, of course, works on the Moslem religion.

A footnote to early Moslem culture concerns the Nestorian Christians who were driven from Syria by the Emperor Zeno about 485. These Christians fled to Persia, where at Nisibis they built up a strong center of Greek culture, complete with libraries of the classics. They attracted scholars from Greece, including some of the faculty of the school at Athens that was closed by Justinian in 529. Thus the Moslems found, deep in the mountains of Persia, a treasure house of Greek science and philosophy that they soon had translated into Arabic. In fact, most of the surviving Greek literature was translated into Arabic by 750, and Aristotle, for example, became so widely studied that literally hundreds of books were written about him by Arabic scholars. The Moslems also obtained Greek works from Constantinople through regular trade channels and captured others in their various wars with the Eastern Empire.

The great period of Moslem literature and learning came under the Abbasid rulers, or Caliphate, from about 750 to 1050. These Caliphs moved the capital of the Moslem world to Baghdad, and during this era the power and influence of Islam spread from Persia around the south shore of the Mediterranean to Spain and even southern France. Actually, Spain and Morocco never recognized the rule of the Abbasids, and their areas of control varied considerably in periods of internal and external conflicts, but culturally the area that accepted Islam became unified. The early Abbasid Caliphs, adopting a religious philosophy that encouraged learning and debate, promoted the establishment of universities and libraries throughout their realm. Early beginnings were made under Al-Mansur (754-775) and Harun al-Rashid (785-809), of Arabian Nights fame, but it was Al-Mamun the Great (813-833) who brought the "House of Learning" or university at Baghdad into prominence. With libraries, laboratories, subsidized scholars, a translating service, and even an astronomical observatory, this institution attracted scholars from Spain to India. Its books were culled from the accumulated scholarship of a dozen languages, and its faculty spoke as many or more. The libraries were open to scholars from all over the world, whether their interests lay in religion or science, poetry, or medicine. Scholarly relations were maintained with all civilized countries of Europe, Asia, and Africa, and contact with western Europe was relatively open, particularly during the periods of peace. Interchange of ideas between East and West continued throughout the Abbasid era, and it is quite possible that during these years the Islamic world received more from the West than it transmitted. In later years this trend was to be noticeably reversed.

By 900, Baghdad was a center of learning that rivaled if it did not exceed Constantinople. Its schools and libraries were models for similar institutions throughout Islam. It was said that Baghdad alone had over one hundred booksellers in 891, and that at the height of its cultural glory it had some thirty public libraries. Other university and public libraries were located all the way from Bokhara and Merv, deep in the heart of Asia on the land route to China, through Basra and Damascus, Cairo and Algiers, to Morocco and Spain in the West. A geographer, Yakut al-Hamawi, who visited Merv in 1228, found no less than twelve libraries there available to the public. Ten were endowed libraries and two were in mosques. One had over 12,000 volumes in codex form and another had been in existence since 494 A.D.

Yakut noted that the lending policies of the libraries in Merv were so liberal that he was able to have 200 volumes to work with in his rooms at one time.

Under the rule of the Seljuk Turks in the later 11th century, Moslem education in the East became more purely theological, but also during this era a more formal university was established at Baghdad. This was the Nizamiyah, founded about 1065, basically a theological seminary, but with other courses also formally taught. It had boarding facilities for students, student scholarships, endowed professorships, and other characteristics of a modern university. A noted hospital was connected with this institution, and both university and hospital had libraries. Though its buildings were ransacked and its students and faculty scattered, the university managed to survive the Mongol conquests and was still in operation in the 15th century.

In Egypt, the Fatimid Caliphs during the 10th to 12th centuries built up a center of culture in Cairo that was to rival any in the world at that time. The Caliph al-Aziz (975-996) protected poets and scholars and established a royal library for their use. Catalogs of this and other libraries in Cairo were compiled, along with subject bibliographies of the known branches of knowledge. Established in Cairo in 972, the mosque-university Al-Azhar survives to the present day.

It was reported, although it was possibly an exaggeration, that the libraries of Cairo, at the height of the city's cultural development in the mid-11th century, contained over 1,000,000 volumes. In 1068, a revolt against the Fatimid ruler Al-Mustansir resulted in the sacking of the royal palace and the dispersal or destruction of its 200,000-volume library. According to one reporter, manuscripts were used for lighting soldiers' fires, and leather bindings of rare volumes served as repairs for their boots. However, the library must have been rebuilt, for when Saladin came into power in 1173 he found it to contain over 100,000 volumes. At an earlier date, a Cairo library was reported to have had its own staff of librarians, administrators, binders, calligraphers, servants, and guards, supported by rentals from property with which it had been endowed. It was supposed to contain over 2,400 copies of the Koran, most of them individual works of calligraphic and book-binding art. Science, particularly astronomy, art, and architecture, flourished under the Fatimids, and literally hundreds of volumes were written by its scholars with the aid of its libraries. Unfortunately the combination of Mongol conquerors and Christian Crusaders was to end abruptly this Egyptian renaissance.

Another place in which Moslem scholarship and learning reached high levels was Spain, where the followers of Mohammed prevailed for several centuries. The Moslems entered Spain after 711, and they built, in Córdoba, Seville, Toledo, and other cities, an advanced civilization that outshone anything in western Europe during the same period. At Córdoba, for example, there was a noted Moslem university, as well as several other large libraries including the royal library, reputed to contain over 400,000 volumes. Its catalog alone consisted of forty-four volumes. Under Al-Hakim II (961-976), this library was reported to have given employment to over 500 people, including many agents sent to all parts of the world to buy books. Al-Hakam gave his own private library to the royal library at Córdoba which had been founded about 850 and greatly enlarged under the rule of Abd-al-Rahman III (912-961). Elsewhere in Moslem Spain there was a total of seventy libraries in the 10th century, several in Toledo. In addition to the royal library, these included libraries in universities in Córdoba, Seville, Málaga, and Granada, among others, and in numerous mosques. Private libraries flourished in Moslem Spain, and it was said that Córdoba was the greatest book market in the western world in the 10th century. Sicily also came under Moslem influence during the 9th and 10th centuries, as did Sardinia and Corsica. From these islands, as well as from Spain, western Europe received translations of classical writings preserved by the Moslems.

Probably at few times in the history of the world have private libraries reached such size and elegance as under the Moslems. The wealth brought by conquest, tribute, and trade developed among them an elite and highly literate upper class. Since bigamy was practiced, and even encouraged for those who could afford it, large families were the rule among the nobility, and among them many younger sons pursued learning and scholarship as a career. Next to war and conquest, these became the most honored professions, and the collecting of libraries both for use and for show, became common among the wealthy. Many of these private libraries reached remarkable size, according to the references we have to them in the works of geographers, historians, and biographers. The library of one Baghdad scholar of the 10th century was reported to require 400 camel loads to move it when he took it from one residence to another. So numerous were these private libraries that one writer has estimated that, as of 1200, there were more books in private hands in the Moslem world than in all libraries, public and private, of western Europe. It was not uncommon for wealthy bookmen to leave their libraries to the people, and to endow these libraries, thus ensuring their continued growth and usefulness.

One interesting aspect of the Moslem libraries is the wide variety of subject matter they contained. With the exception of religious works of other faiths, the Moslems gathered, copied, and translated everything they could, in all subjects, of all times, and in all available languages. Greek and Latin classics, Sanskrit philosophy, Egyptian history, Hindu epics, and medieval French love-poems--all were to be found somewhere in the Moslem libraries, along with biography, science, and pseudoscience, from all times and places. Though most of these libraries were subsequently destroyed, from surviving catalogs and isolated volumes we find evidence of all these and other subjects as well. For example, the library at Fez in Morocco contained the works of the Roman Livy and the Greek Galen, among others. The library at Damascus contained all the known works of Aristotle. A library at Gaza, between Egypt and Palestine, contained many Egyptian papyri, some in hieroglyphics. The Justinian Code of Laws was present in many Moslem collections, indicating the respect that was felt among the Arabs for this great legal collection, even though it differed substantially from their own laws.

Unfortunately, we have little accurate information concerning the physical conditions in the Moslem libraries. The usual book-form was the codex, either of parchment or some other animal skin, or of paper. Rolls were by no means unknown, particularly in the earlier centuries, and in the eastern areas the exotic Asiatic accordion-shaped volumes and even the Hindu palm-leaf *olas* were occasionally seen. As for library arrangement, there are references to the custom of placing different subjects in different rooms in the larger libraries and even of having "subject specialists" in charge of them. In smaller libraries, the books were kept in chests with a list of the contents on the outside. In the larger libraries, the staff list might number hundreds when copyists, binders, illuminators, and other employees were added to those whom we would usually consider as librarians. The latter were often scholars, writers or poets, multilingual, and well paid by patronizing rulers or nobles. However, library administrators are also mentioned, indicating that the management of these large enterprises often called more for a business man than for a scholar. This was particularly true in the endowed libraries where profit-making businesses were involved.

The larger libraries seem to have been cataloged as a matter of normal procedure, and the catalogs took the form of manuscript volumes. References are found to catalogs which filled as many as twenty, or even forty, volumes. These catalogs were apparently arranged by subject, but items were arranged by the order of acquisition within each subject class. Since shelving was by subject in room or chest, the catalog was thus something of a classified accession list, but it apparently served its purpose and was widely used. Many of the Moslem libraries included not only rooms for reading but also rooms for meetings and smaller rooms for discussion and debate.

Particularly in the wealthy private libraries, and in some of the public ones as well, the arts of illuminating and binding reached a high level among the Moslems. Calligraphy itself was an art, and the cursive Arabic script lent itself to beautiful productions. The use of fine vellums, often dyed with exotic colors, and of different colored inks, together with ornate, heavily tooled and embossed leather bindings, produced some of the most beautiful books the world has ever known. Such fine works were, of course, exceptions, but the book itself was thoroughly appreciated and widely used. Although few Moslem libraries were public in the modern sense of the word, most of them, even large private ones, were available to serious scholars. Even outside circulation of books was not unknown, and in many cases extra services were provided, such as free writing materials, copyists, and translators.

Some of the results of the scholarship in these libraries and schools can be seen in the writings of representative Moslem authors. In 987, Muhammad al-Nadim produced a multi-volumed Index of the Sciences, a bibliography of books in Arabic on all branches of knowledge, with biographical notes on the authors. Some idea of the great loss to world literature in the destruction of Arabic libraries can be obtained when it is noted that not one in a thousand of the books al-Nadim described is presently known to exist. Another 10th-century writer, Muhammad al-Tabari, wrote a history of the world in 150 volumes, saying that he had consulted over 10,000 source volumes in writing them. The Egyptian scholar and astronomer Ibn al-Haytham, of the early 11th century, wrote over one hundred volumes on mathematics, astronomy, philosophy, and medicine. Even greater writers, although not so prolific, were the Arabic authors whose works reached the medieval European world. Averroes (Ibn Rushd), who lived in Spain in the 12th century, brought the works of Aristotle back to western Europe with his text and commentaries which were translated into Latin. Before that, the only works of Aristotle known to western Europe were excerpts translated by Boethius about 500 A.D.

Unfortunately, the story of Islamic libraries is all too similar to that of their predecessors in the classical era; they, too, ended in wholesale destruction. Many Moslem libraries suffered in civil wars and in the decline of interest in learning under various rulers at different times. Religious dissension often resulted in conquests that brought on destruction of books relating to the history and beliefs of particular Moslem sects. When Saladin, a Sunnite Moslem, conquered Egypt in 1175, a country where the Shi'ite Moslems had been in power, he is reported to have destroyed whole libraries and distributed the finer works to his victorious followers. After 1100, reactionaries gained control in most of the eastern Moslem world, and the fortunes of Moslem libraries declined sharply. Those that survived tended to center on theology. Learning continued to flourish in North Africa and Spain for two more centuries, but here, too, there was a noticeable decline after 1300.

Not the least important in the destruction of Islamic libraries were the depredations of the Christian crusaders from the 11th to the 13th centuries. In Syria, Palestine, and parts of North Africa, the Christians destroyed libraries as enthusaistically as had the barbarians in Italy a few hundred years earlier. When Spain was reconquered from the Arabs, the great Islamic libraries at Seville, Córdoba, and Granada were destroyed or were carried away by their retreating owners. As late as 1499, Granada was the scene of a bonfire of Arabic manuscripts. In the next century, however, Philip II, in building the Escorial Library, appreciated the value of Arabic sources and brought together all that he could find in Spain, plus others purchased in Morocco. He acquired for this library over 4,000 Arabic manuscripts relating to the history of Spain.

Fire and flood also took their toll of Moslem libraries,

and one particularly large one at Medina was destroyed in 1257 by a fire caused by lightning. The greatest destruction, however, resulted from the raids of the Mongols in the 13th century. From the mountains and steppes of central Asia came the hordes of Genghis Kahn, conquering and destroying everything before them. In the first great sweep to the Caspian Sea and northern Persia, the cities of Bokhara, Samarkand, and Merv were destroyed along with many smaller towns. Samarkand had been a Moslem city for over 500 years, and its schools and libraries were well endowed and well used. The libraries of Merv were justly famous, but all were destroyed along with many of the scholars who were using them. These depredations took place about 1218 to 1220, and after that the Mongols withdrew. In 1258, however, they returned in greater force under the command of Halagu Khan, and this time they reached and destroyed Baghdad. In one week, libraries and their treasures that had been accumulated over hundreds of years were burned or otherwise destroyed. So many books were thrown into the Tigris River, according to one writer, that they formed a bridge that would support a man on horseback. Students and scholars were considered particularly useless to the victors and they were killed by the hundreds.

But what was the effect of that Moslem civilization on the western world and particularly on the libraries of the western world? Since much of their literature was lost, the effect was not as great as if the libraries had been preserved. However, the Islamic libraries, almost as much as those of Constantinople, were a connecting link between the learning of classical Greece and the cultural development of western Europe. One point of contact in particular was Spain. As early as 953, John of Gorce was sent to Córdoba by the German Emperor Otto the Great. Gorce learned to read Arabic and returned to Germany with his saddlebags filled with Arabic manuscripts, including some translations from Aristotle and some Arabic works of science. In 1070, Daniel of Morley, an English scholar, visited Toledo and returned to England with copies of Arabic scientific works. Roger Bacon, English scientist and philosopher of the 13th century, received much of his learning from Arabic sources. Gerard of Cremona, who died in 1187, spent most of his life in Toledo and translated over seventy scientific works from Arabic into Latin. When the Christian Spanish captured Toledo, they found a wealth of Arabic books and, although many were destroyed, others were kept and translated into Latin. The Christian King Alfonso X of Castile had been taught by Arabic teachers, and when he founded the University of Salamanca in the 13th century, it was largely modeled on the Moslem universities, even using translations of the same textbooks. Thus, even before 1250, works of Arabic science and translations and commentaries on the Greek classics had reached western Europe either through Spain or through Sicily and southern Italy. The works of Galen and Hippocrates, Greek physicians, enlarged upon by their Arabic successors, became the textbooks of the earliest European medical schools at Naples, Bologna, Padua, and Paris. Without the knowledge gained from the Moslem world, it is likely that the cultural development of modern Europe would have been considerably inhibited.

Although the Christian Crusades resulted in the destruction of some Islamac libraries, they also resulted in contact, social and commercial as well as military, between western Europe and the eastern Mediterranean, and through that area with the whole of the exotic East from Arabia to China. This contact resulted in an expansion of trade and in the development of new tastes in western Europe, both literary and culinary. With the trade in fine fabrics, rare metals, and tasty foods came the trade in manuscripts that flourished for hundreds of years. Commerce led to economic development, interest in explorations, and the eventual discovery of America. Economic stability helped in the development of nationalism, and laid a foundation for the rediscovery and growth of such ideas as liberty and democracy. But it was in the books that came from Constantinople and from the Moslem libraries and booksellers that western Europe rediscovered the ideas and ideals of the classical world, and with them came the intellectual ferment that marked the beginning of the Renaissance and heralded the dawn of modern history. Thus, in any study of library development in the West, it is necessary to remember that for 1,000 years much of the best in our literary heritage was preserved in the East--in the libraries of Byzantium and Islam.

Additional Readings

The standard reference on the Medieval Library remains the book by that title by James Westfall Thompson, which was first published in 1939. The work contains an essential essay by S. K. Padover on "Byzantine Libraries." Also very useful is Chapter 2 of L. D. Reynolds and N. G. Wilson's _Scribes and Scholars: A Guide to the Transmission of_

Greek and Latin Literature (Oxford: Oxford University Press, 1968). For a fuller history of the period readers should consult A. A. Vasiliev's monumental History of the Byzantine Empire (Madison: University of Wisconsin Press, 1961). Other works of interest are:

Bashiruddin, S. "The Fate of Sectarian Libraries in Medieval Islam," Libri 17 (1967): 149-62.

Mackensen, R. S. "Four Great Libraries of Medieval Baghdad," Library Quarterly 2 (1932): 279-99.

Wilson, N. G. "The Libraries of the Byzantine World," Greek, Roman and Byzantine Studies 8 (1967): 53-80.

Chapter 7

MONASTIC AND CATHEDRAL LIBRARIES

The ravages of conquest and the advent of a barbaric age placed all learning in real jeopardy. With increasing rapidity those concerned with the life of the mind were fleeing the strife-torn cities, and books and learning passed over to the church. For nearly 1,000 years the typical European library was to be the small collection of manuscripts, laboriously copied and jealously guarded, in the many monasteries scattered from Greece to Iceland. Instead of the magnificent temple library, with its thousands of rolls in vaulted marble rooms, the library of the Middle Ages was more often a collection of a few hundred codices kept in a bookchest or two in the corner of a monastery chapel. This decline in books and libraries was typical of the general cultural decline that took place in most of western Europe after the fall of Rome. The remarkable thing is not that so much of classical learning was lost, but that so much was preserved in the most trying of circumstances.

Fortunately for western civilization, the links with the past were never totally lost. Even before the end of the old order there was the beginning of the new, or at least of the institution that was to preserve a part of ancient culture throughout the Dark Ages. That institution was the medieval monastery. Monasteries were already being established in Egypt, in Palestine, and possibly in neighboring areas by the 3rd century A.D., and the idea of the monastery library already existed in those areas. Like the early Christian churches, the monasteries treasured their small collections of scriptures, epistles, and commentaries and gave them an honored place in their chapels.

The exact origins of monasticism are obscure. The

earliest known Christian monasteries seem to have been in Egypt, although the idea did not originate there. Isolated religious communities had been known before Christ, and the recent discoveries in the Qumran caves of Palestine indicate such a development more or less contemporary with Christ. The early monasteries have some relation to the hermit, the dedicated Christian who fled the populated areas in order to live alone to meditate on his sins and to avoid committing more. Perhaps some of these attracted followers and established religious communities, or perhaps the monasteries began as dedicated religious groups, but at any rate separate settlements for men and women were established at an early date and the rise of Christianity is closely associated with the rise of monasticism.

One early Egyptian monastery of which we have some record was founded by St. Pachomius (292-345 A.D.) at Tabennisi in upper Egypt. St. Pachomius had only a small collection of religious works which he guarded zealously. Among the rules he formulated for his monastic group were several relating to the use of books, but in general they were restrictive. The books were to be kept in a cupboard built into the monastery chapel wall and all were to be locked up each night. During the daytime, each monk was allowed to use one book at a time, but it had to be used in the chapel area only and could not be taken to any other part of the monastery. From Pelusium, another Egyptian monastery, we have the letters of the monk Isidore (ca. 390-450). These letters indicate that the monks there were acquainted with Greek and Latin literature as well as with the religious texts.

Monasticism spread to western Europe by the end of the 4th century with early monastic groups around Rome, and an important monastery at Lerins, on the Mediterranean coast of France, was established by St. Honoratus about 410. As the civilized world began to crumble under the raids of the northern barbarians, small groups of devoted Christians withdrew to remote island or mountain areas to worship in relative security. Of all these, one of the most significant was founded by Magnus Aurelius Cassiodorus about 540. Cassiodorus had been secretary to Theodoric, the Ostrogothic ruler of Rome from 489 to 526, and had hoped to found a university in Rome similar to the Museum in Alexandria. He failed at this because of the uncertain conditions of the time, but when he at last retired from public office he used the wealth he had acquired to begin a monastery at Vivarium in southern Italy. His own private library became the nucleus of the monastery book collection, and he spent the remainder of his long life in study and devotion.

Cassiodorus had a strong respect for learning and a reverence for books in general, so his library included many works of classical Latin authors, with a few Greek ones, as well as religious texts. Not content with merely collecting and copying other writers, he also did some effective writing of his own. His most important writing, from the standpoint of library history, was the *Institutiones Divinarum et Saecularium Litterarum*, a lengthy guidebook for everyday living in a monastery. Along with detailed instruction for a religious routine, the author told how manuscripts should be handled, corrected, copied, and repaired, and included what amounted to an annotated bibliography of the best literature of the time. Cassiodorus is also credited with having introduced the idea of intellectual as well as manual labor into the duties of the monks, and hence is largely responsible for the origin of both scriptorium and monastic libraries. Under his direction, a few Greek works were obtained and translated into Latin, and thus he helped enlarge the small amount of Greek literature available in western Europe for the next 500 years. Cassiodorus was a link between the classical and medieval worlds; as a child he had a classical education; as a man he saw the remnants of the old world fade away; and as an elderly scholar he aided in the foundation of the monastic system that was to keep learning alive through the Middle Ages. Historians once believed that Cassiodorus' great library found its way to the monastery at Bobbio after its owner's death. However, recent research indicates that the books were sent to Rome and dispersed by booksellers there.

Contemporary with Cassiodorus, but much more influential in the long run, was the work being done at the monastery of Monte Cassino by St. Benedict and his followers. St. Benedict (ca. 480-543), finding life in Rome too worldly for his tastes, withdrew to the mountains south of the city to live as a hermit. His religious sincerity attracted followers, and in 529 a monastery was founded that was to be the parent house for the Benedictine Order, the oldest and one of the most significant of the several monastic orders. From Monte Cassino, monks went out to establish other monasteries in western Europe, and with them went the *Rules of St. Benedict* for the conduct of life in the monastery. Under these Rules, which were to serve as the essential guide to monastic life for centuries to come, the reading and copying of books was made a regular part of the monastic routine. St. Benedict evidently viewed the copying and reading of books as a spiritual rather than an intellectual task; as a mental treadmill designed to keep the minds of his monks free of worldly thoughts. But his more liberal followers, perhaps influenced by the Instiutiones of Cassiodorus, took a more positive attitude toward books and reading. As the Benedictine order spread, each new monastery constructed contained its library and scriptorium, thereby assuring the preservation of many classical works.

The monastic idea spread gradually throughout Europe, but many of those in northern Europe and even in northern Italy were established not by monks from Vivarium or Monte Cassino, but by missionaries from Ireland as a result of Roman occupation of the British islands. The Romans had conquered the southern part of England by 50 A.D., and that area remained under Roman domination for some 400 years. Roman towns and villas similar to those in the provinces of southern France and Spain grew up, and a cultured society existed side by side with the less civilized Britons. England was never completely converted to Christianity under the Romans, but the natives of Ireland were Christianized under the teaching of St. Patrick and others in the 5th century. By the 6th century, Ireland could boast of many monasteries; and from them missionaries went out to England, Scotland, France, and other parts of Europe. St. Columbia (Columcille, 521-597) left Ireland to found a monastery on the island of Iona off the coast of Scotland, and from this point Christianity spread to Scotland and northern England. St. Columban (Columbanus, 543-615) established monasteries at Luxeuil in Burgundy, at St. Gall in Switzerland, at Wurzburg and Salzburg in Germany, and at Tarantum and Bobbio in Italy. In each of these monasteries, as in the monasteries in Ireland and Britain, books and learning were emphasized, beautiful manuscripts were produced, and secular works as well as religious were included in the libraries.

The monastery and its library first came to England through the efforts of St. Augustine of Canterbury, who was sent there as a missionary by Pope Gregory about 597. Augustine brought with him a small collection of Christian texts, and other books were later obtained from Italy, along with the Rules of St. Benedict, to form a small library at Canterbury. Benedict Biscop, in the 7th century, founded the twin monasteries of Wearmouth and Jarrow in northern England, and built up excellent libraries there. He made at least five trips to Rome, each time obtaining books for his monasteries from sources in Italy and southern France. The Venerable Bede (673-735) was a student of Benedict Biscop and made good use of the libraries in writing his Ecclesiastical History of England. Coelfried, successor to Biscop, continued to build up the libraries of the twin monasteries, and one of his students, Egbert, founded a library at the cathedral school at York.

In France, a monastery of great importance was that at Corbie, established by monks from Luxeuil about 660. A celebrated school was established at this monastery, and its library and scriptorium were among the best in western Europe. In Germany, St. Boniface, an English monk, was establishing monasteries in the 8th century, including those at Fulda, Heidenheim, and Fritzlar. Libraries at each of these monasteries are known to have existed in the 8th century, and a catalog compiled at Fulda between 744 and 749 still survives. The works of the Irish monks stand out in the 7th and 8th centuries, otherwise a bleak era for books and libraries. It was a period of decline in Italy and southern France as the centuries of invasion by the European barbarians were followed by an era of conquests by the Moslems.

One bright cultural spot in the 7th century was Christian Spain. Despite the fact that much of the population was illiterate, there were cultural centers in the larger cities and several religious groups that served as schools or training corps for priests. One of the foremost Spanish scholars of this era was Isidore, Bishop of Seville from 600 to 636, who not only collected a library of the best-known literature of his day but also culled from it to form an early version of an encyclopedia. Just how many books he owned is uncertain, but they must have numbered several hundred since he kept them in fourteen bookcases, or armaria. Each case was dedicated to a particular author. Seven cases were inscribed with the names of religious writers, such as Saints Augustine, Ambrose, and Jerome, while others were dedicated to literary figures, historians, and writers of sacred and secular law. Over each case there was a poem to the author, and for the whole collection Isidore wrote a descriptive poem that included the following passage:

Here sacred books with worldly books combine;

> If poets please you, read them; they are thine.
> My meads are full of thorns, but flowers are there;
> If thorns displease, let roses be your share.
> Here both the laws in tomes revered behold;
> Here what is new is stored, and what is old ...
>
> A reader and a talker can't agree;
> Hence, idle chatterer; 'tis no place for thee!

In his encyclopedia, the Etymologiae, Isidore also provided an early instance of library history by recording all that he could discover on the libraries of the classical era.

The late 8th and early 9th centuries saw the development in western Europe of what is known as the Carolingian Renaissance, under the rule of the Emperor Charlemagne (786-814). Charlemagne himself was seriously interested in learning, knew Latin and even a little Greek, but it was the scholars who flocked to the relative security of his realm, who gave the era its literary significance. He invited learned men from all of Europe to come to his court, and among them was the English scholar Alcuin (735-804). Alcuin had been educated at the cathedral school at York and came to France in 782 to supervise the palace school at Aachen. He sent back to England for books to be copied, and with the encouragement of the Emperor he and his followers established schools and monasteries throughout western Europe.

A most significant outgrowth of this new intellectual activity was the increased demand for books, which stimulated production on a large scale and insured the preservation of much of the Latin literary heritage. Later, as Bishop of Tours, Alcuin set up an outstanding library and scriptorium there. For a half century or so literature and learning flourished, and significant libraries were built up at Corbie and Lyons in France, St. Gall in Switzerland, and Fulda in Germany, among others. Probably the largest of them all was the palace library at Aachen, where Charlemagne filled his shelves with richly bound volumes and even exchanged books with the Eastern Roman Emperor at Constantinople.

The Carolingian revival was dependent upon the security and wealth of Charlemagne's empire for its nurture, but in the 9th and 10th centuries the empire was challenged and eventually devastated by constant attacks by Norsemen, Huns, and Saracens, and once again learning in most of northern and western Europe broke down. The Danish and Viking invasions, which had begun in the late 8th century and continued for some 200 years, destroyed many monasteries and libraries. The coastal areas of England and France were particularly affected, but many secluded monasteries were also damaged by isolated raids or local wars. The Abbey at Tours, for example, was ravaged six times in a little over fifty years. In 867, the Danes overran much of northern England, and York was ransacked. Its books were scattered and its priests and scholars killed or driven away. A library established near Hamburg in the early 9th century was destroyed by Vikings, even though it had been established primarily for the purpose of carrying Christianity to them. Moslems continued to be a threat to the Mediterranean coasts of France and northern Italy, and the same general area was visited by the Huns around 900, with more destruction of churches and monasteries. The early Irish culture that gave rise to the missionaries Columba and Columban was ended in two centuries of Viking raids and conquests from about 850 to 1050. All over western Europe the story was much the same, and where monasteries were not destroyed they often suffered from stagnation and neglect. Only an occasional well-managed or well-located institution managed to thrive through the troubles. One of these was Cluny, founded in France about 910, which not only thrived but led a temporary revival in monastic cultural activities.

The various orders of monks had different ideas concerning books, libraries, and literary labors. The Benedictines, liberally interpreting the rules of their founder, were foremost in the development of monastic libraries and in the copying and distribution of manuscripts. The Benedictine rules concerning libraries were enlarged and clarified, particularly for their monasteries in England, by the *Constitutiones* of Bishop Lanfranc, issued in the 11th century. Among the other orders, the Carthusians and Cistercians also adopted library and reading rules, although they were not as interested in secular works as were the Benedictines. The Augustinians generally collected only a few books but prized them highly, while the Franciscans at first would own no books at all. Later, in the 13th century, the Franciscans began to collect books for their libraries, and the parent house at Assisi developed a comparatively large library within a few years. For all orders, the monastery was generally accepted as a center of learning, and the saying was common that "a monastery without a library is like a castle without walls." Convents for nuns were equally active in collecting and preserving both religious and secular literature, and several nuns became well known in literary fields. St. Paula, who headed a convent in Palestine in the 4th century, was a scholar in Hebrew and Greek as well as Latin. The nun Melania, who founded a convent near Carthage about 420, had earlier gained a living by transcribing manuscripts, and the library of her convent was noted for the beauty of its books. Gertrude, Abbess of Nivelle in 7th-century Belgium, was active in building up the library there, while St. Hroswitha in 10th-century Germany not only collected a library at her convent but also wrote religious poetry and drama.

Throughout the early Middle Ages, Rome remained a source of supply for books needed by the growing monastic collections of France, Germany, and England. The early popes attempted to maintain libraries at their headquarters, and churches and monasteries in and around Rome continued to have significant book collections. According to legend, either St. Peter founded the papal library or St. Clement did so, in 93 A.D. Since most of the early Christian congregations maintained collections of scriptures, and since these collections were often augmented by religious commentaries, lives of the martyrs, church records, and accounts of missionary activities, it is probable that a central collection of Christian literature existed in Rome even before the Church was recognized. However, the first known library for the Church at Rome was that of Pope Damasus in the late 4th century. Damasus is reported to have built a structure to house the library near the theater of Pompey in the Campus Martius and to have modeled it after the Temple of Apollo. An inscribed stone has been found that reads:

> I have erected this structure for the archives of the Roman Church; I have surrounded it with porticos on either side; and I have given it my name which I hope will be remembered for centuries.

Pope Hilary (461-468) is credited with establishing two small libraries for the use of laymen and pilgrims, placing in them approved copies of the scriptures and other religious works. Pope Agapetus, about 535, hoped to establish a school of theology and literature at Rome with the help of Cassiodorus. Agapetus endowed the school with a library for the use of scholars, but in that troubled era it is doubtful that either school or library ever materialized. Pope Gregory I (590-604), himself a prolific writer and collector of manuscripts, was active in building up the papal library and in making it useful to those who needed it. He maintained contact with religious officials and groups from Constantinople to Spain and both loaned and borrowed works to be copied for church collections. In the 7th century there was a papal library in the Lateran Palace where the Pope resided, and when the Church Council of 640 met there, the library was so well organized that the librarian was congratulated by the Council for being able to find any book at any time it was needed by a member of the Council. It was also noted that this librarian could translate Greek into Latin at sight, apparently an unusual scholarly ability at this time. As late as 855, Rome was still a source of manuscripts, but in the following centuries its churches and libraries suffered considerably in wars and political troubles. In the 10th century, there was still a papal library, but it was housed for safety in a specially built tower, the Turris Cartelaria, where it was little used. This collection is last mentioned by Pope Honorious III, who died in 1227, and its contents were apparently scattered or decayed from neglect. From 1309 to 1377, the headquarters of the Pope was at Avignon, in France, and here there was a library for the clergy and also one for a clerical university established by Pope Boniface VIII in 1303. The modern history of the papal library, however, begins with the establishment of a collection in the Vatican by Pope Nicholas V in the 15th century.

The 10th and 11th centuries marked another low period in the development of libraries and literature in western Europe except for a few bright spots, such as Cluny in France and St. Gall in Switzerland. There was a decline of interest in the classics and many monks were even illiterate and allowed the books in the libraries to go untended. The works that were copied were largely theological, and probably there were fewer volumes in all European libraries in 1100 than there had been in 900. Southern Italy was an exception because of its contacts with Byzantine sources which provided it with Greek manuscripts and kept alive its interest in the classics and even in medicine and law. Especially significant was a rebirth of interest in intellectual affairs at Monte Cassino, the first of the Benedictine monasteries, where many important Latin classics, notably the works of Tacitus, Seneca, and Varro were copied and probably saved from extinction. While conditions improved somewhat in the monasteries generally, by the 12th century intellectual life, and the accompanying books and libraries, were beginning to move back toward the city, first to the cathedrals and soon thereafter to the university centers.

The cathedrals, which were the headquarter churches for bishops or archbishops, were far more than merely large churches; they were also religious schools where training for the priesthood took place and often secular training at a lower level as well. In some cases, the cathedrals were in the direct charge of some monastic order, as in England where seven were run by the Benedictines. Others were directly under the Pope, in charge of appointed bishops. Almost all their income came from church-owned lands or from gifts of wealthy patrons. They were usually located near the growing towns and cities and hence were more available to the average student than the more isolated monasteries. Although they had existed since the days of Alcuin, if not earlier, they became more prominent in both religion and education after the 10th century.

The cathedrals and their schools had book collections from the first, but they often differed from the monastic libraries in several ways. Designed for educational rather than inspirational reading, the cathedral libraries generally contained more secular books than the monastic collections. They usually had more consistent means of support, and hence grew steadily and maintained current writings more often than the monastery libraries. The book collections came in time to be larger, more complete, and better organized. Some of the better-known cathedral libraries were those at York, Durham, and Canterbury in England; at Notre Dame, Orleans, and Rouen in France; at Bamberg and Hildesheim in Germany; and at Barcelona and Toledo in Spain. There were sometimes three book collections in a cathedral organization: the main collection, largely theological; the service books; and the school library, containing most of the secular literature. As of the 11th century, all together would contain only a few hundred volumes. Durham's cathedral library had only about 600 volumes in 1200, but included among them were a few medical works. The cathedral at Rouen in 1150 had even fewer volumes, but one-third of them were classical. Canterbury, one of the largest cathedral libraries, possessed about 5,000 books in 1300, but this was exceptional. The 13th century saw a rapid increase in the number of books available, and in the size of all major libraries. The cathedral libraries were never as numerous as those of the monasteries, and in general they were not as important in the cultural history of western Europe, but they served as a bridge, both chronologically and culturally, between the monasteries and the universities, and also brought together the cultural resources that their material wealth could afford.

The monastery or cathedral library up to the 13th century was usually only a small collection of a few hundred volumes or less. It was kept in a book-chest or a small closet in the monastery cloister rather than in a specific library room or building. Later it was connected with, or close by, the scriptorium where the monks copied texts as a part of their regular duties. At St. Gall in Switzerland, in the 9th century, the books were kept in an attic room directly over the scriptorium. A common word for library in the early Middle Ages was armarium, which was literally the book-chest where the books were kept. The librarian, or person who supervised the books, was known as the armarius. Other terms for librarian were bibliothecarius and custos librorum, or keeper of the books. At Fulda, in Germany, the librarian was facetiously called "clavipotens frater," or "brother with the power of the keys" to the books. Early monasteries strove to have a library containing at least one book per monk, but once this ratio was achieved their collections usually grew slowly. St. Gall had 400 volumes in 841; Cluny had only 570 in the 12th century; Bobbio had 650 about the same time, and as late as the 13th century, the monastery at St. Pons de Tomières in France had only 300. With respect to size of libraries, it should be pointed out that the average volume was large and often contained two or more works. Many of them were florilegia, or selections from many authors, giving a wide sampling of literature in a relatively small space. Acquisitions for the medieval library came by copying in the scriptorium, by gifts, and by occasional purchases. Gifts came from entering monks, who often brought with them any books they might own, and from visiting dignitaries, wealthy patrons, and neighboring scholars. Many volumes came as bequests on the death of their owners. Since the leather-bound parchment codices were very durable, more books were lost through wars, fires, and neglect than through excessive use.

The average monastery or cathedral library contained mainly religious volumes. The core of the collection was the Bible, often in large script and in many volumes. Next in importance came the works of the early church fathers with later commentaries on them, the lives of the martyrs and saints, and the service books of the church. Finally, there were Latin textbooks and grammars, a few of the Latin classics, and perhaps a few works of local literature and history. Greek authors were unknown in most of western Europe, except a few in Latin translation, but they were still known in southern Italy. At the monastery of St.

Nicholas, near Otranto, both Greek and Latin were taught from the 11th to the 14th century, and monastic collections in nearby Sicily also contained Greek works. By the 12th century the average monastic library would have been enlarged both in numbers and in range. All of the earlier works would still be present, and there would also be more and better editions of the Latin classics, some civil and canon law, works of the medieval writers from Boethius onward, and even some science, poetry, and drama of the later writers. Local authors would be more prominent in each collection, and works in the local language would be added to the majority in Latin. In format, the books of the 12th century were almost entirely parchment codices. Papyrus had gone out of use and paper had not yet reached most of Europe.

Interlibrary lending was not unknown in the Middle Ages. Books were loaned to be copied and also just for reading, usually between neighboring collections, but sometimes between libraries as far apart as France and Greece or England and Austria. One English library, of the Priory of Henton, loaned twenty volumes in 1343 alone. In 9th-century Germany, when texts were very scarce, the three monasteries of Fulda, Wurzburg, and Holzkirchen interchanged their texts regularly for copying. Books were also rented and pawned. Ordinarily the books were to be loaned only to the residents of the monastic community, and then only one at a time. In some monasteries, the books could be used only in the daytime and in the vicinity of the bookpresses. In others, they were loaned for the year and could be taken to the reader's living quarters or study carrel. Occasionally books were loaned to outsiders, such as neighboring church leaders or rulers, but then some collateral was usually required, either a book or books of equal value, or a deposit of money.

When the size of the medieval library warranted it, the books were roughly classified by subject, and sometimes by size or acquisition. At first the division might be between theological works and secular ones; between Latin works and those in other languages; or between textbooks and more serious tomes. The religious works might be subdivided into Scriptures, commentaries, biographies, and service books. The secular works, particularly in the cathedral libraries, might be divided according to the teaching subjects of the _trivium_ and the _quadrivium_ (grammar, rhetoric, and dialectic; arithmetic, geometry, music, and astronomy). In some libraries, these divisions were designated by letters and these letters were prominently inscribed on the book-chests. Such a broad classification system apparently sufficed as long as the collections were small, but later in the Middle Ages more complicated schemes were planned, if not actually used. Catalogs of the collections, probably more for inventory purposes than for reader use, were kept from the earliest days. These catalogs were in reality merely lists of books, some arranged by author, some by title, and others by a catchword from the title or first line, or combinations of all three. Almost none were in alphabetical order. Such lists have survived from the 8th century onward, and are fairly numerous for the later Middle Ages. Some of these were originally kept on strips of parchment tacked to the side of the book-chest, while others were kept in codex form. Those of the later centuries were longer, more carefully prepared, and had some logic to the arrangement. In the early 15th century, John Boston of Bury, an Augustinian monk, compiled a sort of union catalog of books in all the monasteries of England. He visited hundreds of monasteries, listed the major works in them and then combined them into an alphabetical catalog with locations by numbers.

The librarian, or custodian of the library, was usually one of the monks assigned by the abbot or bishop. Sometimes the position rotated; sometimes an older or incapacitated monk would be given the task. However, since the duties were simple, owing to the small size and infrequent use of the collection, the position of librarian was usually combined with some other duty. In English libraries, the position of keeper of the books was often combined with that of the cantor or sub-cantor (precentor or succentor) who were also responsible for the direction of the choir and the teaching of singing. Rules for one of these libraries read:

> Let not a book be given to anyone without a proper and sufficient voucher, and let this be entered on the roll.

The same rules reminded the librarian that he should know his wares:

> Thou must have full knowledge of what is given to thy charge. The first duty of a librarian is to strive, in his time, as far as possible, to increase the library committed to him. Let him beware that

> the library does not diminish, that the books in his charge do not in any way get lost or perish. Let him repair by binding books that are damaged by age. Let him know the names of the authors.

In some cases librarians were held personally responsible for the safety of the books in their charge and had to replace any that were lost or damaged. Most of the medieval librarians are unknown but a few became famous. Alcuin, for example, was librarian at York for a few years after 780. He described the contents of his library in a long poem which began:

> There shalt thou find the volumes that contain
> All the ancient fathers who remain;
> There all the Latin writers make their home
> With those of glorious Greece transferred to Rome ...

Toward the end of the Middle Ages, in the 14th and 15th centuries, there were many physical changes in the monastic and cathedral libraries. The number of books increased, in most cases from a few hundred to a few thousand. The *armaria*, or book-chests, had given way to book closets and then to small library rooms. By the 15th century, some religious institutions were constructing separate library buildings. The library of Christ Church, Canterbury, constructed in the early 15th century, was a long room 60 by 22 feet, built over a chapel. At Rouen, France, a cathedral library building completed in 1424 was constructed of masonry, 25 by 105 feet. At York, the cathedral library finished in 1421 had two floors, with books upstairs and a study downstairs. As the number of books increased, they were taken out of the book-chest and put onto combination desk-shelves, arranged in the long, narrow rooms so as to catch the most of natural light. Candles or lamps were usually forbidden in the library rooms for fear of fire. Sometimes the collections were divided into two parts, one for general public use, the other for more restricted use. The custom of chaining books to the desks began not with the most valuable ones, but with the ones most used. Later, after the coming of the printed book, many manuscript volumes were chained simply for safekeeping. Various devices were employed to make the books more readily available, such as the book-wheel and the circular desk. The book-wheel was something like a water-wheel with a number of books arranged on it so that a reader standing in one position could consult as many as a dozen different volumes in succession without moving from his original position. The circular, hexagonal, or octagonal desk was a similar arrangement on a horizontal plane. Here the reader usually had to walk around the desk to consult the several books arranged on its top, but in a few instances these desk tops were also attached to axles so that the books could be rotated into a position in front of the reader.

Monasticism flourished and declined at various times and places in western Europe, but generally speaking its libraries represented the heart of western learning for more than 1,000 years. Then, as the cathedral libraries grew and as the universities developed and emerged as full-blown educational centers, the monasteries declined and their cultural significance faded. Their importance lasted for varying times in different countries, but for the most part they had declined or disappeared by the 17th century. Where they remained, their libraries were of little significance outside the monastery walls.

In England, for example, the monasteries were closed under Henry VIII in the 16th century, and their libraries were destroyed or scattered. It is estimated that the 800 or more monasteries must have contained at least 300,000 volumes at the time of the confiscation of monastery properties. Of these, less than two percent are known to have survived. Even private libraries were destroyed by Protestant reformers seeking to wipe out all evidence of the Roman Catholic Church. Some of the finer manuscripts that were taken from the monastery libraries ended up in booksellers' hands, but many of the ordinary ones were used for candle lighters, pot cleaners, and even for scrubbing boots. Agents of the king secured a few of the finer works for his own private library, but the great majority were lost forever.

In Germany, the peasant uprisings in 1524-25 resulted in great losses to monastic libraries, and French libraries suffered in the religious wars in that country between Catholics and Huguenots a century later. In the 18th century it was the libraries of Austria and Scandinavia that suffered, to be followed by others all over Europe in the French Revolution and Napoleonic wars. Besides these disasters, many individual monasteries were lost in fires and floods. Others were neglected or even abandoned as the fortunes of various orders and individual monasteries declined. Poggio Bracciolini, the Italian manuscript hunter of the early 15th century, found priceless manuscripts moldering in an attic at St. Gall.

In other cases, as the monasteries declined or ceased to exist, their libraries were transferred to other collections, church, municipal, or university, and it is usually these that have survived. The library of the Abbey of Cluny, justly famous in the 10th and 11th centuries, had dwindled to just a few manuscripts by the 18th century, and these were housed in the local town hall. They were eventually turned over to the Bibliothèque Nationale in Paris.

Fortunately, the end of the monasteries and the destruction of their libraries came after the invention of printing, so most of the significant texts were in print and few if any unique sources were lost. By that time, even if other forces had not led to the decline of the significance of monastic libraries, the coming of printing would have done so. The ready availability of books by the hundreds and thousands meant that many types of libraries and educational institutions would become available. Nevertheless, the role of monastery libraries in the preservation of western culture cannot be denied. When all other civilizing forces were destroyed or in decline, they kept the love of learning alive, and their little libraries often sheltered the only copies of the works of such great classical writers as Cicero, Varro, and Tacitus. The golden chain of learning wore remarkably thin, but it did not break.

Additional Readings

James Westfall Thompson's The Medieval Library (Chicago: University of Chicago Press, 1939) remains the most comprehensive survey of this topic. A more recent and very useful collection of essays will be found in M. B. Parkes and Andrew G. Watson, eds., Medieval Scribes, Manuscripts and Libraries: Essays Presented to N. R. Ker (London: Scolar Press, 1978). Other items of interest are:

Connolly, B. "Jesuit Library Beginnings," Library Quarterly 30 (1960): 243-62.

Jackson, Sidney. "Cassiodorus' Institutes and Christian Book Selection," Journal of Library History 1 (1966): 89-100.

Ker, N. R. "Cathedral Libraries," Library History 1 (1967): 38-45.

Wormald, Francis and C. E. Wright. *The English Library Before 1700* (London: University of London, 1958).

Chapter 8

THE RISE OF THE UNIVERSITY, THE RENAISSANCE, THE INVENTION OF PRINTING, AND THE GROWTH OF LIBRARIES IN EUROPE TO 1500

The Rise of University Libraries

In the long drama of western civilization, the role of the monastic libraries, and even of the libraries of Constantinople and Islam, was that of preserving the cultural remains of the classical era. The monastery libraries were largely concerned with theology and saved secular works only incidentally, but they did collect and preserve in addition many of the works of the medieval writers. The Byzantine libraries were used as sources by commentators, encyclopedists, codifiers, and compilers of epitomes and summaries, but not very much as sources for original works. The Moslem libraries were somewhat better employed, and particularly in the sciences their users improved upon the Greeks and turned over to western Europe works far advanced in mathematics, medicine, and astronomy. But for libraries to be a great cultural influence, they must be used; their doors must be open to large numbers of scholars and students so the information contained in their volumes can be disseminated to the largest possible proportion of the population. Although the cathedrals with their attendant schools put their libraries to work to a certain extent, it remained for the medieval university to develop libraries that would not only preserve the heritage of the past but also open it up to general use.

Although there were a few schools that could be called institutions of higher learning in the early Middle Ages, it was not until the late 12th century that the university as such emerged. However, long before there was anything like an organized institution, there were groups of students who gathered around a teacher to learn what he had to teach. Many students wandered from town to town and from country to country in search of the best teachers. In some towns, where there were several good teachers, the students would be forced to organize themselves into groups to protect themselves and to obtain better terms from the townspeople and teachers. In turn, the teachers organized for their own purposes, and these student and teacher "guilds" formed the nucleus of the early university. The word university came from the Latin universitas, which at first meant any organized guild or corporation, while the term used for the combination of students and teachers at first was studium generale. For many years there was no prescribed curriculum nor any specific courses or degrees. Gradually, however, rules and regulations were adopted, charters were obtained from king or pope, and formal universities were recognized.

Although institutions for higher learning were known in ancient times, and in medieval Constantinople, it is probable that the immediate inspiration for the early universities in western Europe came from those in Moslem Spain. Christian students had attended these institutions long before there were any established in the rest of Europe. These students brought back books that included Latin translations of Arabic versions of the Greek classics, the philosophy of Aristotle, and the medicine of Galen and Hippocrates, as well as the works of the Moslem scientists themselves. By the early 12th century, there were schools of medicine at Salerno and Bologna in Italy, where the teaching was almost entirely from Latin translations of Arabic texts. But there is also a link between the cathedral schools and the early universities. In Paris, there had developed before 1200 three strong theological schools, at Notre Dame, Saint-Victor, and Ste. Geneviève, and each of these was more or less directly an outgrowth of a cathedral school. Some historians have traced a direct connection in the development of higher education from the schools of Charlemagne's era to the university at Paris, but many of the links are tenuous, and the specific origin of that university, like that of several others, is uncertain.

At Salerno, no university as such developed from the earlier medical school, but at Bologna in 1158 the group of teachers and students was officially recognized by Emperor Frederic as a university. By 1150, the theological schools in Paris were approaching university status, and in 1167 a group of English students there withdrew to form their own school in England--a school that was the beginning of Oxford University. In 1179, the schools at Paris set up requirements for the title of master, along with a regular organization of chancellor, masters, and students, with a system of lectures and examinations. It was thus in fact a university, but the status came officially in 1200, when Emperor Philip August granted a charter. Two other European universities date from the 12th century: Reggio in northern Italy, formed by students withdrawing from Bologna; and Montpellier in France, where a school of medicine was joined by a school of law in 1160. By 1300, there were sixteen other embryo universities established in western Europe, including those at Naples and Padua in Italy, at Orléans and Toulouse in France, at Salamanca and Seville in Spain, at Cambridge in England, and at Lisbon-Coimbra in Portugal.

For many years the universities did not have libraries as such. The teachers or masters had small book collections of their own, and these were sometimes lent to favored students. The students copied the lectures and thus secured textbooks, or bought or rented them from booksellers. The booksellers (*stationarii*) became numerous around the universities, and their bookstocks were essentially rental libraries for the use of the students. The booksellers eventually formed guilds of their own, and both the university officials and the guilds took pains to insure that the texts of books sold or rented to the students were authentic. Probably the earliest "libraries" in the universities, other than the stocks of the booksellers, were those of the student groups or "nations." These groups sometimes lived or ate together or at least had headquarters where books were communally owned and used. Sometimes fees were collected to pay for the purchase or copying of texts for the student library, and there were often gifts from departing students and interested patrons. At Bologna, the libraries of the nations were cared for by student librarians with the title of *conservateur des livres*, and it is probable that similar practices existed at other universities. At Oxford and Cambridge the student groups evolved eventually into "colleges," each with its own faculty, curriculum, and, later, its own library, but on the continent they continued as little more than boarding groups or fraternities. In most European universities, central libraries are a relatively modern development, but the schools and colleges comprising the universities began developing libraries by the 14th century. Whatever the nature of book collections around the universities, whether bookseller, student library, or college library, they were usually quite small before the advent of printing.

The growth of the libraries at the University of Paris and at Oxford will perhaps give a representative picture of early university library development. At Paris, the earliest definite information we have about a library comes in 1250 with the endowment of a college there by Robert de Sorbonne. As part of his endowment, Sorbonne gave his personal library to the school, along with funds for its upkeep. Other gifts of books came to this collection, and its catalog of 1289 listed over 1,000 titles. Appended to this catalog is a physical description of the Sorbonne Library which provides us with some insight into the nature of the medieval university library.

The library room was long and narrow, twelve by forty feet, lighted by nineteen small windows on each side. There were twenty-eight desks in the room. The more valuable books were chained to the shelves, but the chains were long enough to reach the desk. According to the catalog, the books were arranged in major divisions, including those of the trivium and quadrivium, plus theology, medicine, and law. Only four titles were in French, the remainder in Latin. Another catalog compiled in 1338 listed some 1,700 titles in the Sorbonne Library, indicating that growth was slow.

Rules for the use of the Sorbonne Library in the early 14th century are also revealing. Books were to be used only in the building in which the library was housed, and if taken from the library room, they had to be returned before the end of the day. If anyone other than a student or teacher took a book from the library, he had to leave a deposit of equal value. Somewhat later, the library was divided into two sections, one of permanent reference and another of second copies and works of less value which were allowed to circulate. The reference books, many of them chained, were known as the small library, while the circulating collection was known as the great or common library.

In the 14th century and after, other colleges at the University of Paris formed libraries of their own, including one for the Faculty of Medicine, formed in 1391. Many of them were initiated with donations of private libraries, including some given by former faculty members. Over the years, more than fifty colleges and schools connected with the University formed libraries, and it was not until the 19th century that the University as such achieved a central library. When this was done it was formed with the Sorbonne Library as a nucleus.

Although Oxford was recognized as a studium generale before 1200, it was not until 1214 that recognition by the pope gave it full standing as a university. Robert Grosseteste (ca. 1168-1259), Bishop of Lincoln, gave a small library to the Greyfriars at Oxford in 1253, and there was a small library for the general use of the scholars in St. Mary's Church, but most of the college libraries at Oxford were not begun until the 14th century or later. For example, Merton College dates from 1274, but its library was not formally begun until 1377; University College may have had a collection of books for the use of its students as early as 1280, but an organized library is not noted there until 1440; for Balliol College the corresponding dates are 1282 and 1431. Oriel College was founded in 1324, and as late as 1375 owned only one hundred volumes. However, in 1444, this College removed its books from their ancient chests in the chapel hall and housed them in an entirely separate library building. New College, founded in 1380, was the first Oxford College to begin with a library of its own, and after that date most of the colleges began with their own libraries.

The New College Library is one for which we have some early information. The founder of the College, William of Wykeham, Bishop of Winchester, gave 62 volumes for the chapel library and 312 for a common or circulating collection. Of this latter group, an early inventory showed 136 volumes of theology, 34 of philosophy, 52 of medicine, 53 of canon law, and the remainder of civil law. Each fellow at New College could borrow two books at a time and keep them for periods up to a year. He also had a key to the library so that he could use other books there during the day. The books for general reference were chained, and an inventory was taken of all books once a year.

In 1345, Richard de Bury, Bishop of Durham, and a noted bibliophile, planned the formation of a college at Oxford to be endowed with his own private library at his death. Five Benedictine monks were to be placed in charge of the library and all student-monks were to have the right of borrowing books for use in their own rooms. Duplicate copies of books could be borrowed by anyone in the university community, providing that a deposit was left in their place.

Durham College was founded by Richard's successor, but unfortunately the library was apparently sold to pay Richard's debts and few if any of his books were ever received by the College.

The general university library at Oxford had a complicated early history and did not emerge as an effective collection until the 15th century. About 1320, Thomas Cobham, Bishop of Worcester, erected a building at Oxford with a lower floor to be used as a church and an upper floor to be used for an oratory and a general library for all the colleges. Before the library could be organized, Bishop Cobham died, and his books ended up in the Oriel College Library. In 1367, Bishop Cobham's books, having been forcibly removed from Oriel by the university chancellor, were placed for general use in a room above St. Mary's Church. Some of the books were sold at this time to obtain funds for the care of the remainder by the chaplain. The small collection drifted until 1411, when a new Chancellor, Richard Courtenay, took the library under his supervision and guaranteed pay for a chaplain to act as librarian and to keep the library open five hours each weekday. With this stimulus, the collection grew, and with many gifts from Humphrey, Duke of Gloucester, and others, the general library moved into a new location in the 1480s in the new Divinity School Building, where it was known as "Duke Humphrey's Library" in honor of its chief donor. Humphrey, the younger brother of King Henry V, was a learned man himself, and his personal library was probably the finest in England for its time. Among his gifts to Oxford were finely bound copies of the Greek and Latin classics, as well as contemporary French and Italian works. This was the collection that was to be destroyed in the "reforms" of Edward VI in the 16th century.

Elsewhere in Europe more than seventy-five universities were established before 1500, ranging from Seville in Spain to Uppsala in Sweden and from Catania in Sicily to Aberdeen in Scotland. All followed, in general, the organizational pattern of Paris and Oxford, and some type of library was present in all. On the continent, however, the formation of central university libraries was often delayed for several hundred years after the formation of separate college or institute libraries; in fact, the central library is still not a major entity in some European universities. The 15th century saw a few universities with separate library buildings, including Heidelberg in 1442 and Vienna in 1475. The universities in central Europe developed a type of library in the faculty collection distinct from the college or student libraries and the common or university library.

Unlike the monastery libraries, where acquisitions were gained by copying, the early college libraries grew largely through donations. Numerous instances can be cited of gifts of books to the colleges from kings, nobles, bishops, and merchant collectors. Besides those already mentioned, notable examples would include gifts of books in 1336 to Balliol and Merton Colleges at Oxford from Bishop Stephen Gravesend; gifts of 80 books in 1350 to Trinity College, Cambridge, by Bishop William Bateman; and gifts of 250 volumes to New College, Oxford, in 1387 by Henry Whitefield. On the continent, university libraries received similar gifts, as when Bishop Matthias of Worms gave 90 books to Heidelberg in 1410, and Johannes Sindel bequeathed 200 volumes on medicine and mathematics to Prague in 1450. Endowed funds were also given to universities for the purchase of books or the upkeep of libraries, and there is evidence that library fees were collected from students in some cases. Collections remained small, however, as demonstrated by Heidelberg's 396 volumes in 1396 and 840 in 1461, or Cambridge's Queen's College with 199 volumes in 1472. Not until printed books became common did the library book stocks reach into the thousands.

The physical condition of the early university libraries strongly resembled the contemporary monastery collections. The manuscript codices were kept in book-chests in the 12th and 13th centuries. By the late 13th and early 14th centuries they came out of the _armaria_ onto a desk-shelf combination called _pulpitum_. Each of these could hold about eighteen or twenty books, frequently chained but removable to a lower, slanted desk-shelf. At Queen's College, Cambridge, there were 192 volumes on ten desks and four half-desks. In another library, there were 988 books chained to fifty desks. By the 15th century, separate library buildings were being erected--usually long, narrow rooms lighted by many tall windows. The shape of the room was designed to make as much use of natural light as possible, but probably it was also influenced by the fact that prior to being placed in separate buildings, libraries had often been housed in rooms over arcades or open corridors. Inside the rooms, the book-desks were located between the windows, so that the light fell directly on the reading-shelf. Book-stalls or carrels were being used by the 15th century, with tall bookcases of four to six shelves providing separate booths for readers.

The contents of the medieval university library varied considerably from place to place, but there was some uniformity. Most of the books would be in Latin, with a few in the local language, and even fewer in Greek. Religious works would be predominant, including the Bible, the church fathers, theological commentators, lives of the saints, service books, and canon law. The classics would come next, followed by the medieval writers, with some history and local literature. Philosophy, mathematics, medicine, and astronomy, largely in translations from the Arabic and Greek, were more in evidence in later years. Finally, civil law, based largely on Justinian's code, and a few standard textbooks in logic and grammar would round out the collection. By the 14th and 15th centuries there would be more local material and also more science than in the earlier years, but otherwise the collections would vary little from 1200 to 1450. As in the monasteries, the books were shelved roughly by subject, and at the end of a shelf usually there was a list of the books shelved within. Local classification systems were devised in some cases, but for the most part they were little more than a location symbol, referring to desk, shelf, and book number. The catalogs or booklists were arranged more or less alphabetically, but sometimes indiscriminately by author, title, catchword, or size. One library even arranged its inventory list by the first word on the second page, whatever it might be.

Some of the rules and regulations for the use of university libraries sound familiar, but others appear unusual to us now. In some cases, students could take out the circulating books for a month, or even as long as a year; in others, only teachers and advanced students were allowed to remove books from the library; some books could be taken out only if a deposit were left. In one university library, a few books were considered so valuable that they were kept under triple locks, so three officials with separate keys would have to be present before the books could be seen. In 15th-century Oxford, "only graduates and people in religious orders who have studied philosophy eight years shall study in the library of the University...." The same regulations required an oath "that when they enter the common library for the sake of study they will handle the books they consult decently and not inflict any harm on them by tearing out or ruining layers or single pages of the book...." At the Sorbonne in Paris there was a fine for students who left books lying open, and at the University of Angers in 1431 there was a fine for keeping books more than thirty days.

Book selection policy at Cambridge was probably similar to that at other medieval universities:

> No book is to be brought into the Library or chained there, unless it be of suitable value and utility, or unless the will of the donor has so directed; and none is to be taken out of it unless it so happens that there already be a considerable number on the same subject, or that another copy in better condition and of greater value to take its place has been acquired.

Duplicate books were sometimes sold and, on occasion, valuable volumes of little direct use to the students would be sold so more usable titles could be acquired. Library books were sometimes pawned, officially or unofficially, or even taken for debts owed by the college or its masters. Interlibrary lending between universities seems to have been even less common than between monasteries, and often college libraries of the same institution would zealously guard their unique items to prevent their being copied by another.

Librarians did not emerge as a professional class in the early universities. Instead, the keeper of the books was usually a minor faculty member or even a student. Where the colleges were connected with religious orders, the books were in the charge of one or more monks. At Oxford, and probably elsewhere, books were left to the care of the chaplain. Sometimes the librarian was a scholar well versed in the contents of the volumes he guarded, but he was more often a "keeper of the books," charged with their physical care rather than with the responsibility of mastering their contents. In fact, rules concerning the librarian and his duties were often more strict than those imposed upon users of the library. In some cases the library caretaker was personally responsible for every book in his charge and liable for their costs if any were lost or damaged. Inventories were usually made annually and often carried out in the presence of a high college official.

The early university library was in many ways a direct outgrowth of the monastery and cathedral libraries, but it varied from them in one important aspect: it was a working library. There are frequent references to heavily used volumes in the early college libraries, to books that were badly worn and frequently mended, and to the need for replacements. The emphasis of the libraries was on the maintenance of books for use and not on the keeping of volumes for rarity alone. In this sense, the medieval university library might be called the earliest modern library. In the use of these libraries, in the education of the thousands of students who flocked to the early universities, the medieval world was given a new society of learned men. These "graduates" for the most part did not remain secluded in monasteries or dedicated to theology but were trained in civil and canon law, in medicine and philosophy, and they went out into the world and made their knowledge known to others. From the universities and their modest book collections came the learning that was to pave the way for the Renaissance in western Europe. If it was the monastery libraries that preserved knowledge for 1,000 years, it was the university libraries that put that knowledge to use and, in doing so, ushered in the modern era and put an end to the Middle Ages.

The Great Book Collectors and the Rescue of the Ancient Classics

Although monastery, cathedral, and university libraries were the most significant centers of learning during the Middle Ages, there were also private libraries worthy of notice. These libraries were of lasting importance for several reasons. First, they added materially to the amount of literature available at any given time and place, supplementing the institutional libraries. Second, by means of gifts and bequests, they frequently became parts of the institutional libraries, adding considerably to their value. Finally, in the case of the private libraries of the feudal nobility, they often formed the nuclei of future municipal, state, and national libraries. Frequently they were more finely bound, more handsomely written, less worn, and better preserved than their counterparts in the more public collections.

The fate of the many Roman private libraries that existed prior to 500 is worth considering, since it seems likely that at least some of the thousands of manuscripts in the villas of the nobility would have survived. Some of them did, as gifts to monastic and church collections and in isolated family libraries of Italy, Spain, and southern France. Certainly a good percentage of the extant Latin literature survived in western European collections, although some of it was literally lost for decades or even centuries. Early manuscripts were worn out, and those that have come down to us are copies of copies, so textual examination, comparison, and criticism are necessary to obtain anything close to the correct original. Although some of the contents of the late Roman private libraries have survived, most of them were destroyed as definitely and finally as those of the Roman temples.

Though they were rare--at least, modern evidence of them is scarce--private libraries existed in western Europe even in the darkest periods of the Middle Ages. A private library of secular literature in southern France in the 5th century, which included many of the Latin classics, is described in a letter of Rusticus, Bishop of Narbonne from 430 to 461. He depicts what was apparently a provincial Roman villa, equipped with bookcases adorned with portraits of orators and poets. Apollinaris Sidonius, writing at Toulouse in the same century, shows acquaintance with a sizable library of sources. The private library of Isidore, Bishop of Seville, accumulated in the 7th century, has already been mentioned, but Spanish contemporaries of Isidore also had significant collections.

Many other church officials, bishops, archbishops, and cardinals, contributed to medieval library history, either in their own collections or in the libraries they built in their institutions. The Bishop of Passau in the 10th century reputedly prized his library, although it included only fifty-six books. Philip d'Harcourt, Bishop of Bayeux in the 12th century, gave a hundred volumes of his personal library to the cathedral at Bec in Normandy. Richard Gravesend, Bishop of London (1280-1303), owned eighty volumes, including three Bibles, works of the church fathers, canon law, and some works of secular history. John of Salisbury willed his library to the cathedral at Chartres in 1180, while Roger de Thoris, Archdeacon of Exeter, gave his books to the Greyfriars there in 1266. Even parish priests found it possible to own a few books, and Geoffrey de Lawath of St. Magnus in London had a library of forty-nine volumes in the 13th century, including medical works, theology, and grammar. Usually the books owned by religious figures were theological, but there were often evidences of interest in literature and practical subjects as well.

The development of book collections in Italy from the 9th to the 12th century shows an interesting contrast. While northern Italy lagged behind France and Germany in the collecting of libraries during this period, the southern part of the peninsula, along with Sicily, was undergoing a miniature renaissance of its own. Both in the monasteries and at the courts of the rulers there was an atmosphere that encouraged learning and scholarship. This was true despite the almost constant strife with Italians, Normans, Spanish, Moslems, and Byzantines, warring for control of the area. Greek was taught in the monastery schools; libraries were gathered that included Greek works, translations from the Arabic, and Hebrew as well as Latin. Duke Sergius of Naples in the 9th century collected a small library and presented it to the cathedral there. His son, Duke Gregory, could read both Latin and Greek in an era when the latter language was almost unknown in the rest of Europe.

Some women among the medieval nobility were well educated and became scholars and book collectors. A few nuns and abbesses were noted for their interest in books during the early Middle Ages, but after the 12th century it was the wives and daughters of noblemen and rulers who turned to collecting libraries. Clemence of Hungary, wife of Louis X of France, had a library of her own in the early 14th century. Jeanne d'Evreux, wife of Charles the Fair (1322-28), owned a library, largely religious but containing some secular works in French. Jeanne of Burgundy and Blanche of Navarre, both wives of Philip VI (1328-50), brought books of their own to be added to Philip's library. Queen Isabel, wife of Charles VI (1380-1422), had so many books that one of her ladies-in-waiting had to serve as her personal librarian. Margaret of York, English wife of Charles, Duke of Burgundy, in the 15th century, brought a small library of English works with her in 1468, and joined with her husband in continuing to build up the library of the ducal house of Burgundy. A scholar in her own right, she commissioned the translation of Boethius' Consolation of Philosophy from Latin into French, and she brought William Caxton from England to learn the art of printing in Bruges. He later became the first printer in England.

The Jewish minority in Western Europe also produced scholars and book collectors. Under the Moslems in Spain and Sicily, the Jews flourished in a tolerant atmosphere, and many scholars, lawyers, and physicians emerged among them. The Jewish Bible, together with the core of literature built up around it, formed the basis of numerous Jewish book collections, but others went far beyond this theological center and built up large libraries of secular literature.

Jews in the north of Europe were not so wealthy as

those in the Mediterranean area, so they were often hard-pressed to acquire even the necessary books for their synagogues. However, one French Jew, Juda Ibn Tibbon of the 12th century, left a library notable for its contents if not for its great size. Tibbon left his books to his son with concise instructions on how to handle them:

> Arrange them all in good order, so that thou weary not in looking for a book when thou needest it.... Write down the titles of the books in each row of the cases in a separate notebook and place each in its row, in order that thou mayest be able to see exactly in which row any particular book is without mixing up the others. Do the same with the cases. Look continually into the catalog in order to remember what books thou hast. When thou lendest a book, record its title before it leaves the house; and when it is brought back draw thy pen through the memorandum....

Tibbon (1120-70) was a philosopher and scholar who translated books from Arabic into Latin. His motive in building his library was to make it so complete that he would never again have to borrow a book.

Two famous medieval book collectors left works concerning their collecting activities that discussed books they owned or wanted to own. One was Richard of Fournival, Chancellor of Amiens in France, who wrote his Biblionomia in the 13th century. In this somewhat fanciful work he described a "garden of literature" in which tables were covered with manuscripts on various subjects. His largest subject area was philosophy, but medicine, law, and theology were also included in his "garden." There is some doubt as to whether the work describes an actual book collection or is merely imaginary. Also, there is some doubt that it was even written by Fournival, although it is usually ascribed to him. However, it is an excellent account of literary interests of the period and most of the manuscripts described are known to exist or to have existed at one time.

The other bibliophile was Richard de Bury (1287-1345), teacher, officeholder, and later Bishop of Durham. He was an ardent book collector from his earlier years, and when he later became a diplomat in the service of Edward III of England, he visited libraries, scriptoria, and booksellers in many parts of Europe. He bought many books and others were given to him, particularly after he became a bishop. He respected and would accept books in almost any form and on almost any subject. His Philobiblon (or The Love of Books) was completed about 1344, but it was not printed until 1473, and since that date it has appeared in many editions. Basically, it is a book in praise of books, but it also tells how the author collected his library and thus gives an elaborate picture of the book world of his day. Some of his chapter headings were: "That the treasure of wisdom is chiefly contained in books"; "That it is meritorious to write new books and to renew the old"; "Of the numerous opportunities we have had of collecting a store of books"; and finally, "That we have collected so great a store of books for the common benefit of scholars and not only for our own pleasure." De Bury noted that books were the storehouses of wisdom, and he says of them: "There everyone who asks receiveth thee, and everyone who seeks finds thee, and to everyone who knocketh boldly it is speedily opened." One other notable quote from the Philobiblon shows the author's basic belief: "All the glory of the world would be buried in oblivion, unless God had provided mortals with the remedy of books." Richard de Bury's books were supposed to have been given on his death to the Priory of Durham at Oxford, but instead they were probably sold to pay his many debts. Some estimates indicate that Richard de Bury may have possessed as many as 1500 volumes, a very large library for his time, but whatever the number, it is certain that it was the most notable private library in 14th-century England.

The most important private libraries in Europe before 1500, however, were the libraries of the Italian scholar-bookmen who figured prominently in the Renaissance. The Renaissance was ruled by a central concept--humanism--which permeated all areas of intellectual life, but was essentially literary in nature and was firmly grounded upon the study and imitation of classical literature. Scholars everywhere grew increasingly committed to the classical spirit, and many determined to devote their lives to seeking out, recovering, editing, translating, and critically analyzing the works of the ancients.

The movement, basically secular in nature, was spearheaded by men of the world, most of whom were fanatical book collectors. As scholars have frequently noted, their insatiable appetites for the works of the classical authors led to the accumulation of many very important private libraries and stimulated the growth of a book trade which contributed to the breakdown of the Church's monopoly on learning. In time, humanism even gained some influence within the Church, and several noted book collectors of the late Renaissance were ecclesiastics.

From the 14th century through the 16th, Italian merchants, princes, and religious leaders, either in collaboration or in competition, succeeded in bringing to light the majority of the Greek and Latin classics now known to the western world. Some of these classics were discovered in Italy itself, in monasteries, church libraries, or in private hands. Still others were found or rediscovered in the, by then, neglected monastery libraries of France, Switzerland, and central Europe. But of more importance were the volumes brought to Italy from Constantinople, Greece, and the Moslem countries. For centuries these had been lost to western Europe and might have been lost forever if they had not been rescued at that time.

Petrarch (1304-74) was one of the earliest of these Italian book collectors. He collected manuscripts from all parts of Europe and devoted himself particularly to the classic Latin authors. While the reputation of some of his precursors--such as the Paduan judge and lover of classical poetry, Lovato Lovati--has grown in the light of recent research, Petrarch remains the unrivaled champion of the early Renaissance. His rare qualities as book collector and scholar aided him in the quest for the classic Latin authors, and he built the finest private library of his day. He had hoped to see his library made available to the public after his death, but his plans never materialized and his books were scattered.

His contemporary and follower, Boccaccio (1313-75), also played a leading role in the rescue of the ancient classics. While less the scholar than his mentor, Boccaccio wrote widely in a popular vein and did much to stimulate interest in classical literature. It was Boccaccio the book collector who is believed to have been responsible for unlocking the riches of the library at Monte Cassino, and also for spiriting away a number of major works, most notable those of Tacitus, Apuleius, and Varro, to his home in Florence. Upon his death, this magnificent collection of books was given to the monastery of San Spirito in Florence.

A third Florentine completes the triad of great Renaissance book collectors from that city. Coluccio Salutati (1331-1406) had studied with Petrarch when the latter was an old man, and he knew Boccaccio well. Coluccio stands as the humanist who passed the torch from one generation of humanists to another, and several of his disciples were leading figures in the "Great Age of Discovery," in the first half of the 15th century. By 1400 the popularity of the ancient texts, and the unprecedented recognition awarded to those who recovered them, stimulated an enormous interest in the recovery of the classical writers, and many Venetian, Florentine, and Genoese ship captains considered manuscripts to be valuable cargo for their return trips from the eastern Mediterranean. In 1408 Guarino of Verona returned from a visit to the East with a collection of fifty Greek manuscripts for which he found a ready sale. The Sicilian book collector, Giovanni Aurispa, brought in over 200 Greek manuscripts in the year 1423 alone, a feat which amounted to the "transplantation of an entire literature to new and fertile soil." Francesco Filelfo, who went to Constantinople in 1420 as a member of the Venetian legation there, brought home with him about forty Greek volumes, many of which were unknown in Latin translation before that date. The quest for manuscripts led not only to works in Greek but to Hebrew as well. Giovanni Pico della Mirandola, a Christian Hebrew scholar, owned more than one hundred Hebrew works, and his student and friend, Johann Reuchlin, acquired thirty-six more in the same language.

It is noteworthy that much of this collecting was done by individuals rather than by universities, church, or governmental agencies. Many of them were merchants or religious personnel, but the greatest collectors were the Italian princes and their agents. Several men became famous for their ability to locate and obtain manuscripts for pay. Janus Lascaris (ca. 1450-1535), for example, obtained many manuscripts from the East, first for Louis XII of France and later for the Medici family in Italy. Many of these came from the monasteries of Greece, including Mount Athos and others on the Aegean Islands, and among them were scores of previously unknown works. Vespasiano da Bisticci made a profession of obtaining and copying manuscripts, and aided in the building up of several of the famous Italian collections. Poggio Bracciolini (1380-1459) was a collector famous for his discoveries of unknown manuscripts in European monasteries. He is most noted for uncovering lost works of Lucretius and Quintilian.

One important religious collector was Cardinal Bessarion (ca. 1400-1492), a Greek by birth but a longtime resident of Italy. He translated many classical Greek works into Latin and tried to build up the largest Greek library in the world. He had agents searching Greece and Asia Minor and was responsible for rescuing several hundred manuscripts. In 1468 he gave his library to the city of Venice on condition that it be suitably housed and open to the public. This library eventually was built and became the Biblioteca Marciana, or Library of St. Mark.

Among the most important Italian collectors were the members of the Medici family. Cosimo de Medici (1389-1464) hired Vespasiano da Bisticci to collect books for him. At one time, Vespasiano employed forty-five copyists and in twenty-two months produced some 200 books, all elegantly inscribed and bound, for the Medici library. Cosimo's library contained the Bible in several copies, religious commentaries, works of the church fathers, the medieval writers, and also many classical works in philosophy, history, poetry, and drama. In addition to the works he obtained himself, Cosimo also acquired a library of 800 volumes collected by Niccolo di Niccoli of Florence. Tommaso Parentucelli, later Pope Nicholas V, was at one time Cosimo's librarian. Cosimo was himself a scholar who read Latin well and had some knowledge of Greek, Hebrew, and Arabic. Drawing on his collections, he began several libraries including one in the Convent of San Marco at Florence and another in the Abbey at Fiesole.

At his death, however, most of Cosimo's volumes remained in the family library, and this collection was greatly enlarged by his grandson, Lorenzo de Medici (1449-92). Lorenzo the Magnificent, prince, poet, and patron of the arts, had Janus Lascaris as one of his book-collecting agents, and he built up a noble library of religion and the classics. He allowed scholars to use his library and even permitted other collectors to copy his treasures. Nearly half of his books were in Greek and languages other than Latin, and he was one of the first to permit printed books on his shelves. After his death, the Medici family library had a precarious existence, first in the Convent of San Marco, later in Rome, and finally, in 1521, back in Florence. Eventually it was housed in the Biblioteca Laurentiana, a building designed especially for it by Michelangelo.

Federigo, Duke of Urbino (1444-82), was another of the ardent 15th-century Italian collectors. His palace had a series of rooms filled with books, and he invited artists, scholars and writers to use them. He loved the classics but also added to his library the standard church literature and contemporary authors. For many years he maintained a large staff of copyists, and Vespasiano da Bisticci also served him for a time as librarian and book-buyer. At his death in 1482, his collection included 772 manuscripts, of which 73 were Hebrew and 93 Greek. The library room in his palace measured forty-five by twenty feet, and the books were kept in eight presses, with seven shelves each.

The development of the Vatican Library in Rome during the later Middle Ages can be considered along with private libraries since it was largely the result of the activities of a few individuals. Pope Nicholas V (1447-55) who as Tommaso Parentucelli had been librarian to Cosimo de Medici, was responsible for the rebirth of the Vatican Library. The library collected by the popes at Avignon had been dispersed, and after the return of the papacy to Rome no serious attempt had been made to rebuild the collection. When Nicholas became pope, he found only some 350 volumes in various states of repair, and to this he added his own private library. Then he proceeded to add to it with all the resources at his command and with his own wide knowledge of the book world. He sent papal agents all over Europe seeking manuscripts as gifts or for copying. The papal librarian Tortelli helped to build the collection and translated Greek works into Latin. By the time of his death, Nicholas had built the Vatican Library to over 1,200 volumes and made it one of the finest in Italy.

The papacy for the next few years was more concerned with the war against the Turks than with the papal library, but Pope Sixtus (1471-84) not only enlarged the library but remodeled a building for it. In 1475, it included 2,500 volumes, about one-third Greek and two-thirds Latin. In 1484, an inventory of the library in its new quarters found it housed in four rooms and containing some 3,500 volumes. The four rooms consisted of a public Greek library, a public Latin library, a rare book collection of "biblioteca secreta," and the pope's private library. The humanist scholar, Bartolomeo Platina, was librarian in the Vatican after 1475. He cataloged and classified the library, keeping strict records of all use, and opened it to all serious scholars. Although the primary purpose of the library was to collect and preserve works on the history and doctrine of the church, from the days of Nicholas V onward it also contained an increasing number of secular works. Although he probably exaggerated a little, the contemporary Vespasiano da Bisticci was able to say of the new Vatican Library that: "Never since the time of Ptolemy had half so large a number of books of every kind been brought together."

The Emergence of the National Libraries

Though many of the libraries of the late medieval bookmen went into public collections or were scattered, a significant few formed the beginnings of future national libraries. The kings of Naples, beginning with Charles I (1220-85), built up a notable library in that city. This royal collection grew in size and usefulness for some 200 years. In 1485, however, when the French captured Naples, most of the royal library was carried away as spoils of war to join other collections in forming the French royal library. More specifically, however, the French national library began with Charles V, who took a small collection left by his father and installed it, with many additions, in the Chateau du Louvre in 1367. With Gilles Malet as librarian, the French royal library grew to nearly 1,000 volumes scattered through three rooms of the palace. Though largely theological, the library also contained other subjects, including history, law, French literature, and science. There were some works translated from the Arabic. Actually, earlier kings of France had owned books from before the days of Charlemagne, but most of these, like his, were dispersed at the death of the collector. In the wars with the English in the early 15th century, part of the royal French library was captured and carried to England by the Duke of Bedford, but in 1461 Louis XI reestablished a library in the Louvre. In 1472, the library of the Duc de Berry was added to this collection, and still later a part of the collection of the Dukes of Burgundy. About 1500, Louis XII moved the royal library to Blois, where the Orleans family already had a magnificent collection, and added to it the libraries he had captured in Italy. Not until 1595 was the royal library to return permanently to Paris.

In England, the kings also had been haphazard collectors of books since the days of King Alfred the Great in the 9th century. He not only collected books but translated Latin works into Anglo-Saxon, including the writings of Bede and Boethius. After Alfred, various English kings made small palace collections of books, often gifts unopened, but these were considered private property and never became the base of a national library. Not until the 18th century was England to acquire one, in the British Museum.

In Austria, the national library had its beginning in the early 15th century when Emperor Friedrich V ordered all books and archives belonging to the government to be brought to a central location and organized. Books from Constantinople came to this collection as the Byzantine Empire disintegrated, but the library was still not very large when, in 1497, Emperor Maximilian I officially established an imperial library with Conrad Celtes, the humanist poet, as the first librarian. Elsewhere in Europe, the library of the Dukes of Burgundy, augmented by those of some of the Austrian princes, survived intact until the 19th century when it formed the basis for the national library of Belgium. Several German principalities began their libraries with the collections of their rulers before 1500, and in Spain the union of Aragon and Castile in the late 15th century made the foundation of a Spanish national library possible.

One of the most famous of the European royal libraries in the 15th century was that of King Matthias Corvinus of Hungary (1440-90). Matthias had agents throughout Europe buying and borrowing volumes for his library. In that library, which occupied a wing of the palace at Buda, he had twenty or more copyists, illuminators, and bookbinders producing for him beautiful volumes in Latin, Greek, Arabic, and Hebrew. In 1476, he married Beatrice of Aragon, herself an ardent book collector, and between them they gathered a library that for its time was unusually large and beautiful. It was housed in a wing of the palace and divided into two collections, one Latin and the other Greek and Oriental. Various reports credit Matthias with having up to 50,000 volumes, but it is doubtful that he could have had over a tenth of that number. After his death, his books were gradually dispersed and any that were left were probably taken by the Turks when they captured Buda in 1526. Many individual items from the Corvinus library have survived, however, and they now form some of the most treasured items in modern European libraries.

All told, the 15th century was remarkable from the standpoint of library development, much of this progress resulting from the efforts of individuals rather than organizations. Two events helped to shape this development. The first was the coming of the Renaissance, with its emphasis on humanism and the recovery of classical philosophy and literature. Cause and effect are closely interwined here, since the building of book collections undoubtedly helped to bring on and spread the Renaissance. The second event was the development of printing from movable type, which occurred about the middle of the 15th century.

Printing and Libraries

This analysis of the growth of libraries in Europe prior to 1500 cannot conclude without at least brief reference to the invention of printing from movable type. Bacon, in his Novum Organum, announced that three inventions unknown to the ancients had changed the "appearance and state of the whole world," and they were "printing, gunpowder and the compass."

Scholars are just beginning to extend their work on the history of printing beyond questions of origins and development to the far more complex matters related to the impact, influence, and consequences of the invention of printing. The development and spread of the press from its point of origin in mid-15th-century Germany is best left to histories of printing. However, it is important to note that each major development in the book arts has had a measurable impact on the history of libraries. This influence is particularly obvious in the case of printing.

The most dramatic consequence was the marked increase in the output of books, coupled with a substantial decrease in the amount of labor necessary to produce them. Such a combination meant that throughout Europe books were much more readily available to people and generally at a much lower cost. This fact had the result of making more books more readily available to libraries of all kinds, thus contributing to the rapid increase in the size of libraries and a concomitant growth in complexity. In a way, the invention of printing may be said to have given birth to modern librarianship, in the sense that the ever-increasing size of library collections made possible by the printing press stimulated the emergence of a profession charged with the responsibility of organizing and directing these at once large, complex, and valuable national resources.

Additional Reading

A monumental book that provides an essential foundation for any understanding of this period is Elizabeth L.

Eisenstein's The Printing Press as an Agent of Change: Communications and Cultural Transformations in Early Western Europe (Cambridge: Cambridge University Press, 1979). Other works of interest are:

Connell, S. "The Italian Renaissance Library," Journal of the Warburg and Courtauld Institutes 35 (1972): 163-86.

Geanakoplos, D. J. Greek Scholars in Venice: Studies in the Dissemination of Greek Learning from Byzantium to Western Europe (Cambridge: Cambridge University Press, 1962).

Thompson, James Westfall. The Medieval Library (Chicago: University of Chicago Press, 1939).

Wormald, Francis and C. E. Wright, eds. The English Library Before 1700 (London: University of London, 1958).

PART III

MODERN LIBRARY DEVELOPMENT IN THE WEST

Chapter 9

EUROPEAN LIBRARIES: EXPANSION AND DIVERSIFICATION TO 1917

European National Libraries

The growth of libraries in Europe since 1500 has been enormous as compared with the pitifully small collections available during the Middle Ages. The primary cause of this remarkable growth was, of course, the development of printing, which produced more books and cheaper books than could have been imagined a century earlier. Ready access to books also contributed to an increase in literacy levels; a development that stimulated demand for books and encouraged the rise of a substantial book trade. Before 1500 a great book might be available in a hundred manuscript copies, read at most by a few thousand people; after that date, it could be available in thousands of copies and read by hundreds of thousands of people. It has been estimated that in the 16th century more than 100,000 different books were printed in Europe alone, and assuming an average of 1,000 copies each, that would mean a hundred million available to Europeans during that century. The power of the printed word increased a hundredfold the power of the written word, and never again were Europe and the western world to suffer from a lack of graphic communication for the conveyance of facts and ideas.

Of all the libraries of modern Europe, the most outstanding have been the national libraries, those rapidly growing collections dedicated to preserving every book and manuscript which in any way related to the national heritage. Sometimes these collections developed at the expense of other libraries. They may not always have been as influential as some other libraries, notably those of the great universities, but they benefited from the spirit of nationalism and often survived and even flourished while other libraries suffered in wars or depressions. Generally speaking, they had permanency and economic security if not generous budgets and well-trained staffs. Their collective success and survival have meant much to the total history of libraries in the western world.

The French national library in Paris, the Bibliothèque Nationale, ranks among the finest of European libraries. Its development through a series of royal family libraries down through the 16th century has already been traced. After sojourns in castles at Blois and Fontainebleau, the royal library was returned to Paris during the reign of Henry IV (1589-1610). In 1537 it received the "right of deposit" of one copy of each book printed in France, thus being assured a steady supply of new acquisitions at minimal expense. For some years the royal library was housed at the College of Clermont in Paris, but by 1622 it was installed in an old mansion on the Rue de la Harpe. In that year its first printed catalog was issued, listing some 6,000 titles. This catalog consisted of two main divisions, manuscript and print, and each of these was subdivided by language. Under Louis XIV (1643-1715), and particularly under his prime minister, Jean Baptiste Colbert, the royal library grew rapidly. With Nicholas Clement as librarian, the collection was reclassified according to a system of twenty-three main divisions based on the letters of the alphabet. By the 1720s the library was forced to move to a site on the Rue Richelieu, where it soon contained some 80,000 printed volumes and 16,000 manuscripts. These quarters have been enlarged, extended, remodeled, and virtually rebuilt over the years, but the site has remained the same down to the 20th century.

Throughout its history the Bibliothèque Nationale has been favored by the accession of thousands of major works, including many whole libraries. Some of these have been purchased, others were donated or acquired by more direct means. One of the earliest collections added was made up of some 800 manuscripts collected for Catherine de Medici and acquired under the librarianship of J. A. de Thou in the early 17th century. In 1662 the library of Raphael Trichet du Fresne, containing some 1,200 volumes, was purchased. In 1670 the medical library of Jacques Mentel, almost 10,000 volumes, was acquired, and in 1672, agents of the library returned from the Near East with some 630 manuscripts in Hebrew, Syriac, Coptic, Turkish, Persian, and Greek. One of the most exotic acquisitions was a gift of forty-two volumes in Chinese from the Emperor of China by way of a returning French missionary. In addition, book-dealers throughout Europe sent books and manuscripts for consideration, and diplomats in foreign countries sent back gifts and purchases, so the collection in the royal library grew constantly in numbers and value.

The late 18th century saw a rapid growth at the expense of other French libraries. In 1763, for example, when the Jesuits were expelled from Paris, their libraries were seized and the more valuable works added to the royal library. After the beginning of the French Revolution in 1789, the library suffered at first from lack of interest and funds, but it soon was designated the "Bibliothèque Nationale" rather than the "Bibliothèque Royale," and thousands of volumes from the libraries of the fleeing nobility were added to it. Later on, libraries from monasteries, cathedrals, and church schools were seized, and all books that were not duplicates were placed in the national library. The unwanted volumes were destroyed or sent to public libraries throughout France. Thus, though the Revolution resulted in the breaking up of many private and religious libraries, it also brought many treasures into the Bibliothèque Nationale and aided in the establishment of municipal libraries. Moreover, it brought with it the ideas and ideals of national library planning, national bibliographies, and library service for all the people. Still later, the armies of both the revolution and the Empire under Napoleon seized libraries in other parts of Europe and added choice volumes to their national library.

In the 19th century, then, the Bibliothèque Nationale was one of the foremost libraries in the world. By 1818 it contained nearly 1,000,000 volumes; by 1860, 1,500,000; and by 1908 there were more than 3,000,000 printed volumes. Concomitant with the ever-increasing size of the collections was the ever-more-pressing problem of reorganization to cope with the rapid growth. In 1739 the librarian, Abbé Jean-Paul Bignon, a tireless bureaucrat who was both Royal Librarian and President of the Academy of Sciences, divided the library into four main collections: theology, canon law, civil law, and belles lettres. In 1840 a complete reorganization was begun and in that year the author catalog alone totaled eighty-nine volumes. In the 1850s the library building was virtually rebuilt under the architectural guidance of Henri Labrouste. The late 19th century found the library under the able direction of Leopold Delisle (1874-1907) who, although he was a medievalist at heart and strongly interested in manuscripts and paleographical studies, did much to modernize the library and make it available to scholars from all over the world.

Equal to the Bibliothèque Nationale in international importance is the British Museum, which, now a part of the new British Library, remains the national library of Great Britain. This library is not as old as that of France, since the early royal book collections were usually dispersed upon the deaths of their owners, but it has grown rapidly in its two centuries of existence. Although based in part on royal collections, the British Museum has been largely the result of the amalgamation of many private libraries. As early as 1556, the scholar and scientist John Dee suggested to Queen Mary that a royal library should be collected from the scattered manuscripts of the monasteries closed by Henry VIII, but nothing came of the suggestion. Again, a century later, John Dury in his _The Reformed Librarie Keeper_ made a similar suggestion, and in 1694 Richard Bentley's _Proposal for Building a Royal Library_ was even more specific. Perhaps as a result of Bentley's suggestion, the first elements of the British Museum began taking shape in 1700. In that year, the valuable manuscript library of Sir Henry Cotton, together with housing, was bequeathed to the nation by its owner and accepted by William III. In 1707 Queen Anne allowed the royal library to be housed with the Cottonian library, but the two were moved several times, suffered from a fire in 1737, and were never available to the public.

The achievement of a truly national library for England came in the 1750s. In 1753 Sir Hans Sloane, royal physician and a notable book collector, directed in his will that his library and museum be sold to the government for a modest sum on condition that it be suitably housed and maintained. After much debate in Parliament, the collection was purchased and a sum appropriated for a building. Sloane's library contained over 50,000 volumes, but it was overshadowed by another contemporary private collection, that of Robert Harley, which contained as many books plus thousands of pamphlets and manuscripts. Unfortunately, at Harley's death much of his library was sold, but the manuscripts were acquired by the government. To these collections, King George II, in 1757, added his own private library, and the British Museum was formally opened to the public in a rambling mansion known as Montague House on 15 January 1759. The title of Museum was appropriate, since the Sloane collection included many thousands of geological and botanical specimens, but over the years the library has far surpassed the museum in general significance.

Although several minor collections were added to the library in the 18th century, the book collection as a whole grew only slowly until after the Napoleonic wars. In 1817 a major accession came in the purchase of the Charles Burney library of some 13,000 volumes and 500 early Greek and Latin manuscripts. Most important in the Burney library, however, were the files of 17th- and 18th-century British newspapers, bound chronologically and indexed by Burney himself. In 1823 the library of George III was added to the Museum, literally doubling the size of its printed collection. Plans for a new building were begun, and a first wing of this structure was completed in 1828, at which time the library had over 200,000 volumes. The new building was planned originally as a huge quadrangle surrounding an open court, but in the 1850s the Museum was converted into a solid square by making the center court into a bookstack surrounding a circular reading area.

The British Museum has had many outstanding librarians and directors, but probably the most significant was Sir Antonio Panizzi, who came to the staff as assistant librarian in 1831. His energy and interest led him to the position of Keeper of the Printed Books in 1837, and under his administration the library earned the reputation of being the best administered in the world. He supervised the move into the new building in 1838, the building of the central reading room and stacks in the 1850s, the preparation of the first complete catalog and the accompanying catalog rules, the enforcement of the deposit law, the obtaining of special funds from Parliament for the enlargement of the collection, and the beginning of the printed catalog. Finally, in 1856, he was rewarded with the title of Principal Librarian, and he filled this position until his retirement in 1868. His leadership in library affairs was widely acknowledged, and must be considered the most influential librarian of his time.

There are also national libraries in Scotland and Wales. The National Library of Scotland, renamed in 1925, was formerly the Advocate's Library, founded in Edinburgh in 1682. Originally a legal library, it began at an early date to specialize in Scottish literature and history. In 1709 it was granted depository rights for all books published in Great Britain, and under the librarianship of the historian-philosopher, David Hume, it grew to a collection of some 30,000 volumes by the mid-18th century. By 1900, gifts of books and funds increased it to nearly 500,000 volumes. The National Library of Wales in Aberystwyth, founded in

1873, was based on two large private libraries, those of Sir John Williams, a Welsh surgeon, and Edward Owen, a Welsh language scholar, and on the library of the University College of Wales. The library concentrates on Welsh language and literature, containing virtually everything published in Welsh or about Wales since the invention of printing. In a building of its own since 1916, the Welsh National Library also serves as the library of the University of Wales and as a regional library for Wales in the National Library System.

Possibly the largest national library in the world today is that of Soviet Russia, the Saltykov-Shchedrin Library in Leningrad, formerly the Imperial Russian Library of St. Petersburg. Like the British Museum, this collection had its beginning in the 18th century, and like the Bibliothèque Nationale it owes its origins to the spoils of war, in this case a captured Polish library taken by the armies of the Empress Catherine. This library had been built up by the Counts Andreas and Joseph Zaluski before 1740. It was largely western European in language and origin, but it contained a few Russian works and almost everything printed in Polish. In 1740 the Zaluski library was formally turned over to the Polish government and a few years later it was opened to public as the Polish National Library. When Warsaw was captured by the Russians in 1794 and Poland was divided between Prussia, Russia, and Austria, the national library, with its 250,000 books and 10,000 manuscripts, went to the Russians as spoils of war. After the death of Catherine, the library remained inactive until Count Alexander Stroganoff was appointed its director in 1800. He added to it the various small collections owned by the Russian government and organized it into an effective library collection. An early acquisition was the Dubrovsky collection of manuscripts, obtained by a Russian agent in Paris during the French Revolution. Many of these originally had been in the Abbey of St. Germain des Prés, and before that in the monastery at Corbie. At Stroganoff's death in 1811, A. N. Olenin became director of the Imperial Library and it was officially opened to the public. Since the original Polish collection had contained only a few books in Russian, the defect was remedied in 1810 by a legal deposit law that gave the library two copies of every book published in Russia. With a relatively meager budget, Olenin greatly increased the size of the library through exchanges, purchases, and gifts, and at his death in 1843 he left a scholarly collection that was really a national library.

Count M. A. Korf, librarian from 1849 to 1861, was

responsible for the next period of growth for the Russian Imperial Library. During his administration he added some 350,000 printed volumes and 11,000 manuscripts, as well as a large number of prints, photographs, musical scores, and maps. He also remodeled the library building and completely reorganized the book collection, dividing it into departments on the general plan of the British Museum. More important for the library, Korf advertised it and brought it to the public attention so that it not only grew in size but in use and public esteem. By 1860, it was second only to the Bibliotheque Nationale in all the libraries of Europe. Growth was steady, if not spectacular, during the remainder of the 19th century, and a new building was completed in 1901.

Another late comer in the national library field in Europe was the German Imperial Library in Berlin. In 1661 the private library of Frederick William, the Great Elector of Prussia, was opened to the public, but was housed in an almost inaccessible wing of the palace and was not very large. Before his death, Frederick William had built this collection to more than 20,000 volumes, all cataloged and classified by its librarian, Christoph Hendreich. In 1699 the legal deposit system was adopted, which aided the growth of the library in Prussian-printed works. Under Frederick William I of Prussia the library grew to about 75,000 volumes by 1740, and under Frederick the Great to about 150,000 volumes by 1790. The library was moved to a new building in 1780, and after that date the book collection grew fairly rapidly through the purchase or donation of several major private libraries.

In 1810 the library was placed under the Prussian Department of Culture and thus divorced from the direct control of the King. Growth of the collection was henceforth more systematic, and until 1831 the national library served also as the library of the University of Berlin. From 1817 to 1840 Frederich Wilken was head librarian, and his administration was characterized by a remarkable growth of the collection to over 300,000 volumes. The political unification of Germany in the 1870s brought new importance to the former Prussian National Library, which now became the German Imperial Library. Since there were other and larger libraries in the new Germany, such as the former national libraries of Bavaria, Saxony, and Hanover, the Imperial Library concentrated on building up its collections of foreign publications from all parts of the world. By 1890 the library contained over 800,000 volumes, and by 1909, when it moved into a new building, it had over 1,250,000 works, including one of the finest collections of incunabula in the world, and more than 33,000 manuscripts.

There are other state libraries in Germany that in many respects are also "national" libraries. For example, the Bavarian State Library at Munich has a longer history and at times has been larger than the Prussian State Library. Formed in the 16th century from the library of Duke Albrecht V of Bavaria, this collection grew with such acquisitions as the Schedel Library from Nuremburg and the J. J. Fugger collection from Austria. Many Bavarian monastic and church libraries were taken into the State Library in the 19th century, making it one of the treasure houses of Europe for manuscripts and incunabula. By the 20th century it contained over 1,000,000 volumes.

Italy, like Germany, has several national libraries, including two with the title of National Central Library, at Rome and Florence. The National Central Library at Florence originated in 1747, with its main book collection the 30,000-volume library donated by Antonio Magliabecchi to the city in 1714. Magliabecchi, a noted bibliophile and one-time librarian for the Duke of Tuscany, left his books for the good of the "poor people of Florence." During the latter half of the 18th century, books from several suppressed monasteries were added to the collection, and during the 19th it continued to grow with major gifts and bequests. By 1859, it contained nearly 100,000 volumes and over 3,000 manuscripts, but the nature of the collection was more that of a rare books museum than of a public library. After the formation of the Kingdom of Italy in 1861, the Florence Library was united with the Palatina Library formed by the Grand Duke of Tuscany, and the resulting collection became the National Library. Growth was rapid after this date, and by 1930 it contained over 2,000,000 printed works, 22,000 manuscripts, and many thousands of letters, music scores, maps, and ephemera.

The Victor Emmanuel Library at Rome is also designated a National Central Library, and there are six other national libraries located at Bari, Milan, Naples, Palermo, Turin, and Venice. The library in Rome opened in 1876 with much of its original collection of books seized from monasteries and religious houses closed in 1873. Closely connected with the Victor Emmanuel Library is the Biblioteca Casanatense, an endowed collection of some 300,000 volumes, strong in medieval history and theology.

The National Library at Milan dates from 1763, when a private library of Count Carlo Pertusati was purchased by the government and placed at the service of the public. It enjoyed the sponsorship of Empress Maria Theresa of Austria and received several large gifts through her interest. In the 19th century it grew steadily, concentrating its acquisitions in the fields of Italian drama and the history of Lombardy. The national library in Venice is the famous Biblioteca Marciana, originally begun with the collection donated by Cardinal Bessarion in 1468. Although it contains only about 800,000 printed volumes, its manuscript collection of some 13,000 volumes is invaluable and includes some of the rarest early medieval codices in existence. The national library at Turin is one of the most recent to be so designated, having been formerly a university library formed in 1720. It is housed in an 18th-century palace remodeled for library purposes. At Naples the national library was founded in 1804 and based on the private collection of Cardinal Seripando. Housed in a former royal palace, it contains today 1,500,000 volumes and 10,000 valuable manuscripts. Collectively, the national libraries of Italy form both a cultural heritage and asset that will rank with the national libraries of any of the western nations.

The smaller nations of northern Europe all have national libraries, as do those of eastern Europe and the Balkans. In many ways their histories are inextricably linked to the great wars that swept Europe in the 20th century, and thus they are better treated in Chapter 11 of this work.

The national libraries of Europe collectively represent a magnificent cultural heritage in graphic form. By definition their role is nationalistic in nature, and these libraries are devoted to collecting, organizing, and preserving the graphic records and artifacts reflecting the history of their respective nations. They are frequently the most impressive libraries in their countries and national librarians like Abbé Bignon in France and Antonio Panizzi in England must be ranked among the most influential librarians of all time.

The focus of the national libraries has insured their existence in even the most difficult of times. They have benefited from the copyright privilege, which provides that one copy of every book copyrighted in their respective countries shall be deposited in the national library. Furthermore, they have generally been the beneficiary of substantial government support, and they have been able to demand large-scale philanthropy unknown to most university and public libraries.

Their administration has generally reflected their principal goal--to collect and preserve their cultural heritage. Thus, great emphasis was placed on the acquisition and organization of materials. This explains why national libraries have become known as great research libraries and bibliographic centers, earning at the same time a reputation for conservative use policies and a general aloofness from other library affairs.

Nevertheless, it should be emphasized that by the onset of World War I, the first of two wars that were to drastically affect the European library scene, the great national libraries were well established and could boast the most magnificent collections in Europe.

European University Libraries Since 1500

By 1500, the universities were well established in Europe. Although they differed widely in organization from country to country and even from institution to institution, the universities were on the whole a powerful cultural influence in the era that represents the bridge between medieval and modern. Libraries also differed considerably from university to university. In some there were major central or university libraries; in some the college libraries were all important, with little or no central collection; in others the emphasis was on faculty or departmental libraries. In any case, the early university communities depended heavily on the "stationers," or booksellers and book-renters who gathered around every campus.

After 1500, the size of libraries increased considerably. One reason for this, of course, was the invention of printing, which made available large numbers of cheap books. Another reason was the availability of books and manuscripts from the libraries of suppressed monasteries. From the 16th century through the 19th, in various parts of Europe at different times, monasteries were closed, and in many cases their literary treasures eventually found their way to the shelves of university libraries. Much of the material thus received was theological, rare and scholarly, but the important point is that it was preserved in working libraries where it could be put to use.

At the University of Paris, the most important and the largest of the college libraries was that of the Sorbonne.

From about 2,500 volumes, mostly manuscript, at the end of the 15th century, the Sorbonne collection grew slowly through periods of successive prosperity and decline paralleling the fortunes of the University as a whole. By the beginning of the French Revolution in 1789, it contained some 25,000 printed volumes and 2,000 manuscripts. In 1792 the University was closed, and in 1795 its library was seized and divided, with the printed volumes going into public libraries and the manuscripts to the Bibliothèque Nationale. When the University of Paris was reopened after the Napoleonic era, a new Bibliothèque de la Sorbonne was established, and in 1861 its name was changed to Bibliothèque de la Université. Since then its growth has been steady, so that by 1900 it was approaching 1,000,000 volumes in all of its departments. In 1897 the Sorbonne Library was moved into new quarters with a reading room seating 300 persons and two stack rooms of five floors each.

Besides the Sorbonne, which now serves as the library of the college of arts and sciences, there are the libraries of the colleges of law, medicine and pharmacy, the Bibliothèque Ste. Geneviève, and the newly created science library, the Bibliothèque d'Orsay. The library of the Faculty of Medicine dates from the late 14th century, and its holdings by 1500 numbered only about 1110 volumes. In 1500 the system of chaining the most used volumes to the reading desks was adopted and was used for nearly 300 years. During the French Revolution, the medical library profited to some extent because it was combined with the library of the Royal Society of Medicine, and the entire collection was moved into a new building to serve the medical college. By 1900 it contained about 180,000 volumes and was one of the best medical libraries in Europe. The library of the Faculty of Law was formed in 1772 and included some 80,000 volumes by 1900; that of the Faculty of Pharmacy was not begun until about 1882 but owned 50,000 volumes by 1900.

The oldest library now under the University is that of Ste. Geneviève, dating from the 12th century. Originally the library of the Abbey of Ste. Geneviève, it remained small until the 16th century. Numbering some 40,000 volumes by 1710, it was then a semi-public library, noted as being open to "all honest men who requested admittance." Apparently the librarian at that time had staff problems much as modern librarians do, since he reported that a gift of books received seventeen years earlier had still not been cataloged. Though it lost some of its rarer manuscripts during the French

Revolution, Ste. Genevieve's library survived as a whole, and by 1860 its holdings had grown to more than 160,000 volumes and 5,000 manuscripts. After years of separate administration as a government-owned library, it was placed under the administration of the University of Paris where its strong collections of history and social sciences make it a most valuable part of the university library system.

There are some thirty other major college and university libraries in Paris, and several hundred scattered throughout France. Most of the early French universities were church-related and did not survive the Revolutionary era, so most modern institutions date from the 19th century, particularly the 1870s era of the Third Republic.

Down to the 19th century there were really only two universities in England--Cambridge and Oxford. The libraries of these two venerable institutions were already centuries old by 1500, but the religious troubles of the following century severely crippled them. When Henry VIII ordered the dissolution of the monasteries and religious orders in 1537, it marked the beginning of one of the most tragic episodes in the history of libraries. Henry, irritated with the church in Rome and jealous of the wealth and influence of the church in England, ordered the monasteries closed and had their properties divided among the king's friends. As was so often the case in history, the valuable libraries of the monasteries suffered destruction simply because they were housed in an institution under attack. Consequently, thousands of invaluable and irreplaceable books and manuscripts were wantonly destroyed. At first, with acquisitions from some of the closed monastery collections, the university libraries benefited to some extent, but later their contents, too, were "censored" and nearly erased altogether. Many books were seized by agents of the king and sold as waste paper, although some volumes found their way to collectors on the continent and a few were saved by bookmen in England. In the 1550s, Edward VI's Royal Commissioners almost completely destroyed the remainder of the libraries at Cambridge and Oxford. At the latter, even the library shelves were removed and sold. After this purge of libraries, about the only ones left in England were those of the older cathedrals. A contemporary writer, John Bale, approved the end of the monastic orders but deplored the destruction of the libraries:

> If there had been in every shire but one single library, to the preservation of those noble works,

> it had been well. But to destroy all without consideration is and will be unto England forever a most horrible infamy.

The central library at Oxford was reborn between 1598 and 1602 when the indefatigable Thomas Bodley refurnished it with two library necessities: stacks and books. Bodley had traveled on the continent many times, both as a private citizen and as a government envoy, and he knew the best sources of books and manuscripts. Thomas James was selected as the first librarian of the new library that was to become known as the "Bodleian." James issued the first printed catalog of the library, numbering about 2,000 titles, in 1605. When Bodley died in 1613, he endowed the library further and its growth since that date has been continuous. Some of the college libraries at Oxford had survived the purges of the mid-16th century, others were reconstituted, and as new colleges were formed, each of them began with a library of its own. Wadham College was founded in 1612, with a library formed the following year. Pembroke College, founded in 1624, was fortunate in having a library from the beginning. The Bodleian Library moved into a new, separate library building in 1612, and several of the college libraries also acquired new quarters, either in separate buildings or in wings or halls of classroom buildings. By 1620 the Bodleian claimed 16,000 volumes, and by 1700, nearly 30,000. During the 17th century, it had obtained two important gifts, a collection of 1,300 manuscripts given by Archbishop Laud and a library of 8,000 volumes donated by a lawyer, John Selden. In 1714 a physician, John Radcliffe, endowed a library of science and medicine at Oxford with a building of its own. In the mid-19th century, this library and building were given to the trustees of the Bodleian and became a part of the main library. By 1900 the Oxford University libraries contained over 800,000 volumes and 41,000 manuscripts.

Although the Cambridge University libraries fared better in the 16th century than those at Oxford, the central library there still had only 300 printed books and 150 manuscripts in 1582. Moreover, Cambridge had no benefactor such as Sir Thomas Bodley. After the Restoration of Charles II in 1660, Cambridge received some royal attention and the library received several notable gifts and bequests from the King's friends. Henry Lucas left a collection of 4,000 volumes to Cambridge in 1666, and Bishop Tobias Rustat gave £1,000 for the purchase of books. In 1755, Cambridge moved its library into a new building, and though its growth was not spectacular until the latter half of the 19th century, it contained nearly 1,000,000 volumes by 1900. The college libraries at Cambridge also grew steadily, several of them acquiring separate buildings in the 17th century. By the late 19th century, Trinity College, in a building designed by Sir Christopher Wren, boasted a library of over 90,000 volumes, but the other college libraries were smaller. They, too, have received many significant collections over the years, most notably the Samuel Pepys library given to Magdalene College.

Although Oxford and Cambridge were for centuries the only universities in England, others were established in Scotland and Ireland. The University of Glasgow, founded in 1453, had a notable library almost from the beginning, while St. Andrews University, founded about the same time, dates its central library from 1610. The library at the University of Edinburgh was founded in 1583, largely with funds and books donated by Clement Little, a wealthy merchant-lawyer. A fourth Scottish university, at Aberdeen, was founded before 1500, but its earliest library records date from the 1630s and its collection never equaled the others in size or importance. In Ireland, the library of Trinity College in Dublin began with a gift of books by the English Army after a victory over the Irish in the Battle of Kinsale in 1601. By 1604 this collection contained 4,000 volumes, and it grew steadily to become in time the most important library in Ireland. James Ussher, later primate of Ireland, directed the early growth of the collection, and on his death in 1655 willed his own library of 7,000 volumes and 600 manuscripts to it. Other major gifts were received over the years and by 1900 it contained over 300,000 volumes and 2,000 manuscripts.

In Germany, several university libraries had been established before 1500, including those at Cologne, Erfurt, Freiburg, Greisswald, Heidelberg, Leipzig, Munich, Rostock, and Tübingen. They were followed in the 16th century by Marburg, Würzburg, Königsberg, Wittenberg, and Jena. Small at first, but supplemented by additional college and institute libraries, they were often formed or enlarged by books taken from a closed Dominican monastery. The religious wars of the 16th century spelled disaster for some libraries, but benefited others. The 17th century brought the Thirty Years' War, when many German libraries were ravaged by invading armies, and by 1700 both universities and libraries had reached a low ebb. However, the 18th century brought better conditions, with Göttingen's University library, for example, growing from 12,000 volumes in 1737 to 150,000 in 1800. Especially important was the closing of the Jesuit institutions, which resulted in the transferral of many books to the universities in the 1770s.

Although the French Revolution and Napoleonic wars brought more disruption to the German universities, they soon overcame these handicaps. Not only did the central collections increase in size in the 19th century, but the same was true for the many separate college, faculty, and institute libraries. By 1875 the university libraries at Göttingen, Heidelberg, Leipzig, Breslau, and Strassburg contained from 300,000 to 400,000 volumes each, and were among the best research libraries in the world. Not only were their book collections excellent but their librarians were recognized leaders of the emerging library profession, providing influential examples for librarians of other places and later eras to follow. New ideas in librarianship either originated in German libraries or were quickly adapted to German needs. After the unification of Germany in the 1870s, the university libraries continued to flourish and new buildings were soon required to accommodate the rapidly increasing bookstocks.

In Italy, where the medieval university began and flourished, the period since 1500 has seen less progress than the auspicious beginnings promised. Although fifteen strong universities existed in 1500 and several new ones were added in the 16th century, a period of decline soon set in and very few were added before 1900. In most Italian universities, central libraries were not begun until long after the universities' establishment, and in a few cases none ever were established. Instead, institute and departmental libraries were forced to provide most library service in the Italian university, many of which are large and valuable. Padua did not have a central library until 1629, and Bologna not until 1712, but later universities, such as those at Messina and Sassari, had central libraries from the beginning. Most of the collections have grown more from gifts than from planned purchases, and this partly explains the lack of popularity of the central collections.

Italian university libraries probably suffered less from wars in the 16th and 17th centuries than those of northern Europe, but their growth was slow. Even by the 19th century, collections usually numbered fewer than 100,000 and in many cases, although these constituted valuable research materials, they were of little use to the average student. Lack of staff, crowded quarters, and poor organization also added to Italy's library problems. Unification of the nation in the 1860s brought increased emphasis on education and most of the universities were taken over as state institutions. Steady growth was the rule for their libraries in the early 20th century, and there were few losses in World War I.

In Russia, university libraries are a different story. There, universities were late in beginning and grew slowly until the 20th century. Since the Russian Revolution, however, the university libraries have grown tremendously, both in size and numbers, and they constitute today an important part of the overall library program in the Soviet Union. The oldest university in Russia proper is the University of Moscow, founded by M. V. Lomonosov in 1755. The universities of Vilnius and Lvov, now in the Soviet Union but formerly in Lithuania and Poland, were founded in 1570 and 1681 respectively, and in the 19th century others were founded at St. Petersburg, Kazan, Kharkov, Kiev, Dorpat, and Odessa. University libraries were small in the early 19th century, but the central collections were usually supplemented by both student and departmental collections. Moscow University Library grew most rapidly, receiving over one hundred major gifts of private collections. The University of Kazan Library was fortunate in having the mathematician Nikolai Lobachevski as librarian from 1825 to 1835, and he made of it the best-organized library in Russia, complete with full catalog and his own classification system. In 1834, the library was moved to a new building and shortly afterward a card catalog was initiated--one of the earliest in Europe.

The development of Russian university libraries in the late 19th century is readily illustrated by the rapid growth of their book collections between 1876 and 1910. During that period, Moscow University Library grew from some 150,000 to over 300,000 volumes, and other collections grew as follows: St. Petersburg, 50,000 to 125,000; Dorpat (now the University of Tartu), 125,000 to 400,000; Odessa, 40,000 to 250,000; and Kazan, 100,000 to 242,000. By the beginning of World War I, there were thirteen major universities in Russia with some 3,000,000 volumes in their libraries for their 43,000 students. This does not generally count the books available in libraries other than the central collections.

European university libraries evolved steadily during

the period treated here. Originally small collections supporting rather limited academic programs, they came by 1900 to represent the "heart of the university"--collections designed to play a major role in the university's newly defined objective of seeking the truth through original research. The invention of printing and the development of an extensive and well-organized book trade greatly facilitated the collection of books and other materials. As collections grew, those charged with the responsibility of managing the library found more and more of their time being absorbed in matters relating to the acquisition, organization, and use of their materials.

Books, now readily available, and no longer hoarded by "bibliomaniacs," came to be viewed as instruments to be used rather than simply artifacts to be preserved or guardedly consulted. The chained libraries of the early 1600s, where the books were chained to their respective locations, gave way in time to libraries where both faculty and students could consult the library's resources in the building and, in some cases, even remove the books from the library.

The burgeoning size of the collections and the increased use fostered by liberalized circulation policies required librarians to spend more and more time considering questions related to the housing and organization of their collections. Library organization was generally based on the provision of a shelflist, or accessions list, as an inventory record, and the publication of a printed subject catalog for the use of patrons. By 1900 the growing size of libraries and the increasingly insistent demands of readers for improved access to collections had given rise to the card catalog--usually divided into an alphabetical author catalog supplemented by a classed or topical catalog.

Classification schemes were studied and the latter part of the 19th century witnessed a number of major developments, many of them emanating from the United States. By 1900 many university libraries could boast their own buildings, but a significant feature of the European scene remained the existence of a number of more or less autonomous departmental or institute libraries on each campus; European university libraries rarely evidenced the centralization so common to their American counterparts. Most significant, however, was the emergence of the university as a major center for research and the education of scholars; a development that placed increasing responsibilities upon university libraries to meet the research needs of their users.

The Emergence of Public Libraries

While academic libraries underwent a rather steady development from "houses of treasures" to utilitarian research centers all over Europe, little of this consistency of development can be discerned for public libraries during the same period.

One problem was the variety of ways in which "public" was defined in Europe, and for that matter in America, during the period under discussion. In some countries "public" simply meant "not private," while in others it came to mean something more like the modern American and English usage: open to all on an equal basis, supported by public tax funds, and administered as a public trust.

Furthermore, the student of library history must remember that governments have frequently taken a pronounced interest in public libraries, and their interest has rarely been altruistic in nature. That is, they have usually become involved in public library affairs because they saw the library as playing a potentially positive role in the process of government. Again, this involvement was provoked by widely varying considerations in different European countries. In many, especially the totalitarian nations, the purpose has been to disseminate selectively information thought conducive to the continued welfare of the State. In others, especially those favoring a democratic political style, the emphasis has been on the free flow of information. As a result, the development of public libraries in Europe projects a complex and diverse picture upon the historical canvas.

Before considering this development, it is necessary first to define what we mean by "public library." Certainly the national libraries were publicly owned in the later centuries, although they may have begun as private libraries of kings or nobles. Also, many of the universities--almost all of them in later years--were owned by the governments, so they were public in ownership at least, and many were open to general use. On the other hand, many private libraries were open to the public, or at least to individual scholars. What we mean today by the public library is the general library that is not only publicly owned but also open to any citizen who desires to use it. More particularly, we mean by the public library the municipal or regional circulating library. In this restricted sense, the public library does not appear on the European scene until the late 19th century, and in many respects it is a 20th-century development. However, public reference libraries were available in most large cities of Europe throughout the period covered, and no consideration of public library history in Europe can be complete without acknowledging them.

These public reference libraries began in many ways--as a gift of a private library, through the transfer of a monastery or cathedral library to public use, or as a professional collection. No matter what its origin, the growth of such libraries between 1500 and 1900 was usually slow. Where progress was made in times of peace and prosperity, collections were often destroyed or dispersed in times of war. The libraries were usually poorly housed (although a few of them were in architecturally elegant surroundings) and had inexperienced or uninterested "library keepers" rather than librarians in charge of them. Hours of opening were few and the contents were of such a scholarly nature that not many people used them. It was a rare librarian who saw in the public library something more than an antiquarian collection.

The history of public libraries in France is typical. In the 16th century, a number of town libraries were established in the larger cities but they were seldom more than reference collections in the city halls. Lyons, for example, had a "Bibliothèque de la Ville" in 1530 and Aix-la-Chapelle in 1556. These were often theological collections given by, or taken from, local monasteries or churches, and they were poorly housed and little used. Paris had several semi-public collections, such as the Mazarine Library, and others connected with churches and colleges, but before the French Revolution there was little in the way of public library service elsewhere in France.

The period from 1789 to 1815 saw a social and economic revolution in France accompanying the French Revolution and the Napoleonic era, and the effect on libraries and educational institutions was tremendous. In 1789, shortly after the Revolution began, all religious libraries were declared national property and the books and manuscripts were confiscated. In 1792, there was a general confiscation of books belonging to the nobility or other citizens who had fled France after the Revolution began. It is estimated that as many as 8,000,000 books were confiscated and gathered into general book deposits at several points in France. Although many were lost or damaged in this process, several hundred thousand of the more valuable volumes ended up in the Bibliothèque Nationale and the remainder were set aside for new district libraries to be established throughout France. Most of these libraries were in fact established, at least in name, but the books assigned to them often languished in warehouses for years, and even when opened the libraries were poorly managed and rarely used. In some cases the books were sold and the funds put to other use. By the 1820s the larger French cities had municipal libraries that were fairly respectable in size, but they were usually poorly housed. Amiens, for example, had 46,000 volumes housed in an upper floor of the courthouse, and Rouen had 40,000 volumes on the second floor of the city hall.

In the 1830s France experimented with the idea of public libraries for adults located in the public schools, but this idea did not catch on, and the majority of adults continued to read books purchased or obtained from lending libraries. The subscription library, begun in England by the 18th century, had its counterpart in France, but it was not very successful outside of Paris and the larger cities. After 1850, a few publicly supported "popular" libraries were opened in Paris. By 1908 there were about eighty of these. There was no central public library, but the collections were centrally supervised. Most contained only a few thousand volumes and were housed in rented rooms or in unused areas of municipal buildings. They were open only a few hours each week and reached but a small portion of the public.

In 1904 a new stimulus to public library service in France came with the activities and writings of Eugene Morel, who attempted to introduce in France the American and English conception of the public library. This resulted in some increase in the numbers and use of the popular libraries, as for example in the Department of the Seine, outside of Paris, where some fifty communal and village libraries were formed before 1914. They were, however, directed almost entirely toward recreational reading and reached only a few adults. Shortly before World War I, a survey of public libraries in France showed that the library situation there was deplorable. Unfortunately, the war came before any improvements were made.

Across the Channel, in Great Britain, the development of public libraries has been unlike that in France. The 16th century began with the great loss of libraries brought on by the closing of the monasteries and the dispersal of their collections. The 17th century saw the revival of the university libraries and the growth of a few notable cathedral and private libraries, but little was done in the direction of public library service. Several municipally owned libraries were founded in the 17th century, but they could hardly be called public libraries in the modern sense of the word. Most of them were the result of books left to the towns upon deaths of prominent citizens. Norwich, for example, had a collection given to the town in 1608, and some of the original volumes are still in the Norwich Free Public Library. In 1615 a city library was opened in Bristol through gifts and efforts of Dr. Toby Matthew and Robert Redwood. Leicester dates its public library from 1632, and the Chetham Library in Manchester was a gift of Sir Humphrey Chetham in 1653. The contents of these early libraries were heavily theological or classical, were not allowed to circulate, and hence were little used. In some cases they were stored away for years at a time. In the late 17th century, some parish churches made small gift collections available for public use, and the private grammar schools made primitive beginnings toward library collections.

In the 18th century a few publicly owned libraries were added, but the three major additions to library service were the parochial libraries, the subscription or social libraries, and the circulating libraries. The first were largely the work of one man, Dr. Thomas Bray, who, late in the 17th century, had taken part in the formation of the Society for the Propagation of the Gospel in Foreign Parts. This group was mainly interested in providing ministers for the English colonies in America, but Dr. Bray went further and attempted to supply those ministers and their parishes with books for religious training and inspirational reading. Finding that many English parishes were in need of the same support, Dr. Bray and his associates founded similar church libraries in parishes throughout England. These parochial libraries were almost entirely theological, small, and suffered more from neglect than from overuse. However, they provided the local ministers with some professional reading, and possibly a few of the parishioners with some rather heavy fare.

The commercial circulating libraries were entirely different. They were established by booksellers, usually on a purely commercial basis. Edinburgh is said to have had a circulating library as early as 1725, and others were definitely in business in London and other large cities before 1750. These "libraries" would be called rental collections today, but they provided the general public, or all who could afford the small fees, with popular reading matter. By 1800, most of the larger towns in the British Isles had circulating rental libraries, and some of them remained profitable down into the 20th century. Rental fees at these collections were usually small, not over a shilling per month. William Lane of London was one of the most enterprising of the circulating library founders. He established chains of bookstores with circulating collections in them, and then published books, fiction and popular nonfiction, to fill them. Charles Edward Mudie established Mudie's Circulating Libraries in the 19th century and at one time had over 25,000 subscribers in London alone. These libraries, with their blatant appeal to the romantic and erotic interests of the lower and middle classes, were labeled "evergeeen trees of diabolical knowledge" by the playwright Sheridan, and drew increasing criticism from conservative members of the elite society who feared that they would contribute to the corruption of the morals of the masses. Paperbacks and public libraries virtually replaced the commercial circulating libraries in the 20th century, but the "two-penny library" was still popular in the early 1900s.

The latter part of the 18th century saw the development of the subscription library, a natural extension of earlier and more informal "book clubs." A group of the more well-to-do readers of a community would form a "lyceum" or "reading society" with a library for the use of members only. Shares in the library were frequently sold, and fees were paid by the month or year. The quality of the reading matter was generally more serious than that of the circulating libraries. The Society Library of Dumfries, Scotland, was begun around 1745, and the Liverpool Lyceum about 1758. By 1900 the subscription libraries were common. They were usually housed in rented halls or rooms, with a keeper on duty at certain hours, but by the mid-19th century many had acquired their own buildings. Some of them grew to respectable size and provided a large part of the "public library" service available before 1850. One of the most famous and successful of the subscription libraries is the London Library, established in 1841 and boasting Carlyle among its founders. At the turn of the century it contained over 500,000 volumes and still thrives today. Another interesting survivor is the Leeds Library, founded in 1768 and limited to 500 subscribers throughout its long existence.

For the benefit of the workers and small tradesmen who could not afford the subscription libraries, benevolent individuals and groups formed "mechanics' institutes" that included in their programs libraries of vocational and inspirational reading matter available at small rental fees. Fiction and more-popular non-fiction volumes were later added. Probably the first of these libraries was the Birmingham Artisans' Library, formed in 1795. The Glasgow Mechanics' Institute, formed in 1823, not only had a library but conducted classes and later became a recognized educational institution. Other mechanics' libraries were founded at Edinburgh, 1821; Perth and Liverpool, 1823; and Aberdeen and London, 1824. The idea spread to the smaller towns, and by 1850 there were reported to be nearly 700 in the British Isles. Some of them lasted only a few decades, but many were eventually to become public libraries, or their books were given to local public libraries after the passage of the Public Libraries Act. The role of the subscription libraries and the mechanics' institute libraries as forerunners of the free public library cannot be overlooked. They demonstrated the desirability of libraries that were relatively large and readily accessible to large numbers of people. At the same time, the inadequacy of voluntary support for library service was becoming readily apparent to library advocates. The patronage of the mechanics' institute libraries was limited, but it probably included a majority of those who would have been interested in using a free public library, and they helped in promoting the idea of library service and in providing a ready-made reading public when free libraries were established.

Modern public library history began in Great Britain in 1847, when Parliament passed an act appointing a Committee on Public Libraries to consider the necessity of establishing libraries through the nation. That famous committee, ably presided over by William Ewart and vigorously supported by public library pioneer and library historian Edward Edwards, reported in 1849; noting the poor condition of library service then available, it recommended the establishment of free public libraries in all parts of the country. The Public Libraries Act, passed in 1850, allowed cities with populations exceeding 10,000 to levy taxes for the support of public libraries, and subsequent laws extended the act to Scotland and Ireland and to smaller towns. In 1870 the Public School Law, which made communities responsible for the establishment and maintenance of free public schools, increased the number of readers and consequently the demand

and need for free public libraries. By 1877 more than seventy-five cities had taken advantage of the Library Act to establish free lending libraries, and by 1900 the number had passed 300. Andrew Carnegie's philanthropy provided library buildings for many of the municipal libraries, and in fact the buildings were sometimes better than the collections they housed.

Although public libraries in Great Britain were relatively poorly supported and understaffed until after World War I, they met a definite need, and as generations of school children accustomed to public library service grew up, both use and support of the public libraries increased. Fortunately, the growth of public libraries came at a time when many large private libraries were being broken up, and many of the latter were bought by or given to public institutions. In this manner some of the public libraries in the larger cities, although founded late in the 19th century, came to have collections to rival many of the older collections on the continent and compare favorably with university and research libraries.

Since 1500 Germany has been the home of some of the world's greatest libraries, but, although many of them have been owned by the government and open to limited public use, they have not been public libraries in the modern sense. Probably one reason has been that Germany was divided into a number of small kingdoms and principalities until 1870, and each of these governmental units tended to promote one large "national" library rather than several smaller public ones. Also, library tradition in Germany has always been directed toward the scholarly research library, whether university or public, and the English-American idea of a popular circulating library has been slow to win acceptance.

Municipally owned libraries, however, had an early beginning in Germany. Several had already been established before 1500, but after that date town libraries were established in Ulm (1516), Magdeburg (1525), Lindau (1528), Hamburg (1529), Augsburg (1537), Eisleben (1542), Luneberg (1558), Grimma (1569), and Danzig (1580). These "libraries" were usually small collections of theological works, poorly cared for and little used. Martin Luther, in 1524, urged that public libraries be established to encourage the spread of Protestantism, and many small collections were instituted in churches and town halls. In the 17th century there was little progress in German public libraries, and those already established were often neglected. During the Thirty Years' War, which caused great loss of life and property, many libraries changed hands, but the small public collections were hardly worth taking as spoils of war. More royal libraries were established in Germany during this century, and although they began as private collections they often ended up as public reference libraries.

Eighteenth-century Germany saw the development of what were then the greatest libraries in Europe, in the royal or court libraries and in the universities. Concentrating on scholarly materials, these libraries secured and preserved large numbers of books, pamphlets, and manuscripts on all subjects. As monasteries were closed or declined and lost interest in their libraries, their books and manuscripts were frequently obtained by the scholarly libraries and thus preserved for future generations. Many magnificent private collections were also bequeathed or given to the court and university libraries. The scholarly reference library became the standard in Germany during this century, and popular libraries for the general reading public were never seriously attempted.

In the 19th century, a beginning toward popular circulating libraries was made. The town of Grossenhain, for example, opened a library for the circulation of books to the general public in 1828, and, about the same time, systems of village libraries were begun in Saxony and Württemberg. In the 1840s, an attempt was made to open popular libraries (Volksbibliotheken) in Prussia, and by 1850 four such libraries were opened in Berlin. After 1870 the Society for Extension of Popular Education promoted popular libraries, and a few were established with support from both the Society and the local government. Some industries established popular factory libraries for their employees. A public circulating library was opened in Kiel in the 1890s, and by 1900 there were twenty-eight popular libraries in and around Berlin, containing from 3,000 to 10,000 volumes and appealing largely to the workers. In 1907 the Berlin Municipal Library was formed to act as a central library for the many popular libraries already functioning, and it grew steadily until the coming of World War I. Little attention was paid to public library service for children, although there was a public children's library in Berlin. Elsewhere in Germany before 1914, small popular libraries were established by educational and charitable organizations, but it was difficult to obtain municipal support for them. In Hamburg, where the

Stadtsbibliothek was a valuable reference library of over 600,000 volumes, a separate Volksbibliothek was established only in 1899.

By the mid-20th century the Russians were probably the most library-minded people in the world, if their library statistics can be believed. However, this has not always been the case. As of 1500, Russia was not far removed from its period of Mongol control and was still deep in medieval feudalism, far behind even eastern Europe in cultural progress. Russia had experienced neither a Renaissance nor a Reformation and was easily 200 years behind western Europe in general development as of 1800. Public libraries in the modern sense of the word were unknown until late in the 19th century, and even church and monastery libraries were scarce. Odessa had a municipal library founded in 1837, there was one in Kazan in 1866, and in Kharkov by 1886. These were the non-circulating, research type of public collection. Some semi-public society libraries were also opened in the larger cities, while in rural areas, by the 1890s, public schools were maintaining small collections of books for adult readers. The library at Kazan, for example, was supported by a private organization although it was open as a public reference library until the 1920s, when it became the basis for the national library of the Tatar Republic. In 1880 the Russian government statistics reported 145 public libraries throughout the nation, containing together almost 1,000,000 volumes. By 1905 the figure reported had increased to 5,000 free public libraries, but it was noted that many of them had very few books, some as few as fifty volumes. By 1915 there were reported to be 800 public libraries in Russia large enough to be in charge of a full-time "library keeper," with more than 20,000 smaller book collections at the community level. The municipal library in Odessa at this time had some 200,000 volumes, while that at Kiev had over 600,000. Obviously, the idea of public library service in Russia is not solely communist, but neither was censorship and state control. Both of these enemies of free libraries were strong under the Czars, and freedom of speech and press were only slightly greater before 1917 than after.

Italian libraries are a different story. The great Renaissance libraries, private and public, led the way for all European libraries into the modern era, but unfortunately library progress slowed considerably in Italy after the 16th century and did not keep up with northern Europe. Many of the large private collections ended up in libraries open to the public, but they were often museums of books rather tnan public libraries. Some such public reference libraries were established in the 17th century, but more in the 18th and 19th. Although these collections sometimes contained valuable manuscripts and rare books, they were usually short of funds and poorly staffed so their public services were almost nonexistent. In the late 19th century some of them became more conscious of serving the public and opened reading rooms. By 1900 Bologna's public library had some 200,000 volumes, with others at Brescia, Ferrara, Padua, and Palermo, for example, being only slightly smaller. The suppression of monasteries in the 1860s added to the bookstock of many of these "biblioteches communales."

Popular reading rooms and circulating libraries in Italy are more a product of the 20th century. By 1908 there were some 300 small "biblioteches communales" and "biblioteches popolares" and in that year a Federation of Popular Libraries was established to promote public libraries. Some progress was made, but World War I intervened, and even in the 1920s the popular libraries were usually housed in wings of public buildings or in upstairs rooms over stores or offices.

In summary then, public library development in Europe between 1500 and 1917 was erratic, characterized by some three and one-half centuries of indifference and less than a century of active interest. The nature and extent of public library development in the various parts of Europe varied greatly and was to become even more confusing with the rapidly changing political situation which developed out of the two World Wars. Nevertheless, by 1914 most European nations had arrived at the point where they agreed that some form of publicly supported library service was desirable.

Governments cited a number of reasons for this consensus, including the need to provide a harmless form of recreation for the masses; the need for controlling the sources of information available to the people; the need to compete effectively with the circulating libraries and their high circulation of "unhealthy" fiction; or the need to provide the free access to information required if a democratic republic was to function properly. But once the consensus on the need for public libraries was achieved, a number of other factors influenced the extent to which libraries were developed in the various European nations--most significantly, the economic resources available, the extent of literacy, the political stability of the country, and the commitment of the government to libraries. The ways in which these factors, plus the horrible destruction of two World Wars, conspired to influence public library development in Europe after 1917 will be discussed in a later chapter.

Private Book Collectors and the Rise of European Libraries

Our attention in this book must focus increasingly on the ever-more-complex and extensive development of "public libraries"--that is, those libraries publicly owned, or at least open to the public with or without restrictions on their use. However, the strictly private library is also a part of library history and must be briefly considered, if for no other reason than the significant role the private collector and the fruits of his labors played in the foundation of many of the great libraries discussed in this chapter.

Several points deserve mention. The private collector with means often had a better chance to build up a well-rounded library or a definitive subject collection than did a public library. With no "public" to serve, the private library could be built to a point nearing perfection and maintained at that point without fear of loss or wear. Unfortunately, the death of a book collector often resulted in the sale or dispersal of his library; only rarely did a family maintain an ancestral book collection through several generations. When the private library was dispersed, it might be given or sold to a public library, or it might find its way into the hands of other collectors. Eventually, however, many of the finest private libraries were obtained and preserved intact in public hands.

While the medieval book collector was most often a member of the nobility or clergy, many of the great collectors after 1500 were wealthy merchants or professional men. However, book collection has not been the monopoly of any one group, and people from all walks of life have been ardent bibliophiles. The development of printing undoubtedly broadened the field of book collecting; with the lower cost of the printed book, virtually every educated man was in a position to collect a small library and most of the writers and thinkers of the period did so. At least part of the stimulus for book collecting came with the Renaissance as it spread northward from Italy, and although it may be said that modern learning relied most heavily on the books in publicly owned libraries, it certainly was encouraged by the widespread availability of books in private libraries.

As we have already demonstrated, great book collectors played a major role in the development of many of Europe's most significant libraries. What, for instance, might have been the nature of the British Museum collections without the addition of the Cotton, Sloan, and Harleian libraries? It is difficult to imagine the great national libraries achieving such significance without the acquisition of the many private collections that became available to them either through purchase, confiscation, or benefaction. The debt owed by society in general to private collectors of books and manuscripts can hardly be overestimated. Although their range of interest is often narrow and their holdings are for years removed from the public view, the end results of their collecting have proven to the benefit of all mankind. Whether donated or sold as a unit to a public or research library, or split up and resold to other collectors, books have not been destroyed. Moreover, they are often kept in far better condition in private libraries than they would have been in public ones. Without the prodigious efforts and costly collecting, and even the personal vanity of the book collector, many of our most valuable literary treasures certainly would have been lost.

Additional Readings

With this period in library history we witness the proliferation of libraries and also a significant growth in the literature treating the development of libraries. As a result, the following list of additional readings is highly selective. Those interested in pursuing the literature further can utilize James G. Olle's Library History: An Examination Guidebook 2nd ed. (London: Clive Bingley, 1971), which is a critical guide to European Library history with an emphasis on British library history. The more recent literature is covered in issues of the journal Library History which is published in Britain twice a year. For brief summaries of library history in each of the nations covered in this chapter the reader can also turn to the ALA World Encyclopedia of Library and Information Services (Chicago: American Library Association, 1980).

Altick, Richard D. The English Common Reader: A Social History of the Mass Reading Public, 1800-1900 (Chicago: University of Chicago Press, 1957).

Camp, John F. "Libraries and the Organization of Universities in France, 1789-1881," Library Quarterly 51 (1981): 170-91.

Clarke, Jack A. "French Libraries in Transition," Library Quarterly 37 (1967):366-72.

________. Gabriel Naudé, 1600-1653 (Hamden, Conn.: Archon, 1970).

Danton, J. Periam. Book Selection and Collections: A Comparison of German and American University Libraries (New York: Columbia University Press, 1963).

Darnton, Robert. "Reading, Writing, and Publishing in Eighteenth-century France: A Case Study in the Sociology of Literature," Daedalus 100 (1971):214-56.

Hassenforder, Jean. Développement Comparé des Bibliothèques Publiques en France, en Grande-Bretagne et aux Etats-Unis dans la Seconde Moitié du XIXe Siècle (1850-1914) (Paris: Cercle de la Librairie, 1967).

Kaufman, Paul. Libraries and Their Users (London: n.p., 1969).

Kelly, Thomas. Early Public Libraries: A History of Public Libraries in Great Britain Before 1850 (London: The Library Association, 1966).

________. History of Public Libraries in Great Britain, 1845-1975 (London: The Library Association, 1977).

Miller, Edward. That Noble Cabinet: A History of the British Museum (London: Andre Deutsch, 1974).

Preedeek, Alfred. A History of Libraries in Great Britain and North America (Chicago: American Library Association, 1947).

Wehmer, C. "History of German University Libraries," Library Trends 12 (1964):496-506.

Chapter 10

LIBRARIES IN AMERICA TO 1850

Latin American Library Beginnings

Long before the establishment of the Jamestown Colony in Virginia or the arrival of the earliest settlers on the St. Lawrence, there was already a highly developed Spanish culture in parts of Latin America. A number of the earliest explorers of that area are known to have packed a few precious books among their belongings when making the hazardous journey to the New World. However, by far the most bookish of the early settlers were the churchmen--especially the Jesuits and Franciscans--who lived and worked in parts of Latin America as early as the middle of the 16th century.

Scholars have provided us with detailed studies of the rather extensive development of libraries in colonial Latin America, and their work clearly demonstrates the way in which the private collections, just as in Europe, came in time to form the nucleus of the first university and public libraries. For instance, in 1767, when the Jesuits were expelled from Latin America, their many fine libraries eventually found their way into the university and national libraries.

The 18th century, however, represents a troubled time for most parts of Latin America, and we have been able to find scant evidence of a "public" library development during this period. It seems clear that books were available in libraries, and for sale, at the universities in Peru, Argentina, Guatemala, and Cuba, but specific details are difficult to locate. Thus Latin American library history for the most part begins with the 19th century and the end of colonialism.

Most of the Latin American countries that achieved independence formed national libraries early in their existence, partly as a matter of national pride. These collections were often made up largely of sequestered private or religious libraries and, once gathered together in some public building, they were largely forgotten. Throughout much of the 19th century they remained more like museums than libraries. Brazil's national library was founded in 1810, but as late as 1900 it had only about 200,000 volumes. Chile's national library dates from 1813, and Argentina's from 1810, while Uruguay claims 1816, Venezuela 1833, Peru 1821, and Mexico 1833, as the dates of their earliest national collections. Some university libraries claim 18th-century beginnings, such as those of the University of Havana, 1728, and the Central University of Quito, 1787. The early 19th century saw more universities established, and also a trend toward public libraries, especially in the larger colonies. Brazil established state libraries, in the 1850s and 1860s, notably those at Aracaju for Sergipe State in 1851, and at Curitiba for Parana State in 1857. These remained generally small and often combined functions of archives and library at the same time. Emphasis was largely on preservation rather than use, and lack of interested librarians kept the 19th-century Latin American library poorly organized and uninviting. Foundations were being laid, however, for a few significant libraries of the future, especially in the national collections.

Private Libraries in the United States

In the 19th century the Reverend John Milburn reflected that:

> Men must have bread before books. Men must build barns before they establish colleges. Men must learn the language of the rifle, the axe and the plough, before they learn the lessons of Grecian and Roman philosophy.

What the Reverend Milburn failed to note was that while bread was considered vital for the preservation of the body, a few books were often viewed as equally vital for the preservation of the soul. It is clear that many pioneer families would have deemed it foolish in the extreme to set out for a strange and faraway country without their Bibles, hymnals, and prayer books. Furthermore, while the rifle, axe, and plough were essential tools of the farmer and hunter, books were considered equally essential tools by the many lawyers, doctors, preachers, and educators who settled in early America.

Of course, even though books were considered necessities by many pioneer families, people did find it imperative to institute certain economies when they moved to the New World, or when they followed the sun toward the progressively retreating American frontiers of the 18th and 19th centuries. Thus we should not be surprised to find that the libraries found in the English colonies of America were generally small and "purposive" in nature.

Small private libraries existed from the very first in the Pilgrim and Puritan colonies in Massachusetts. Of the Pilgrims, the Reverend William Brewster left a library of over 400 volumes when he died in 1643, many of them obtained after he came to the New World. Governor William Bradford owned some eighty volumes; the Plymouth minister Ralph Partridge had almost as many, and even Captain Miles Standish owned about fifty books. Most of the Pilgrims' books were religious, but there were also some history, travel and political science, a few literary titles and classics, and a few practical works such as those on agriculture and military science owned by Standish. Governor Bradford's library contained some works in French, while William Brewster owned some volumes in Latin and a Hebrew grammar. Of seventy wills of Plymouth citizens still extant for the period 1620 to 1690, only twelve failed to mention books.

Among the Puritans on Massachusetts Bay, the ministers and doctors usually had small private libraries, ranging from a dozen volumes to as many as several hundred. Governor John Winthrop brought a collection of both legal and religious works, but its size and specific contents are not as well known as those of some of his followers. In 1669, the Reverend Benjamin Bunker left about eighty volumes of religious works, while his contemporary, Jonathan Mitchell, left 108 volumes of religion, seventy-four of classics, and eleven of science, mostly medicine. Other professional men of 17th-century New England usually had small book collections at least, but this is also true of many merchants, farmers, skilled craftsmen, and even fishermen. Generally, the smaller the number of books owned, the more religious their nature, and the owner of a single volume usually possessed a Bible. Wills and inventories of estates are the most readily available sources of information concerning colonial book possessions, but wide acquaintance with books is also apparent in the surviving letters, speeches, and papers of the early settlers.

The largest library in mid-17th-century New England was probably that of Governor John Winthrop, Jr. of Connecticut. As early as 1640 this collection numbered over 1,000 volumes, and after his death in 1676 it was preserved and enlarged by his son and grandson. Remnants of the collection given to the New York Society Library in the 19th century indicate that it was cosmopolitan in nature, with books in Latin, French, Dutch, Italian, Greek, and Spanish, as well as English, and on subjects as varied as religion, history, travel, philosophy, law, and literature.

In the latter years of the 17th century, the largest New England private library was that of Cotton Mather, the author and minister. His father, Increase Mather, had owned some 675 volumes in 1664, but many of them were lost in a fire in 1676. Cotton Mather's library contained about 2,500 volumes by 1700, and before his death in 1728 it had reached some 4,000 volumes. Both of these libraries were largely theological, but the son's in particular contained many volumes of history, geography, and philosophy, with a few titles in scientific fields. Since he wrote over 400 books and pamphlets himself, it is easy to see that he not only collected books but made good use of them as well.

Although the libraries mentioned were exceptional in size, small collections were not unusual in the New England home. To aid the buyers of books, there were booksellers in Boston by the 1670s, and both before and after that date many New Englanders ordered books from England. In addition, itinerant book hawkers visited the smaller towns, carrying a few books in their packs and taking orders for others.

Seventeenth-century Virginia also had its private libraries, especially in the homes of government officials, lawyers, ministers, and planters. Surviving wills show that blacksmiths, carpenters, and ship captains also owned books. Robert Hunt, Oxford graduate and chaplain with the first colony in 1607, brought books with him which were burned in a fire in 1608. John Wingfield, one of the earliest arrivals at Jamestown, brought books with him, and John Pory, Secretary to the Colony a decade later, spoke highly of his books as "being in solitude the best and choicest company." Thomas

Bargrave, a minister, left his library for the use of a proposed Indian school in 1621, and James Lobe, a former ship's surgeon, left in his will a "cedar chest full of books." Some women also left libraries, although the collections may have been made by their husbands. In 1673 Mrs. Sara Willoughby left a library that was largely religious in nature, but included Aesop's _Fables_ and a practical title: _Directions for Planting Mulberry Trees_. Toward the end of the 17th century, larger book collections could be found in Virginia. In 1690, William Fitzhugh's library was kept in a room which he called his "Study of Books," and it contained works on history and medicine as well as law. Ralph Wormeley, the Secretary of the Colony who died in 1701, left 375 books, quite general in nature, while the Presbyterian minister Francis Makemie left a library of 992 titles, some of them "handsomely bound." Wills mentioning books, sometimes by list of titles, sometimes merely as "parcels of old books," are numerous for the period after 1650, and one writer estimates that there must have been 1,000 book collections worthy of being called private libraries in 17th-century Virginia. Subjects included in the libraries ranged from theology to farming and from the classics to almanacs. They indicate a high degree of literacy for at least a part of the population, but it should be pointed out that probably half of the adult population, as of 1700, was illiterate.

In the 18th century the private library became more common, particularly among professional people, government officials, and large plantation owners in the South. In New England there were such noted private libraries as that of Thomas Prince, a Boston minister whose avocation was the study of New England history. He formed an important library of books and manuscripts relating to New England and deposited them in the Old South Church in Boston before his death in 1758. These books later became the property of the Boston Public Library. In Newport, Rhode Island, the minister and lawyer Abraham Redwood built up a private library that formed the nucleus of the Redwood Library in 1745. James Franklin had a small library in his Boston newspaper office around 1725. It was stronger than usual in the relatively contemporary English drama, poetry and essays. In the middle colonies, John Sharp of New York built up a large collection of books which he gave to the city in 1713 for public use. It was largely theological and there is little record of its use until it became a part of the New York Society Library in 1754. The Reverend Alexander Innes left a sizable collection of books at his death in 1713, and these were donated to the Anglican churches of New Jersey and New York. Samuel Johnson, an early president of King's College in New York, built his library around English literature, the classics, and history. One of the finest private libraries in New Jersey was that of Richard Stockton, a signer of the Declaration of Independence. Because of his patriotic activities he was a marked man to the British and his home and library were destroyed in 1777.

Probably the most important private library of the middle colonies was that of James Logan of Philadelphia. This Quaker gentleman, who had served as lieutenant governor and as chief justice of Pennsylvania, collected more than 3,000 volumes before his death in 1751. His library was strong in mathematics, astronomy, and science in general, but it also included many of the classics and works of history. Logan hoped to make his library available to the public and before his death a building was erected for it, with books circulating to serious readers "under certain circumstances." Logan was one of the most outstanding scholars of the colonies, reading Greek, Hebrew, and French, and as much at home in Latin as in English. The Loganian Library was closed during the Revolution, but in 1792 it was joined with the Philadelphia Library Company. Benjamin Franklin also had a notable private library of his own, in addition to his activities in connection with other libraries. He bought books frequently on his trips to Europe, usually books that he wanted to read or use. At the time of his death in 1790, Franklin owned more than 4,000 volumes, covering a wide range of topics. Willed to his grandson, Franklin's books were scattered, with many of them coming on the market in 1801, when they were sold by a Philadelphia bookseller. Fortunately, many of Franklin's volumes were recognizable as such, and about 1,000 of them can now be located in various libraries.

Thomas Chalkley gathered a small library on the history and doctrines of the Quakers, which he donated in 1742 to help form the Friends' Library. This specialized collection was to become the most important library on the Quakers in America.

In the South, the largest private library of the later colonial period was that of William Byrd II of Westover, Virginia. Byrd's father had built up a large estate and had started to collect books, but it was the son who, before his death in 1740, enlarged the library to nearly 4000 volumes. Byrd was a planter, lawyer, and public official, as well as a writer, and his library reflected the cultural level and interests of the well-to-do planter. Almost a fourth of the collection was made up of works of history, with another fourth in classical literature, and about ten percent each in English literature, law, and science. There were a number of volumes in French and Latin, and theology was represented by a few works of the church fathers, some volumes on the Church of England, and some current books of sermons. For at least a few years Byrd had a librarian in charge of his books--William Proctor, who also served as tutor for the Byrd children. Byrd's library was well used, not only by his family, but by numerous friends as well. Other Virginia planters also had libraries numbering in the hundreds of volumes. The large plantation owners were not alone in acquiring books; most ministers, lawyers and doctors had at least small professional collections, and many farmers and merchants owned more than the usual Bible and almanac. In the smaller collections, as evidenced in wills, inventories, and sales, books of practical value such as those on farming, surveying, or law joined with sermons and inspirational works to make up the majority.

As conditions in the more heavily settled regions of the colonies became more stable, books became more readily available. Bookstores were established throughout the New England and Middle Atlantic colonies, and some few were established in the South, although the latter region, due to persistent transportation problems and lack of towns of size, acquired most of its books directly from English dealers. After the obvious difficulties encountered by bookmen during the Revolution were behind them, sizable libraries were built throughout the colonies.

Each generation of pioneers, however, experienced essentially the same problems in acquiring and building libraries as they followed the frontier west. First on the eastern slope of the Alleghenies, then in the Ohio Valley, the Mississippi Valley, and finally in the Far West, settlers were forced to work hard and long to establish themselves in their new homes. Such hard work left little leisure for reading, and the hard financial times left little money for the purchase of books. Nevertheless, an examination of wills and probate court records relating to the estates of these pioneers reflects a situation similar to that which we have described on America's first frontier. Many of the early pioneers owned books; most of the book collections were small and religious in orientation; the professional men almost always owned a collection of books relating to their work; and in a few cases large and impressive libraries were collected under the most difficult of conditions.

Not to be ignored in this discussion of private libraries is the development of the privately owned book collection that in size, value, and arrangement warrants the name of library. A collection of books in itself, no matter how large, is not necessarily a library, but when those books are well selected, arranged in some logical order, cataloged or not, but usable by the owner and/or by others, then they constitute a library and deserve recognition as such. The United States has been fortunate throughout its history in having a sizable number of citizens who collected and preserved books, and doubly fortunate that many of those book collections have ended up in publicly available libraries. Just when a collection becomes a library is debatable, however. The United States Census of 1870 reported a total of 107,673 private libraries in the nation, admitting that its figure was incomplete. Since the average size of these "libraries" was only about 235 books, and since there was no way of indicating just how many of the books were in reality texts, pamphlets, children's books, or catalogs, this figure tells us little. Time and place, as well as number of volumes and their nature, must be considered in determining a library worthy of note. For example, 300 books in frontier St. Louis in 1805 is notable; the same number in Boston at the same date is not, unless the collection consisted of extremely rare works.

Many of the private libraries built up in the colonial period were dispersed or destroyed during the American Revolution. Libraries of patriots were destroyed or scattered by the actions of the British and Tories, as in the case of Joseph Hooper of Massachusetts, whose 500-volume library was burned with his home. In Philadelphia, private libraries were scattered when British soldiers occupied the abandoned homes, and the same thing happened on southern coastal plantations occupied by the enemy. On the other hand, many libraries belonging to wealthy Loyalists were confiscated and sold by revengeful patriots, particularly toward the end of the war. But the coming of peace after the Revolution, together with pride in a new nation, encouraged the collection of private libraries, particularly of Americana, and by the early 19th century many notable collections had begun.

The early presidents all had private libraries of some

size, custom apparently followed by many other state and national leaders. President Thomas Jefferson, who was to gain a reputation as the greatest bibliophile ever to occupy the White House, inherited a small library from his father, but a fire in his home in 1770 destroyed this collection. Although he mourned the loss, Jefferson noted that these books were easily replaced, since they were mostly legal works and texts. He immediately began building up another library that numbered 2,640 volumes by 1783, and 6,487 when he sold it to the Library of Congress in 1815. Between 1815 and his death in 1826 he collected yet a third library of nearly 1,000 volumes.

The first half of the 19th century witnessed the activities of several important book collectors who concentrated on books in the general field of Americana--history, travel, biography, and literature. One of the earliest of these was John Allan of New York (1777-1863), who amassed a notable collection of Americana and also collected early illustrated works and examples of early American printing. His library was sold in 1864 for almost $38,000. Isaiah Thomas (1749-1831), historian of printing, collected a library of early Americana, including many early newspapers. This collection went to the library of the American Antiquarian Society, which he had helped to establish in 1812. John Carter Brown (1797-1874) is one of America's best known book collectors, since his library was kept intact and passed on to Brown University in 1900. As a relatively wealthy man, he was able to acquire many rare items and on occasion to purchase whole collections. It was particularly strong in early Americana, travels, and explorations; at the time of its first catalog in 1865, it contained some 5,600 titles, many in several volumes. The Brown Library was later added to by his widow and sons and has grown considerably since becoming the property of the university. Today it is one of the finest collections of Americana in existence. Peter Force, editor and historian, began collecting books in the 1820s, and became such an avid collector that he often mortgaged his property in order to increase his library. Centering his interest on American history, he collected books, pamphlets, broadsides, newspapers, periodicals, and manuscripts until he owned more than 60,000 items in all. In 1867 his heirs sold this collection to the Library of Congress, thereby more than doubling that library's holdings in its field. James Lenox (1800-1880), able to retire from business at the age of forty, spent the latter half of his life building his immense and valuable library. In 1870, convinced that his library was too large for any individual to own, he gave to the people of New York both his books and his large collection of paintings, and later a building to house both. He subsequently gave more books and funds for book purchases, but his original gift contained some 15,000 volumes. Much of his library was Americana, particularly before 1850, but he also had a large collection of Shakespeareana, English literature, and Bibles. Not all of the book collectors of the early 19th century were in the Northeast, however. Almost every section of the country had its ardent collectors, and many of their libraries fortunately have been preserved.

College Libraries

The history of the college library in America stretches back into the 17th century, nearly as far as that of the first private collections. Indeed, America's first college could be said to have begun with a collection of books. Harvard had been founded in 1636, so that young men could be trained for the Puritan ministry without returning to England, and it acquired its name in 1638 when the Reverend John Harvard gave the college some 280 books and a small endowment. Other gifts of books followed, including one of forty volumes from Governor John Winthrop in 1642, but the college library grew slowly. Its holdings were largely theological, and even in 1723, when the first catalog was printed, it contained only 3,500 volumes. In addition to about 2,000 religious works, there were titles in history, geography, classics, science, and languages, represented in that order.

In 1764, when Harvard College was more than 125 years old, the library contained fewer than 5,000 volumes, and in that year it burned, with almost all of its book collection. After this tragedy, friends of the college came to its aid and the Massachusetts Legislature voted funds to replace the burned building. In addition, a popular subscription raised money for the purchase of books, and with the aid of other gifts the library was back to its former size by 1775. Something of the nature of a colonial college library can be gathered from the library rules at Harvard in 1765: The librarian was required to keep the library room open and heated only on Wednesdays, and only junior and senior students could take books from the library. If these rules sound strict, they were an improvement over the earlier ones which had allowed only seniors to have library privileges. After 1765 Harvard boasted an "undergraduate library," which was a collection of duplicates and more popular works set aside for the use of students. Perhaps the real intent of this move was to restrict student use to a smaller and more replaceable collection, preserving the majority of the library for faculty use.

A college and a college library were planned for the new colony of Virginia as early as 1620. A collection of books was gathered in the colony and others were sent from England to provide a library for "Henrico Indian College," to be established near the present site of Richmond. The Indian uprising of 1622 put an end to these charitable plans and Virginia did not acquire a college until William and Mary was founded in 1693. This founding was largely the result of the determination of the Reverend James Blair to provide for the training of Anglican ministers in the college, and he appropriately became its first president. A few hundred books were gathered for the use of the college before 1700, but most of these were destroyed in a fire in 1705. The library was reestablished with a few gifts, but the private library of the Reverend Blair provided most of the reading for the first few decades. In 1742 the will of Governor Alexander Spotswood gave the college about 200 volumes, and the next year, upon the death of Blair, his library, or most of it, officially became the college library. Even so, it is doubtful that the college owned more than 2,000 volumes before the Revolution. Younger faculty members usually "kept" the library a few hours per week, and for some years only clerks were in attendance. No books circulated, and apparently only the faculty used the college library to any extent, while students generally relied on their texts and lecture notes.

New England's second college also began with a collection of books. The eleven ministers who in 1700 organized a society for the formation of Yale College in New Haven, Connecticut, each donated a few books, and in the next decade other donations increased the collection to nearly 1,000 volumes. In 1714, the Reverend Elihu Yale, for whom the college was named, gave 300 books to its library, and in 1733 the Reverend George Berkeley of London sent a gift of some 1,000 volumes, including many valuable folios. By 1742 the Yale library contained about 2,500 volumes, and the college president, Dr. Thomas Clap, in that year began to reorganize and catalog the collection with the aid of a tutor. He divided the library into sections, roughly according to size, and numbered each book in each section, giving to each a fixed location. Next he drew up three catalogs, or booklists: one alphabetically by author, one arranged as the books on the shelf, and a third by broad subject matter, using about twenty-five headings. By 1765 Yale's more than 4,000 volumes were still heavily theological, although there were many on history, classics, philosophy, and mathematics. Literature and science were neglected; there were few books published in America; and, in fact, there were few titles published after 1725.

Like other colonial colleges, the College of New Jersey was begun about 1750, but its library had only some 1,200 volumes as late as 1764. Governor Jonathan Belcher of New Jersey gave his library in 1757, about 475 volumes, and other gifts came from friends in America and in England. When Dr. John Witherspoon became president of the college in 1768, he added 300 volumes to the library, but it still contained fewer than 2,000 when it was virtually destroyed by British soldiers during the Revolution. The University of Pennsylvania (then the Academy) had its library beginnings about 1750 also. Despite the enthusiastic support of Benjamin Franklin and library fees charged to students, its book collection was not very large before the Revolution. King's college (later Columbia University in New York) was begun in 1757, and its major library patron was a Reverend Bristowe of London, who donated some 1,500 volumes. Joseph Murray of New York, one of the college's founders, also left it his library and an endowment, so that by 1764 the collection was large enough for the appointment of its first librarian, who was also the professor of mathematics. Columbia's library, too, suffered at British hands during the Revolution, but some of the pilfered volumes were later restored. Rhode Island College (later Brown University in Providence) began about 1765, with some books collected by the Reverend Morgan Edwards, but still had only some 250 volumes in 1772. Other gifts were received, however, and the collection grew slowly. Fortunately, the Rhode Island students also had access to the volumes in the Providence Library Company, founded in 1753. In 1766, Queens College (later Rutgers) was founded in New Brunswick, New Jersey, but apparently its library, prior to the Revolution, consisted largely of the books belonging to its faculty. The last colonial college was Dartmouth, where classes started about 1770 and where a library had begun several years earlier. Eleazar Wheelock, who founded the college as a school for Indians, had begun to round up books as early as 1764. Fortunately, Dartmouth in New Hampshire was little disturbed by the Revolution, and with other gifts being received, a librarian was appointed in 1779 to arrange and administer some 1,200 volumes. In general, colonial college libraries were small, made up almost entirely of gifts, managed on a part time basis by an instructor, open only a few hours weekly, and little used, especially by the students.

The few college libraries formed during the colonial period suffered during the Revolution; in fact, higher education in general was set back seriously by the conflict leading to independence. Still another decade of uncertainty was to follow the Peace of Paris in 1783, but by the 1790s there was a definite improvement in colleges and college libraries and a few new colleges were begun. Growth was slow, however, for most college libraries, until after 1850, and the colonial tradition of opening the library only a few hours a week, with close restrictions on the use of books, was hard to outgrow. Not until after the Civil War, and indeed not until the late 19th century, did modern libraries really begin to develop in the nation's colleges and universities.

Though forced to move from Cambridge to Concord during the early part of the Revolution, Harvard College saved its library and even added to it with funds allocated by the new state legislature and with books confiscated from fleeing Loyalists. It revived during the 1780s, and a foreign visitor, Francisco de Miranda of Venezuela, described it as "well arranged and clean ... contains some 12,000 volumes, English generally, although not badly selected." By 1790, it had reached the place it was to keep as the nation's preemininent academic library. The printed catalog of that year shows a strong emphasis on theology, but an increased interest in English literature and more titles by 18th-century writers. History, travel, and philosophy were important but there was very little in the field of science. The only periodical was the Gentleman's Magazine. By 1827 Harvard's library totaled over 25,000 volumes, and by 1840, when it was moved into a building of its own, it contained 40,000 volumes exclusive of pamphlets. The building was a bequest of former Massachusettes Governor Christopher Gore (1758-1829), and although it was constructed with the expectation that it would meet the needs of the college for a century, it was outgrown in less than twenty-five years. By 1856 it contained 70,000 books and 30,000 pamphlets. Much of this growth came through gifts, and some of the more important ones are worth mentioning. In 1818, the library acquired the American history collection of the German historian, C. D. Ebeling, totaling about 3,000 volumes relating to America, with some 10,000 maps and charts forming the most complete cartographic collection on America then in existence. The libraries of two presidents, John Adams and John Quincy Adams, came in part to Harvard, and over a period of many years Senator Charles Sumner gave some 1,300 volumes, 15,000 pamphlets (many very rare), and some 250 valuable maps. All told, between 1780 and 1840 more than 1,000 noteworthy gifts of books were received, not counting the many gifts and bequests of funds for the library endowment.

Besides its main college library, Harvard also had several significant departmental and special libraries before 1860. The Law School Library had its beginning in 1817, when Governor Gore presented his own library to the school. Many other gifts were added, and in 1863 this collection alone had 13,000 books. The Divinity School Library dates from 1825, and by 1863 this collection, augmented by some 4,000 volumes from the religious library of Professor Gottfried Lücke of Göttingen, also totaled over 13,000 volumes. The Library of the Phillips Astronomical Observatory began in 1847, and before the Civil War there were also libraries in the Museum of Comparative Zoology and the Lawrence Scientific School. Besides these, there were also student society libraries, such as those of the Procellian Club, the Hasty Pudding Club, the Christian Brethren, and St. Paul's Society.

About Yale's library in 1784, Señor Miranda was not complimentary. He noted that it was "nothing special: two or three thousand volumes." However, the numerous gifts of funds and books, the library grew slowly from 4,700 volumes in 1808 to 21,000 volumes in 1850, and 78,000 in 1875, not including pamphlets. There were also several special libraries, including the Law School Library founded in 1845, and the Theological Seminary Library. Two student society libraries, the Linonian and the Brothers in Unity libraries, were actually begun before the Revolution. In 1860, the Linonian had 12,000 volumes; the Brothers in Unity was somewhat smaller. The Yale Library moved into a new building in 1846, after having been housed previously in rooms or wings of several college buildings.

Several other New England colleges were formed in the half-century after the Revolution, and in general they followed a familiar pattern. The gift of a small collection of books started off the college library, and later gifts of endowment funds and books provided a little growth. Only in about the middle of the 19th century did much support for the library come from the college authorities, with the appointment of a regular librarian and a definite budget. Williams College in Massachusetts began in 1793, and a year later its library had fewer than 400 volumes. By 1876 it could boast of only 17,500 volumes, with an additional 10,000 in two society libraries. Wesleyan University in Middletown, Connecticut, began its library in 1833, based on the collection of Thomas Chapman of Camden, New Jersey. In 1868 Isaac Rich of Boston gave funds for a library building, and a few years later this building housed 26,000 volumes, an excellent collection in the 1870s. Bowdoin College Library in Brunswick, Maine, began with the college, but received its real start in 1811, with the gift of some 4,000 volumes from James Bowdoin, the son and namesake of the Massachusetts governor of the 1780s. Bowdoin College was particularly fortunate during its first half-century, and its library reached some 18,000 volumes by 1875. Amherst College Library began with a single case of books in 1821, but with gifts of books from friends and subscription drives among the alumni, the library grew to some 30,000 books by the 1870s. In that decade, Amherst was fortunate in having as assistant librarian a young man named Melvil Dewey, who was recataloging the library with what he called the decimal system of classification.

In 1800 the Dartmouth College Library numbered only 3,000 volumes, and at one time it was reduced to selling rare volumes in order to purchase new and more usable ones. After its student society libraries were added, the Dartmouth Library reached some 50,000 volumes by 1875. Brown University began its post-Revolutionary existence with a library that consisted of about 500 old, moth-eaten and mildewed volumes that had been stored during the war. With several major gifts of books and funds from the Brown family of Newport and other alumni and friends, it reached some 45,000 volumes by 1860, housed in the Doric architecture of Manning Hall.

In the Middle Atlantic States, the University of Pennsylvania Library was one of the foremost in the antebellum era. Beginning its post-Revolutionary period with a gift of books from the King of France, a series of fairly large gifts increased its holdings steadily until, by 1860, it had about 20,000 volumes. There were also medical and law libraries on the campus as well as two student society collections. Other college libraries in Pennsylvania before 1850 included Dickinson College in Carlisle, founded in 1783; Washington and Jefferson College in Washington, founded in 1802; and Allegheny College at Meadville, founded in 1820. Each of these remained small in size, having only 7,000 to 8,000 volumes as late as 1875, although each was fortunately supplemented by one or more student society libraries. In New Jersey, Rutgers College Library remained small, reaching only 7,000 volumes by 1870, while Princeton (still the College of New Jersey) was more fortunate in reaching 30,000 volumes by 1875. Princeton's library was burned almost completely in 1802, but numerous gifts, including $1,000 for books given by President James Madison, an alumnus, aided in its growth over the years. In 1873 Princeton's library moved into a new octagonal stone building with a book capacity of 100,000 volumes, donated by John C. Green of New York City.

In New York, Columbia College library developed with a relatively small central collection and several departmental libraries. With the gifts of the private libraries of several of its presidents, and of such notable New Yorkers as Supreme Court Justice John Jay, the central library totaled some 16,000 volumes by 1860. The reason for the slow growth of college libraries during this period can be seen in Columbia's library book budget: about $175 in 1825 and only $500 as late as 1862. As late as 1870 Columbia added only 325 volumes, including fifty bound periodicals.

In the South Atlantic States, the colonial college of William and Mary was joined after the Revolution by the state colleges of North Carolina, South Carolina, and Georgia. In Williamsburg, the college that had provided colonial Virginia with both political and intellectual leadership suffered a decline after the Revolution and grew only slowly. After 1825, the new University of Virginia in many ways replaced William and Mary, and its library, as planned by Thomas Jefferson, became one of the finest in the nation. Jefferson personally selected the first consignment of books for the University library and spent the last year of his life (1825-1826) working with them. He died soon after the University was formally opened, but his effect on the institution was long felt. President James Madison also gave the University of Virginia Library a large gift, including some 2,500 volumes and $1,500 in cash. Another large donation came in 1838 when Christian Bohn of Richmond gave the Library about 4,000 books and 1,500 engravings. It had been housed almost from the beginning in the Rotunda Building, also designed by Jefferson, one of the most handsome college structures in the South.

North Carolina's University Library at Chapel Hill began in 1795 with a small collection including fourteen volumes donated by the governor of the state, William R. Davie. Other donations followed, and in the 1820s the college president sent to England to purchase nearly 1,000 volumes for the library, along with apparatus for a chemistry laboratory. In 1850 the library moved into a separate building constructed in the form of a Greek temple, and at that time it contained about 7,000 books. The library of the University of South Carolina at Columbia began shortly after the founding of the University in 1805. Though most gifts to the library were relatively small, it did receive from the State more support than most contemporary publicly owned college libraries, and the book collection grew steadily. In its own building after 1841, the main library was supplemented by a student society library of 1,250 volumes.

West of the Appalachian mountains, the first "college" to be established was Transylvania University at Lexington, Kentucky, in 1798. It grew only slowly at first, but after 1820 it became a full-fledged university with law and medical schools. In that year $14,000 was raised for the library and other equipment, with the result that a collection of some 4,000 volumes was soon gathered. Most of the college libraries of the Ohio and Mississippi valleys date from the second quarter of the 19th century. St. Louis University Library began in 1829, and by 1875 had 17,000 volumes, with an additional 8,000 in the student society libraries. The Indiana University Library began in 1829, with a collection of books purchased by its first president. Gifts were scarce, but small appropriations were occasionally available and state and federal documents helped fill the shelves. The first catalog was printed in 1842. A fire destroyed most of the library's 5,000 volumes in 1854. Marietta College, in Ohio, founded in 1835, raised some $8,000 in subscriptions from friends and alumni in 1850 to add to the college library, and by 1870 it had some 15,000 books, with another 10,000 in the society libraries.

By the middle of the 19th century, then, hundreds of colleges had been established in the country, with libraries which varied greatly in collection size and the nature and extent of services. However, a few generalizations seem to be justified. In his now famous _Notices of Public Libraries in the United States_ (1851), Charles Coffin Jewett described the Nation's college libraries in the following way:

Our colleges are mostly eleemosynary institutions.

> Their libraries are frequently the chance aggregations of the gifts of charity; too many of them discarded, as well nigh worthless, from the shelves of donors.

He noted that this was not true of all our libraries, but sadly, it aptly characterized most of them.

No matter where it was located, the typical college library before the Civil War was small, usually having fewer than 25,000 volumes, made up almost entirely of gifts, with little or no direct financial support from the college administration. Open to students only a few hours per day, or even per week, its bookstock consisted almost entirely of old books, reference works, and standard editions. Little attempt was made to make the library attractive or inviting to students, and in fact the student was not expected to use it very much. If the collection was housed in a separate building, that structure was usually classic in design and little fitted for library purposes.

Generally, a member of the faculty was charged with responsibility for supervising the library, a task one was expected to assume with no reduction in other duties and no increase in pay. One is not surprised to find that these new "librarians" were often reluctant recruits who approached their duties with distaste and impatience. Consequently, hours when the library was open for use were short; rules were strict and inflexible; and the librarian was often viewed with a mixture of fear and disgust by the students. Some few librarians, like Charles Coffin Jewett of Brown, were dedicated and informed professionals, but such men were rare indeed in antebellum America.

While questions relating to the acquisition and organization of library materials were beginning to garner attention from professionals like Jewett, most librarians found that they could deal with the small collections under their charge with a minimum of imagination and effort. If the collection was classified, it was usually by a locally devised system, and the only catalogs were printed or manuscript lists, kept by author, location number, and/or broad subject.

College libraries, with their small and inadequate collections, limited hours, and prohibitive circulation policies were of little use to the college student. Fortunately, students had recourse to the literary society libraries that developed on most college campuses in the first half of the

19th century. These societies were primarily debating societies and their interests ranged across all areas of academic and public concern. As these debates were expected to be learned, as well as rhetorically correct, the students immediately recognized the need for substantial libraries from which to mine their material.

Since the college library of the antebellum period offered little support for the contemporary and popular reading interests of the society members, the societies quickly developed libraries which in many cases rivaled or far excelled their respective college libraries in size and usefulness. At Brown, for instance, the leading society was the Philermenian, founded as the Miskosmiam Society in 1794, reorganized and renamed in 1798. The members of the Philermenian gathered for fortnightly meetings to listen to debates, hear their fellows read speeches and poems, and judge declamations. In 1798, the society began to collect a library, and by 1821 it contained 1,594 well-selected volumes. In 1833 the Philermenian Society library and the library of a rival group--The United Brothers--contained in aggregate some 5,600 well-used volumes, and their collections eclipsed by far in usefulness and value the 6,000 volumes in the university library.

Predecessors of the Public Library

Probably the first attempt at a public library in the colonies came in 1656, when Captain Robert Keayne, a merchant of Boston, willed his book collection to the town for a public library, stipulating that the town build a suitable building to house it. Boston at least partially met this condition, building a Town House with a room for the books, but it is doubtful that they were used much. A catalog was made in 1702, a few other books were added, and the collection met its end in a fire in 1747.

In 1656 Governor Theophilus Eaton of Connecticut left some ninety-five volumes to the town of New Haven for the use of a proposed college. The college never materialized, and the town council, after worrying over the books for several years, finally sold them to a minister in 1689. They had been kept in the town schoolhouse during the intervening years, so they might be considered a public collection, whether or not used. Concord, Massachusetts, was also concerned in 1672 with "some books that belong to the towne," but how many there were, or how they were used, the records fail to say. Although evidence of publicly owned book collections is scarce, that of publicly used church libraries in the era around 1700 is firm. The King's Chapel Library in Boston, for example, was founded in 1698 with books given by the Bishop of London, and several colonial New England wills refer to ministerial libraries being left to churches for the use of the public.

The Reverend Thomas Bray, the Anglican clergyman who sponsored parish libraries in England, was particularly interested in establishing libraries in the colonies, and between 1695 and 1704 he was responsible for establishing some seventy libraries in America. Bray divided these libraries into three types: 1) the five provincial libraries, which were large libraries established in the major city of each province; 2) thirty-nine parochial libraries, which were smaller collections given to Anglican parishes; and 3) some thirty-five layman's libraries, which were distributed to ministers, and which contained books that were loaned or given outright to the residents of the area. The provincial libraries were the largest of the three types, and the most significant collections were established in Annapolis, Maryland, and Charleston, South Carolina.

Early library laws in Maryland and South Carolina were passed by the provincial legislatures to secure and maintain the Bray libraries. At least one of the Bray collections (Annapolis) was intended as a general public library and contained some 1,100 volumes. It was maintained by the provincial government in the State House from 1697 until 1704, when it burned. Some books were saved and united with those of a local school, surviving into the 20th century as a prized collection of the St. John's College Library.

Other parish libraries stemming from the activities of Bray and his associates were formed in New York, Pennsylvania, North Carolina, and South Carolina. A collection of books sent to Bath, North Carolina, in 1700 numbered 166 bound volumes for the use of the ministers and 800 books and pamphlets for the use of the general public. Oddly enough, the books for the ministers were more general than those for the public, since the latter were almost entirely theological or inspirational. A Bray library sent to Charleston led to the passage of a legislative act in 1700, placing a minister in charge of the library and giving detailed instructions concerning its use. With such an auspicious beginning it seemed likely that the parish libraries would grow and eventually become active public services, but no provisions were made for adding new books, and, after the death of the Reverend Bray, interest in parish libraries declined and most of them disappeared. A few books originally in the parish libraries have survived in public or church collections, and they serve as a reminder of a library venture that preceded by two centuries the rise of the public library.

As conditions grew more stable in the colonies, and as the people gained increased leisure for recreation and study, many bookish individuals began to cast about for a way in which the increased demand for books might be satisfied. The solution--the social library--seems to have been the child of the fruitful mind of one of America's greatest intellects, Benjamin Franklin.

His voracious appetite for knowledge and his desire to improve himself and others led him to organize his now famous Junto in Philadelphia in 1728. The group's purpose was to nurture honest and decorous debate and thought, and to contribute in any way possible to the betterment of mankind. The club, made up of twelve young Philadelphians primarily of humble origins, was dedicated to the ideal of the search for truth. Franklin expressed this basic belief in intellectual freedom when he wrote that "when Truth and Error have fair Play, the former is always an overmatch for the latter."

In their search for knowledge and understanding his friends in the Junto were constantly frustrated by their lack of books. In an attempt to solve this problem Franklin suggested in 1730 that the members of the Junto all bring their books to the little room where the group was then meeting and by thus "clubbing our Books to a common Library, we should ... have each of us the Advantage of using the Books of all the other Members, which would be nearly as beneficial as if we owned the whole." However, the experiment was short-lived because some of the members felt their books were not being properly cared for, and also because of the inconvenience of the arrangement.

But the intelligence of "clubbing" as a means of providing increased access to books was readily obvious to Franklin, who in 1731 "set on foot my first Project of a public Nature, that for a Subscription Library." This library, founded in 1731 and chartered in 1742 as the Library Company of Philadelphia, was the first established in this country--

in Franklin's words, "Mother of all N. American Subscription Libraries now so numerous." He was especially proud of these libraries and was confident that his library was imitated by other communities and that "These Libraries have improved the general conversation of the Americans," and have made the "Common Tradesmen and Farmers as Intelligent as Most Gentlemen from other countries." Scholars have been skeptical of Franklin's claim that the Library Company spawned all the other social libraries of the period, but recent scholarship has demonstrated convincingly that Franklin's creation was indeed very influential in the establishment of other libraries throughout the Colonies.

Once established, the social library form became a popular means by which local communities could supply their reading needs. This library type, which definitely represents a significant predecessor of the public library, in the years after 1731 came to take on a number of forms, all grouped for convenience under the label "social libraries." However, for our purposes, it would be well to pause for a moment to consider the term's various mutations. Franklin's Library Company of Philadelphia was what is known in legal terms as a joint stock company; that is, each member of the library company owned one or more shares in the corporation, and his shares could be bought and sold like stock in any company.

This "proprietary" form became the basic model for the creation of social libraries, but in time other social libraries came to need support beyond the original funds derived from the sale of stock in the company. Thus they began to collect annual fees in addition to requiring purchase of stock, and in time even allowed individuals who were not shareholders in the corporation to "subscribe" to the library (thus the origin of the label "subscription" library) on a year-to-year basis, or for even briefer periods of time.

A third major refinement of the original proprietary library form was the athenaeum, an organization founded along social library lines but which emphasized the provision of scholarly newspapers and magazines as its essential service, while also sponsoring frequent cultural and recreational programs as another aspect of its activities. Furthermore, the athenaeum was frequently the most expensive--stock ranged as high as $300 a share as compared to an average among social libraries of $1 to $4--and thus was the most aristocratic of the social library forms. The first, established in Boston in 1807, remains the most impressive of them all, and provided the model for many more, including those still in existence in Salem and Philadelphia.

Finally, a further development of the social library form came in the early 19th century when interested individuals established what were known as "mechanics'" and "mercantile" libraries. Ray Held, in his history of libraries in California, attempted to classify social libraries by who used them, concluding that one could divide social libraries into two groups: 1) those established by individuals who intended to make personal use of them; and 2) those established by individuals who intended them for the use of others. The mechanics' and mercantile libraries fall into the latter group, and represent the rise of libraries founded by benevolent leaders for the use of the "people." In this case, wealthy businessmen and industrialists supported the establishment of mercantile and mechanics' libraries throughout the industrialized cities of America in order to "promote orderly and virtuous habits, diffuse knowledge and the desire for knowledge, improve the scientific skill," and generally make effective citizens and productive workers of the mechanics working in America's factories, and the mercantile clerks training for management of her commerce.

The organization of the social library was usually very simple. In the smaller ones, there was little or no attempt to arrange the books except in general classifications, but in the larger collections more serious attempts were made at cataloging, ranging from simple manuscript accession records to printed alphabetical or classified lists. Housing for the collection might be in a public building, a member's home or business, or, for larger collections, in a separate rented or owned building. Hours of opening ranged from a few hours one or two days per week to fairly regular schedules of eight to ten hours daily. An attendant, volunteer or paid, charged books and checked on their return in the smaller collections, but the larger ones had more or less full-time "librarians." As early as 1793, a pamphlet had been written to advise the book selectors for social libraries on the best methods of obtaining books and the best books to be chosen. This was the Selected Catalogue of Some of the Most Esteemed Publications in the English Language Proper to Form a Social Library, written by Thaddeus Mason Harris, who had served for a short time as a librarian at Harvard. His booklet was one of the earliest American works on book selection, and as such it is interesting. He divided all books into three classes: memory, reason, and imagination. The first class included all phases of history, biography, and travel; the second, science, philosophy, and religion; and the third, poetry, drama, fiction, and art. In all, he recommended only eighty-one titles, but these were well selected for the time and purpose. Ordinarily, the smaller social libraries bought only a few new books each year, but collectively they made up a major book market, so the book publishers and dealers soon came to offer them special discounts to secure their trade.

The social library proved an efficient means for meeting the growing reading appetite of America's rapidly increasing population. However, it was characterized by a fatal flaw--the principle of voluntary support--and as Jesse H. Shera has noted, "the shifting sands" of voluntary support were proving inadequate to the task of supporting the widespread and efficient library service so desired by library advocates throughout the nation. Especially troublesome was the tendency of social libraries to fail during hard financial times. The depressions of 1819, 1837, and 1857 all pressed severe economic deprivation upon the nation, and people were forced to withdraw support from all sorts of cultural and recreational activities, including social libraries. As a consequence, many American communities lost their library service every time the region experienced difficult financial times. Such instability was simply unacceptable to those who believed that libraries were essential, for whatever reason, to the success of the Republic. Their efforts to discover a form of support which would be capable of bringing stability and energy to library service led them eventually to the idea of supporting libraries with public tax funds.

Thus the many variations on the social library model first formulated by Franklin and his young friends in Philadelphia constitute a significant chapter in the unfolding story of the rise of the public library. Indeed, when the public library was established in the latter half of the 19th century, it either absorbed the local social library or, in many cases, actually found its origins in the gift of the collection belonging to the social library. At any rate, social libraries had limited futures once public libraries were established in their respective communities, and only the most unique, or those boasting the most impressive of traditions--like the Library Company of Philadelphia--are still in existence.

The nation's social libraries were generally promoted

as serious sources of knowledge for those who desired to improve themselves. They did not, at least openly, cater to the public taste for romance and popular fiction, choosing instead to purchase only the best nonfiction and some few classic works of fiction. The public's voracious appetite for romance was filled by libraries designed as commercial ventures and aimed at stocking only the most popular and exciting of the new fiction. These libraries, called "circulating" libraries, made their first appearance just prior to the American Revolution.

Maintained usually by printshops or bookstores, these "libraries" made available rental books for a small fee, either a book at a time or a number of books over a given period of time. Possibly the first of these rental collections was opened by William Rind in Annapolis, Maryland, in 1762. He proposed to allow his customers the use of two books at a time for an annual fee of twenty-seven shillings. His venture was unsuccessful and it was discontinued in 1764. However, the idea caught on and by 1765 or a little later, there were rental collections in Boston, Philadelphia, New York, and Charleston. One in Boston, begun by John Mein, was particularly ambitious and published a catalog of some 1,200 titles available for rent at the rate of twenty-eight shillings a year for all that one could read, one volume at a time. Unfortunately, since Mein was a Loyalist, as the Revolution approached he was forced to leave the city. In New York, Samuel Loudon's circulating library offered some 2,000 titles to discriminating readers in the early 1770s, and some of his most popular volumes were poetry. The circulating library was to have its greatest success in the half-century after the Revolution, and it should be noted that most of the enterprises that rented books also sold them. Booksellers were common in the larger towns before 1775, with Philadelphia having at least twenty-five sellers of books advertising before that date. Their basic bookstock usually consisted of primers and other textbooks, prayerbooks, and dictionaries, with the local laws and almanacs being regular items. Besides these, the average buyer could find sermons, current political tracts, and some literature, but the heavier works found in most private libraries were probably ordered from England.

While the purely commercial circulating library increased in numbers after the Revolution, its cultural importance was probably negligible when compared to the social libraries. For one thing it was restricted, as was the bookstore of which it was usually a part, to the larger towns. It depended upon a reading public somewhat different from that of the social library--more on the casual reader than the serious one. It was usually small, but occasionally in old, established stores it reached several thousand volumes. Caritat's Circulating Library in New York City, opened in 1797, had over 5,000 volumes in its catalog of 1804, including more than 1,000 titles of fiction. Even more than the social library, the circulating library reflected popular reading tastes, but unfortunately there are few surviving records of the bookstocks of those commercial ventures, much less any counts of their actual use. An interesting example of a circulating library was the "Book Boat" that flourished on the Erie Canal for a generation after 1830. Going from Albany to Buffalo and back, the boat would tie up at a wharf for a few hours or even a few days at a time, and rent its literature, varying from sermons to joke books, at two cents an hour or ten cents a day. The rental collections were less important in the general development of public libraries than the social libraries, but they provided a needed service and they have left their descendants in the public library pay collection and the drugstore rental shelf.

While the social and circulating libraries must be considered significant predecessors of public libraries in this country, it is important to note that another significant forerunner of the public library was the school district library. Writing in his Third Annual Report for 1839, Horace Mann, then Secretary of the Massachusetts Board of Education, stated the credo for such libraries--a credo that was to be utilized again (in a slightly different form) by the founders of America's first public libraries:

> After the rising generation have acquired habits of intelligent reading in our schools <u>what shall they read</u>? for, with no books to read, the power of reading will be useless; and with bad books to read, the consequences will be as much worse than ignorance as wisdom is better. What books, then, are there accessible to the great mass of the children in the State, adapted to their moral and intellectual wants, and fitted to nourish their minds with the elements of uprightness and wisdom?

It was this question that prompted educators, intellectuals, and eventually legislators to seek for a way in which such reading might be furnished to adults as well as children, and one solution was to establish libraries associated with the school-districts so common to the seaboard states.

This type of library apparently originated in New York state but spread widely throughout New England and the Middle West. New York's Legislature passed an act in 1835 that made it permissible for school districts to levy taxes for school libraries. This law brought little response, but a second one passed in 1838, which provided state funds to match local levies for books, was more successful, and in three years more than 400,000 books were placed in the schools of the state. This idea grew until by 1850 there were nearly 1,500,000 books in New York's school libraries. However, without proper staff and quarters many of the books were lost or allowed to deteriorate. The interest in the libraries was high at first but soon declined, and state laws later allowed the library funds to be spent for other purposes. In Massachusetts, a school-district library system was established in 1837, and 2,084 such collections were reported there by 1850. In all, they contained only about 100,000 volumes, or an average of about fifty books each, and here again the movement was hardly a success. Connecticut followed Massachusetts in 1839, and Rhode Island in 1840, and in a few cases in these states the collections eventually became working school libraries. Several Middle West states, including Michigan, Indiana, and Ohio, passed school-district library laws before 1850, but in general they were not very successful.

The school-district libraries were a failure partly because of their contents and partly because of the way in which they were handled. They usually consisted of textbooks, general works, and a smattering of inspirational literature, with little attention paid to their selection. The majority were above the reading level and beyond the interests of all but the most advanced students, and though they were theoretically available to the adults of the community, they were not widely used. Several publishing firms took advantage of the school-district library laws and compiled sets of works, poorly selected, printed, and bound, but sold on commission through local representatives. These sets often took up the entire funds available, and their drab appearance and dry contents did little to promote their use. For lack of adequate quarters in the school buildings, the library books were often stored in the homes of teachers or school board members, and an investigation of the New York school-district libraries in the 1850s found many of the books molding in closets, cellars, and attics. In a sense, the school-district library was an attempt at both public and school library service, and in both it was a failure. It was premature, poorly supported, and consequently unsuccessful, but it established the precedent of public support for library services and paved the way for better school and public libraries at a later date.

Another form of library service to children which deserves notice is the Sunday School library--perhaps the most numerous and least-known library type in 19th-century America. Practically every church, especially in the North and West, could boast a small collection of books designated as the "Sunday School" library. At times they represented fairly substantial general collections, but more often they contained only religious and inspirational works. Where other sources of reading material were not available, especially in frontier areas, they were frequently consulted by children and adults alike; but the specialized nature of the collections and their general neglect soon led to their decline.

In addition to the school-district and Sunday School libraries, children did have access to books through several other kinds of libraries. One source of reading for children came in the form of the libraries attached to the many private schools and academies established in the country prior to the Civil War.

Some academies were established during the colonial period, but little is known of their libraries. The Boston Latin School, for example, is supposed to have been founded in 1635, but nothing is known of its library until the 19th century. There definitely was a library there in 1844, when the Boston Latin School Association was formed to support it, and by 1875 it had some 5,000 volumes. In New York City, Public School No. 1 had a small collection of books in 1810, and by 1820 the city was appropriating $50 per year for library books in each school. In Virginia, the state legislature chartered Rumford Academy in 1804, with authority to promote a lottery to raise funds for a library, but apparently it was not successful. In frontier Missouri, St. Louis Academy boasted a library in its 1818 advertisements, and the Academy of the Sacred Heart had a library in 1827. Abbott Academy at Andover, Massachusetts, was established in 1829 and had a well-organized library by 1842, but in 1875 it still contained only 1,500 volumes. The academy movement was strong in New England and the Middle West by 1825, and in the South by 1850. In Ohio, there were no fewer than 171 academies and institutes founded between 1803 and 1850. In most cases, little is known of their libraries, but from the remains of a few that have survived, or where printed catalogs are available, it is apparent they were often gift collections, poorly selected and seldom used. Moreover, the academy libraries were usually cared for by a faculty member, and any organization or cataloging was usually haphazard. Hours of opening were few and emphasis on reading other than textbooks was usually lacking. However, many of the teachers in the academies often had book collections of their own that were more pertinent to the needs or interests of the students than the school libraries, and usually available to the students. Also, in the stronger academies, there were often literary society libraries that were small but well used.

Besides the academies, there were also a few public libraries offering books particularly for children in the early 19th century. The library founded by Caleb Bingham at Salisbury, Connecticut, in 1803 was specifically designated for children from nine to sixteen years of age, although it seems to have been used generally by adults as well. In 1804 Dr. Jessey Torrey started a library for young people in connection with the New Lebanon, New York, Library Soceity. Some of the subscription libraries contained books for children, and there is evidence of a Children's Library Society in Louisville, Kentucky, in 1810, and in Richmond, Virginia, in 1823. The West Cambridge, Massachusetts, Juvenile Library was started in 1835, but it was open only a few hours each Saturday. Three books per family could be taken out for thirty days. The apprentices' libraries, YMCA libraries, and the Sunday School libraries each provided some service for children and young people. The apprentices' libraries were usually available to boys over eleven or twelve, as were the YMCA libraries, and the Sunday School collections tried to win juvenile readers with sentimental stories of unbelievably good little girls and boys. Circulating rental libraries also contained some titles of interest to older children, but books available to children in public collections before the Civil War were generally scarce.

The Emergence of Special Libraries

In a sense, many of the libraries discussed to this point could be defined as special. However, in modern usage we tend to consider special libraries to be relatively small collections with carefully defined clienteles, with an explicit and sharply focused mission. Given these characteristics it is possible to survey the first two centures of American library history and identify examples of libraries that might legitimately be labeled "special."

For instance, the Pennsylvania Hospital Library in Philadelphia, probably the first medical library in the United States, began in 1763. Similarly, the Library of the American Philosophical Society, founded in 1743 in Philadelphia, may well be the oldest special library of any type in the nation, unless the parochial libraries sent over around 1700 by Dr. Thomas Bray for the use of Anglican ministers could be so considered. Since there were few libraries of any type antedating these, it may be said that special libraries have as venerable a history as any others in the United States.

Early theological libraries were almost always associated with colleges and schools of divinity. Apparently, the oldest strictly theological collection was that of St. Mary's Theological Seminary, founded in Baltimore in 1791. There was also a Presbyterian Theological Seminary in Beaver County, Pennsylvania, established in 1794. It began with a library of some 800 volumes collected by the Reverend John Anderson. By 1825 twenty-one more theological libraries, most of them in seminaries, had been established, and by 1875 there were over 120. The library of Andover Theological Seminary, Andover, Massachusetts, although larger than average, is typical of the growth of the theological collection. The seminary was founded in 1807, opening in 1808 with a small library which grew slowly from gifts and purchases until by 1875 it possessed over 34,000 volumes, not including some 12,000 pamphlets. Besides several large gifts, in 1858 Andover was able to purchase the library of Dr. C. W. Nieder of Berlin, containing some 4,000 rare and valuable works. The seminary library issued a printed catalog in 1819, and another in 1838, with a supplement in 1849. From 1818 to 1866 it occupied a room in the college chapel, but in 1866 it moved into a separate building that had been donated by three Andover citizens. The majority of theological libraries were smaller than that at Andover and ranged during the 19th century from 2,000 to 15,000 volumes in size. In addition to the strictly theological libraries, there were also strong theological collections in most of the early college libraries. Harvard's Divinity School, for example, began its own library in 1825, and owned 17,000 volumes by 1875. Also many churches had small libraries, although they were usually more like study collections for the ministers than actual libraries.

The legal profession was an early developer of special libraries. Since his tools of trade were law books, the colonial student of law usually added to his textbooks the provincial laws and legal handbooks and thus developed a small private law library out of necessity. Some of these were undoubtedly used by other lawyers, as were also those in the offices of provincial officials. These could hardly be considered special libraries, however, and it was not until after 1800 that the first law libraries emerged. Philadelphia's Law Association Library opened in 1802, and Boston's Social Law Library in 1804. As their names indicate, they were extensions of the social library concept to groups of lawyers, enabling them to buy collectively more law books than they could afford individually. County law libraries, semi-public in nature, were established in New York and other Northeastern states by the 1840s. Sometimes they were initiated by public legislation, as in Massachusetts, and at other times by local law associations. Still another type of law library in the 19th century was that of the law school, or law department in a college. Harvard University's Law School Library was founded in 1817 and contained over 15,000 volumes in 1875. In that year, twenty-one other law schools reported libraries, most of them with fewer than 10,000 volumes.

Historical libraries were popular in the 19th century, and these also varied considerably in size. The Massachusetts Historical Society was probably the earliest to be formed, having been chartered in 1791, but it was followed by several others in neighboring states early in the next century. By 1850 most of the states had historical libraries, a few receiving government funds and the remainder depending upon supporting societies. In either case, acquisitions consisted largely of gifts, free government publications, and exchanges with other historical groups. Some towns and counties supported local historical societies, but in most of these the libraries were small and neglected. By 1875 there were some eighty historical-society libraries from Maine to California and from Alabama to Wisconsin, varying in size from only a few hundred volumes to the New York Historical Society's 60,000. The Rhode Island Historical Society Library in Providence is typical of historical libraries prior to 1875. The Society was organized in 1822 and had about

150 members, with a $5 admission fee and $3 annual dues. Beginning with a few gift volumes, its library contained about 6,000 volumes and 30,000 pamphlets by 1870. The collection was primarily on the history of Rhode Island, secondarily on New England and the remainder of the United States. Many of its volumes were obtained by exchange of its publications with similar societies in other states. The Society owned its building but had no paid employees, and its library, with volunteer "librarian," was open only to members and their guests for a few hours each week. Some historical societies were sponsored by, or related to, religious organizations. The Friends' Historical Society of Philadelphia and the Presbyterian Historical Society of the same city are examples. Each of these had libraries of several thousand volumes in the 1860s. Although most of the historical libraries were poorly financed, their collections often contained many valuable volumes, and their publications made notable additions to the published historical literature of the United States.

Somewhat akin to the historical libraries were the scientific-society libraries that developed in the larger cities during the early 19th century. From its colonial beginnings, the library of the American Philosophical Society in Philadelphia grew slowly, but its additions in science and philosophy were almost invariably valuable. By 1875 it contained some 20,000 volumes and about as many pamphlets. Also in Philadelphia was the Academy of Natural Sciences, founded in 1812 and by mid-century proclaimed as one of the best in its field, with 30,000 volumes and 35,000 pamphlets. The Franklin Institute was founded in the same city in 1824, as a group particularly interested in the physical sciences, and its library was only a little smaller than the other two. In Boston, the American Academy of Arts and Sciences (founded 1780) and the Boston Society of Natural History (1831) each had libraries of more than 10,000 volumes by 1875, while the Massachusetts Horticultural Society (1829) had a library of about 2,500 volumes. In New York there were such scientific libraries as those of the American Geographical Society, founded in 1852, and with 10,000 volumes in 1875; and the New York Academy of Sciences, founded in 1818, with only 3,500 volumes at the later date. In 1885 New York City had at least thirty-three special libraries of note, including nine medical and hospital libraries, six law libraries, eight scientific libraries, four theological libraries, two historical libraries, and one insurance library.

Special medical and hospital libraries were fewer and

smaller than those in other subject fields in the 19th century, possibly because the literature in the field of medicine was relatively small. After the Pennsylvania Hospital Library, five other medical libraries were begun before 1800, and by 1860 there were twenty-three medical libraries, varying in size from 1,000 to 10,000 volumes, most of them in the Northeast. In New York the Hospital Medical Library was begun in 1796, and by 1875 had over 10,000 volumes, while the Academy of Medicine Library there had accumulated only 3,000 volumes since its founding in 1846. Philadelphia's College of Physicians Library, dating from 1789, had 18,750 volumes in 1875, and was, next to the Library of the Surgeon General's Office in Washington, the largest medical library in the country. Elsewhere, there were libraries of hospitals, medical schools, and societies in almost every state by 1850, although most of them were small.

Libraries Serving Government

As the national libraries in Europe are among the major libraries of the world, so in the United States the nation's greatest library is a government agency, the Library of Congress. Originally intended as the reference library for the national legislative body, this institution has had a long and varied history, but it has emerged in the 20th century as the national library in all but name. The Library of Congress is not the only major library operated by the United States government, and, besides the federal libraries, there are also many important ones belonging to the states. Altogether, the government libraries in the United States represent a major portion of the library resources available to the American people. They are designed primarily for the use of government officials and employees, but many of them are also open to the general public, and directly or indirectly, their valuable resources are available.

The history of the Library of Congress begins with the history of the United States. The new government, from 1776 on, made use of several book collections in New York and Philadelphia, particularly those of the New York Society Library and the Philadelphia Library Company. A few books were owned by the Continental Congress and its successors, but no definite move toward an actual library came until after the government moved to the new capital at Washington, D.C., in 1800. In that year, Congress appropriated funds for the purchase of books, and a first order for 740 volumes was placed in London. In 1802, a room for the Congressional Library was set aside in the new Capitol, and President Thomas Jefferson appointed the Clerk of the House of Representatives to be the first librarian. Jefferson also aided in the selections for this first library, but it had only grown to about 3,000 volumes by 1814. In that year, during the war with Great Britain, the Capitol was burned by an invading army and the embryo Library of Congress was destroyed. After the war there was considerable debate as to how the library could be reconstituted, and former President Jefferson solved the problem by offering to sell his excellent private library to the government. After much debate the offer was accepted, and in 1815 the collection of 6,500 volumes was purchased, giving the nation a library that was much superior to the one that had burned.

George Watterson was appointed as the first full-time Librarian of Congress, and temporary quarters were found for the new library until 1824, when permanent quarters were completed in the new Capitol. By this date, Congress was appropriating about $5,000 per year for the library, and through purchases, gifts, and government publications the bookstock was growing steadily. In 1832 part of the legal collection in the library was removed to form a library for the Supreme Court, but this remained under the jurisdiction of the Librarian of Congress for some time. By 1850 the library had reached some 50,000 volumes, second in size only to Harvard University's library. Once again, a fire in the Capitol destroyed much of the library in 1851, including about two-thirds of the original Jefferson collection.

At mid-century, the Library of Congress was considered to be little more than a collection of books of use to members of Congress; its emergence as the "National Library" was to come under the persistent and enlightened leadership of Ainsworth Rand Spofford, who served as Librarian of Congress from 1864-1897. However, there was a library in Washington at mid-century that was billing itself as "national" in scope. That library, which constituted part of the newly formed Smithsonian Institution, was directed by America's most prominent librarian, the determined and controversial Charles Coffin Jewett.

When Jewett was appointed librarian at the Smithsonian in 1847, he fully intended to make the Smithsonian Library the national library of the United States. However, he reckoned without the influence and eventual victory of the secretary of the Smithsonian, the prominent scientist Joseph Henry, who was determined to allocate the Institution's limited resources to the support of scientific research and publication programs.

At first Jewett appeared to be making some headway. He was able to bring about the passage of a copyright deposit law which stipulated that one copy of each copyrighted work was to be deposited at both the Smithsonian and the Library of Congress. He worked diligently to make the Smithsonian the "centre of bibliographical knowledge" in the country, and pioneered a number of venturesome, but frustrating, cooperative cataloging programs. Finally, he published his famous _Notice of Public Libraries in the United States of America_ (1851), which is now recognized as the pioneer attempt to survey and assess the Nation's library resources.

Before too many years had passed, the strong-willed librarian and the determined secretary of the Smithsonian clashed over policy, and Jewett was forced to resign, moving to Boston where he later became the first superintendent of that city's new public library. Secretary Henry promptly proceeded to dismantle Jewett's national library plans, and in 1866 the Smithsonian's 44,000-volume collection was transferred to the Library of Congress, making the LC collection the largest and most impressive in America.

Most of the states also maintained one or more government libraries. Even before the Revolution, there were collections of legal works available in the provincial legislative halls for the use of officials and legislators. Virginia had a small library in the office of the provincial secretary as early as 1661; at least fifty books have survived that belonged to the colonial government before 1776. In that year Thomas Jefferson suggested a bill for a state library for Virginia, but nothing came of it until 1828, just two years after Jefferson's death, when the state established a state library and gathered into one location all the books then belonging to the state's offices. In 1831 the Virginia State Library in Richmond had 5,500 volumes, and in 1856, 17,500.

Pennsylvania's state capital had a small library as early as 1777, and the other colonies probably had at least collections of law books for the use of their officials and legislators, but it was not until after 1800 that most of the states began to form official state libraries. South Carolina had one by 1814, Pennsylvania by 1816, New York and New

Hampshire by 1818, and most of the Eastern states by 1840. Michigan's state library began in 1828, and Illinois' in 1839, with most of the other Midwestern states forming libraries by 1850. Territorial libraries often preceded state libraries in the more western states.

The early state libraries were usually made up mainly of legal works and official government publications, but from the beginning there were many historical or geographical works. These acquisitions mostly came from gifts, via exchanges of state publications with other libraries, and through receipt of federal publications through acts of Congress. The use of the libraries was ordinarily restricted to state officials, and even they sometimes had to leave deposits to borrow books. Librarians were generally political appointees. Some of the state libraries, however, were from the beginning for general public use, as that of New York, which was established as a "public library for the use of the government and of the people of the state." Financial support for the early state libraries was usually erratic and most of them grew very slowly. Shortly after the Civil War there were forty-six state and territorial libraries, but only ten of them had over 30,000 volumes and the largest was that of New York with 95,000.

Canadian Libraries

The history of Canadian libraries parallels to some extent that of the United States, but there are notable differences. First, there are the French origins of eastern Canada and the continued domination of French language and culture in Quebec. Then, there is the long colonial status of Canada and the close political and cultural ties with Great Britain, even after the achievement of Dominion and Commonwealth status. Finally, there are the vast distances, the sparce population, the slow development of transportation, and the long winters, all factors that accentuate the other difficulties in socialization and communication. Nevertheless, the development of Canadian libraries has been steady, and today they are comparable to those of Europe and the United States.

There seems little doubt that books accompanied some of the earliest French explorers to Canada. Certainly men such as Marc Lescarbot, Samuel de Champlain, and the Sieur de Monts had small libraries even on their earliest visits to Canada. Lescarbot, at least, is reported to have made some of his volumes available for use by others. Also, the early missionary priests brought books with them, and as early as 1635 there was a small library attached to the earliest Jesuit "college" founded in Canada. But, for the French fur trapper and trader in the wilderness, and even for the Acadian farmers in Nova Scotia, books were virtually unknown. Small religious collections and the private libraries of priests and officials made up the sum total of books in French Canada for 150 years, or until after the British took over in 1763.

Even before the British flag flew over the St. Lawrence, the Hudson Bay Company had carried it into the fur country of northern Canada, and a few boxes of books were available to traders at the Company's outposts; and even the early explorers into western Canada, whether overland or via the Pacific, carried a few books with them. Once the English were firmly settled in Quebec, Governor Frederick Haldemand promoted the establishment of the first subscription library in 1780, providing books in both French and English for subscribers who could afford to pay £5 down and £2 per year. A little later, in Upper Canada (Ontario), Governor John Graves Simcoe gave his private library of legal and historical works to the Legislature of that Province in 1791. Stimulus for education, and secondarily for libraries, came from the Loyalists who had fled from the United States during and after the American Revolution. Most of these people represented what had formerly been the upper class of New England and the Middle Atlantic colonies, and although they had seldom been able to bring their libraries with them, most of them were accustomed to owning books, and as soon as possible they began to establish private and social libraries. A social library was formed in Montreal by 1796 and another in Niagara by 1800, with perhaps a dozen others before 1820 in various Canadian towns and villages. The College of New Brunswick was founded in 1795 and King's College in Nova Scotia by 1802. Each of these institutions had small libraries, but like their neighbors in the United States, they depended primarily on gifts for their first few decades.

By the 1830s, the social libraries were joined by Mechanics' Institute libraries, semi-charitable agencies patterned after similar organizations in England. Providing lecture series and other educational encouragement for the working classes in addition to libraries, these Institutes received not only approval but some financial aid from provincial governments. Among the earliest such libraries were those at Montreal, York, and Halifax, and by 1850 some forty others had been established, although not all survived. In 1851 the Canadian Parliament passed legislation regulating the establishment of mechanics' institutes and similar libraries, allowing a government grant of £50 each annually. When many of the institutes failed to report properly on the use of the funds, they were discontinued in 1860. Many of the institute libraries survived, however, and after the Confederation of Canada was formed in 1867, several of the provinces provided small grants to them. Some eventually became public libraries, while others survived into the 20th century as "association libraries," a type of subscription library. The services were at best minimal, but they provided an element of library service for those interested, particularly in the smaller towns.

After 1846, Ontario and eastern Canada tried the school-district library, similar to those then under way in New York and New England. Operated by the schools but intended for public use, these libraries were part of the program for general public education planned by Egerton Ryerson. By 1874 there were 1,344 such libraries in Ontario, containing some 266,000 volumes, or an average of about 200 volumes each, according to the annual report of the Ontario Department of Education. They were bought through the Department of Education from a selected list, and were generally more suitable for adults than for children. Joseph Howe, in Nova Scotia, was similarly involved in establishing schools and libraries in the 1840s and 1850s. In Quebec, parish libraries were established in much the same manner. On the whole, the success of the school-district libraries was more apparent in Ontario than elsewhere, but they were far from providing anything like public library service. They did form a beginning by acquainting a few users with worthwhile reading material, and in their public support they set the precedent for both public and school libraries of the future.

A few other developments in Canadian library history, prior to Confederation, are worthy of mention. The Library of Parliament was founded in 1815 in Ottawa, and in 1841 it was joined by a smaller collection from Lower Canada or Quebec. Unfortunately, in 1855 a disastrous fire occurred that destroyed most of the books, but they were quickly replaced and by 1882 the Parliamentary Library contained nearly 100,000 volumes. From the late 18th century, provincial legislative libraries existed at least in name, but they were usually small legal collections under the care of a clerk until late in the 19th century. Private libraries of more than a few volumes were scarce in early Canada, but records of several notable ones have survived. Jonathan Odell, Provincial Secretary of New Brunswick from 1784 to 1812, left a library of nearly 1,000 volumes, probably the largest private library in Eastern Canada at that time. Robert Addison, a missionary sent out by the English Society for the Propagation of the Gospel, brought some 1,250 volumes with him to Niagara in 1792. They were largely theological, and were apparently made available to other Anglican ministers and to interested parishioners. Even out on the Pacific coast, early explorers and fur traders brought along a few books. Dr. John McLoughlin, agent for the Hudson Bay Company, at the mouth of the Columbia River, maintained a large collection of reading matter in the early 19th century for his own use and for his frequent visitors. When the Red River Library, the first to be founded in the Province of Manitoba, was begun in 1847, its core was a private collection donated by Peter Fidler, a trader and land speculator. Other government officials, professional men, and businessmen gathered sizable collections, many of which later came to rest in public and college libraries.

Conclusion

The development of libraries in America, North and South, projects an ever-more-complex mosaic upon the historical canvas. However, certain similarities are evident. First, it is clear that a certain percentage of the residents of each new settlement in the New World possessed the ability to read and had brought a few precious books with them when they journeyed to their new homes. Furthermore, they set about importing reading material from their native lands, and, ultimately, producing newspapers, magazines, and books locally.

Furthermore, as conditions stabilized, as the population grew, and as the amount of leisure time available to many people increased, the small privately owned collections began to prove inadequate for the information and recreational needs of readers. By the early 19th century nearly all of the settled regions of America had experimented with various forms of the "public" library--all designed to make books and other reading material more readily available to an ever increasing number of readers.

At the same time, academic institutions were being established throughout America, and, reflecting the practice common to European civilization, they were nearly always equipped with some semblance of a library. While the collections were generally small, ill-housed, and little used, they nevertheless represented the seeds of contemporary American academic libraries.

But much was yet to be done. In 1850, while the need for a form of "public" library was viewed as essential by many literate individuals, the idea of a "public library" open to all, supported by tax-funds, and administered as a public trust was only just gaining some attention. Similarly, while academic libraries were common ingredients in the educational recipe, they were to gain a truly significant role in American education only during the last few decades of the century. Other library types remained in a similar embryonic stage.

And yet, much had been accomplished, and the stage was set for momentous library developments in America. Before these can be considered, however, we must turn our attention back across the Atlantic, to survey the rise of the modern European library.

Additional Readings

The literature of American library history has proliferated substantially over the past twenty years. Fortunately, there are a number of useful bibliographic guides available to those seeking guidance. Most valuable in this regard is American Library History: A Bibliography, Michael H. Harris and Donald G. Davis, Jr. (Austin: University of Texas, 1978), which lists some 3,500 items on the subject. This bibliography is brought up-to-date by the essays on "the year's work in American Library History," published in the Journal of Library History. A valuable guide to the older literature in library history is now available in Libraries in American Periodicals Before 1876: A Bibliography with Abstracts and an Index, Larry J. Barr, Haynes McMullen, and Steven G. Leach, (Jefferson, N.C.: McFarland and Company, 1983). Also of real value is the Dictionary of American Library Biography, (Littleton, Colo.: Libraries Unlimited, 1978), which contains over 300 biographies of prominent historical figures in American librarianship. Finally, Elizabeth Stone has compiled a useful chronology, American Library Development, 1600-1899 (New York:

H. W. Wilson, 1977). The works listed below represent a highly select list of works on pivotal aspects of early American library history.

Briggs, F. A. "The Sunday School Library in the Nineteenth Century," Library Quarterly 31 (1961): 166-77.

Brough, Kenneth. Scholar's Workshop: Evolving Conceptions of Library Service (Urbana: University of Illinois Press, 1953.

Clayton, Howard. "The American College Library: 1800-1860," Journal of Library History 3 (1968): 120-37.

Cole, John Y. For Congress and the Nation: A Chronological History of the Library of Congress (Washington, D.C.: Library of Congress, 1979).

Davis, Richard Beale. A Colonial Southern Bookshelf: Reading in the Eighteenth Century (Athens: University of Georgia Press, 1979).

Ditzion, Sidney. "The District School Library, 1835-55," Library Quarterly 10 (1940): 197-219.

________. "Mechanics and Merchantile Libraries," Library Quarterly 10 (1940): 197-219.

Harris, Michael H. The Age of Jewett: Charles Coffin Jewett and American Librarianship, 1841-1868 (Littleton, Colo.: Libraries Unlimited, 1975).

Kaser, David. Books for a Sixpence: The Circulating Library in America (Beta Phi Mu, 1980).

Korty, Margaret B. "Benjamin Franklin and Eighteenth Century American Libraries," Trans. of the American Philisophical Society, New Series 55 (1965).

Ranz, James. The Printed Book Catalogue in American Libraries, 1723-1900 (Chicago: American Library Association, 1963.

Shera, Jesse H. Foundations of the Public Library: The Origins of the Public Library Movement in New England 1629-1855 (Chicago: University of Chicago Press, 1949).

Chapter 11

MODERN EUROPEAN LIBRARIES

It is quite appropriate to end a discussion of early American library development with the middle of the 19th century. For it was the second half of that century which witnessed the rise of the library types and library services which characterize contemporary American libraries. Similarly, it would seem appropriate to begin our consideration of modern European libraries at the conclusion of World War I, since the war that wreaked havoc across much of Europe also had a major impact on library development.

On 28 June, 1914, the assassination of the nephew-and-heir of the Austro-Hungarian emperor touched off a cataclysm that was to have profound implications for the world, including the development of libraries. Immediately obvious were the problems of staffing and financing of already established libraries, both severely proscribed as men were called to military service and money spent on peacetime activities was channeled increasingly into the war effort. Later developments included the destruction or capture of major library resources, such as the destruction of the Library of the University in Louvain on 27 August, 1914, and the gradual but increasingly mindless destruction of libraries as the fates of war sent first one army and then another charging across the face of Europe. Finally, the war provided the Russian communists with the opportunity of reconstituting the now Soviet world in a hitherto unknown fashion; a fact that was to have an extremely influential effect on the development of libraries in that part of the world.

Given these justifications for assigning the beginning of the modern phase in European libraries to the conclusion of World War I, how is the topic to be approached? This question has proven exceedingly difficult for library historians, for unlike the rather uniform nature of library development in the Americas, especially North America, the European library scene virtually defies generalization. This serious difficulty is further complicated by the fact of World War II, which had a devastating influence on Europe and led, in effect, to the emergence, in many countries, of radically altered forms of government, a development of great significance to libraries in those countries.

In short, the history of European libraries after the conclusion of World War I is not unlike a giant mosaic made up of many pieces of varied sizes and irregular shapes--a mosaic that, due to its size and complexity, defies ready interpretation. And yet, the requirements of a book of this type demand an attempt to discover the figure in the carpet, the essential threads that dominate the pattern.

The Continued Development of the National Library

In Chapter 9 it was noted that Europe's greatest libraries were her national libraries. This fact is even more apparent when we examine the history of these libraries in the 20th century. France's Bibliothèque Nationale, Britain's British Museum (now part of the British Library), Russia's monolithic state library in Leningrad, and the new national library in Moscow, the Lenin Library, represent the greatest libraries in their respective countries, in Europe itself, and, indeed, rank among the finest in the whole world.

Their growth has not been without trials and setbacks. The two great wars, economic fluctuations, and changes in governmental patterns have all contributed to the challenges faced by those charged with the responsibility of managing these ever-more-complex and important national resources. A brief examination of the history of some of these libraries will help us to appreciate their development.

As noted earlier, the European national libraries were well established and generally thriving prior to World War I. In addition, their decidedly nationalistic emphasis and their stature as the best-financed and staffed libraries in their respective countries allowed them to survive and, in some cases, to benefit from the War. The Bibliothèque Nationale is a case in point. While it suffered seriously at the hands of invaders during both world wars, the library, due to its symbolic and real significance to the French nation, enjoyed a rapid and substantial growth after each of the conflicts. Bookstocks were increased at a rapid rate, more people were employed by the library, and financial support rose significantly. Today the Bibliothèque Nationale enjoys the reputation of being France's finest library and ranks as a major library resource in all of Europe. Like other European libraries, it has suffered of late from the financial instability so prevalent in Europe, but it remains the bibliographic and professional library center in France, and perhaps in all of Europe.

A similar consistent growth is evident in the history of the British Museum Library in the 20th century. Recently, observers of the national library scene have been impressed by the bold and imaginative creation of the British Library in the short span of time from 1967 to 1972. This new national library system consists of four main divisions: the Lending Division (National Central Library and National Lending Library of Science and Technology), located in Boston Spa; the Reference Division (the British Museum Library and its various departments) in London; the Bibliographic Services Division; and the Central Administration Division. The objective of this unified and expanded service is:

> to provide the best possible library services for the United Kingdom ... preserving and making available for reference at least one copy of every book and periodical of domestic origin and of as many overseas publications as possible ... providing an efficient central lending and photocopying service in support of the other libraries and information systems of the country; and providing central cataloguing and other bibliographic services related not only to the needs of the central libraries but to those of libraries and information centres throughout the country and in close cooperation with central libraries overseas.

This new national library format promises to meet the needs of the readers of the United Kingdom, despite the severe economic problems besetting the country, and to greatly enhance the reference and lending-library services available throughout the nation.

In Russia, the Revolution of 1917, stimulated by the panic and political chaos engendered with the outset of World

War I, resulted in the long run in the improvement of the national library. After a few months of disorganization and uncertainty the former Imperial Library was declared a national collection, and its holdings were enriched by the acquisition of many collections formerly owned privately by the Russian nobility. Under the new Soviet government this enormously enlarged library was designated the Russian Public Library, but it was later labeled the Saltykov-Shchedrin State Library. Its growth has continued unabated, and today its holdings number over 20,000,000 volumes. Its importance has also grown in time, and its activities in all areas of library, bibliographic, and documentary services has increased in kind, although it serves now primarily as the national library for the Russian Federation.

While the State Library in Leningrad may be called the Russian National Library by virtue of its descent from the former Imperial Library, the Lenin State Library in Moscow replaced it as the official national library and is even larger in size. Its predecessor was the collection of books housed in the Rumyantsev Museum, founded in 1862, which numbered nearly 1,000,000 volumes prior to the Revolution. After 1917, it, too, was enlarged with books confiscated from private and other libraries, and a substantial amount of money was expended for new books. Today it contains over 30,000,000 cataloged items, including books, pamphlets, and periodicals. Taken together, the two Russian "National Libraries" represent one of the largest and most progressive national library systems in the world, and their influence and control over library affairs in communist Europe is unrivaled.

Another example of national library development in Europe can be found in Germany. After World War I, the title of the Berlin library reverted to that of Prussian State Library, and its collection grew to more than 2,500,000 by 1930, with 55,000 manuscripts and over 400,000 maps. At that time it was receiving some 20,000 periodicals and cooperating closely with other major libraries, while continuing to be a bibliographic center for the entire nation. Among its many strong points were an almost unequalled collection on music and music history, and a collection on the history of World War I containing over 100,000 items. Under such librarians as Adolph von Harnack, Fritz Milkau, and Hugo Anders Kruess, the influence of the Berlin Library was felt throughout the library world.

During World War II the holdings of the Prussian

State Library were evacuated from Berlin, with some parts going to various smaller towns where it was felt they would be safer. After the end of the war, and the division of Germany into East Germany and West Germany, the holdings located in West Germany were brought together into the library of the University of Marburg. Despite crowded conditions, this West German Library, as it was designated, had grown to some 2,000,000 volumes by 1966. The Deutsche Bucherei at Leipzig, which had served Germany from 1912 to 1945 as a non-lending depository library and bibliographic center, was located in East Germany after World War II. A West German counterpart was developed at Frankfurt when the Deutsche Bibliothek was founded in 1946; it obtained a new and modern building in 1959, by which time it had some 300,000 volumes. Designed more for preservation than for immediate use, this library serves West Germany as a national bibliographic center.

All the countries of modern Europe have national libraries, although a few go by another name. In nearly every case these libraries represent the finest libraries in their respective countries, and generally they boast of the largest collections, the most impressive quarters, and the best qualified and most influential staffs. Their charge is admittedly nationalistic, and, as a result, use policies are often characterized by restrictions that reflect the goals and political philosophies of their respective governments. Nearly all of these libraries are afflicted with serious space and staff shortages, incurred as a result of the consistent and rapid growth of their collections. Despite their problems the national libraries of Europe represent a magnificent cultural heritage in graphic form.

University Libraries in Contemporary Europe

Each of the countries of modern Europe have at least one institution of higher learning, and these institutions all possess some kind of library. But, not unlike the situation with the national libraries described above, there is more variety than standardization; more differences than similarities. Nevertheless, the nature of academic library development in 20th-century Europe can be illustrated by a selective look at what appear to be representative countries. Most of these libraries have struggled with the recurrent problem of the frequent destruction of their holdings and the disruption of services caused by the two world wars. Not infrequently, the history of a major academic library is characterized by a cycle of growth, destruction, rebuilding, destruction, and a second major rebuilding.

Academic libraries in France were large and well housed prior to World War I. During that war a number of these libraries, such as the library at the University of Nancy, were destroyed. In World War II, the University of Caen, including its fine library, was destroyed by bombing, and a number of other libraries were destroyed or damaged in the invasions of northern France. After each war these libraries were rebuilt and French university libraries have enjoyed a steady growth since the end of World War II. Financial difficulties and the consistent pressures to expand, to handle the ever increasing collections and meet new demands for services, remain the basic problems facing French academic libraries.

English higher education, once the monopoly of Oxford and Cambridge, has expanded with increasing rapidity in the 20th century. These new libraries were generally spared any serious difficulty in World War I, but faced a severe test in the bombing of England during World War II. Today a number of major universities exist across England, and they are generally served by large and modern libraries. The University of London is typical, with its impressive library numbering over 4,000,000 volumes. Oxford and Cambridge continue their leadership in academic library areas, although the libraries at both institutions are characterized by extreme decentralization. Both libraries, which contain in aggregate substantial research collections, are counted among the finest university libraries in the world.

The 20th century has seen both great disasters and great progress for German libraries of all types. Although university libraries were not physically damaged during World War I, they suffered from lack of staff, funds, and foreign publications. The needs of science and industry, emphasized by the war, encouraged the growth of technical institutes and colleges in the 1920s, but the uncertain political and economic conditions, with inflation followed by depression, prevented much progress. During the years after 1933, while Germany was under the dictatorship of Adolf Hitler, the university libraries were subjected to close governmental control, although in general the scholarly libraries did not suffer from book purges and book burnings as much as the public libraries. Funds were still short, however, and staff members too few. An indication of the low ebb of library progress can be seen in the fact that not a single new university library building was constructed in Germany between 1914 and 1950.

World War II brought tremendous physical destruction in the Allied air raids on Germany. The university libraries at Bonn, Breslau, Frankfurt, Göttingen, Jena, Kiel, Munich, Munster, and Würzburg were either destroyed or heavily damaged, and many staff members were killed. At Jena, for example, sixteen staff members were killed in one bombing raid. At Hamburg over 700,000 volumes were destroyed--almost the entire collection of the combined State and University Library there--while at Frankfurt over 600,000 volumes were destroyed and at Würzburg over 350,000. Other institutions suffered less seriously, but the combined losses totaled millions of volumes. Some valuable manuscripts and early printed books were saved by sending them to areas less likely to be bombed.

After 1945 Germany was divided into eastern and western zones, with the former becoming a communist state under the control of Soviet Russia. Here, the universities of Jena, Leipzig, and Rostock, for example, have been converted into centers of communist learning and their libraries have become part of a nationwide system dedicated to both research and indoctrination. At first the libraries were purged of all pro-Nazi or anti-communist literature; but later, with the emphasis on books and learning that is an earmark of communist countries, the empty shelves were filled with proper communist literature and these universities have rapidly regained their position in the library world, at least in number of volumes. In the 1970s the six major universities in East Germany together held over 8,000,000 volumes, with that of Leipzig being the largest.

In West Germany, the postwar period has seen remarkable recovery and advances in university libraries. A new university, the Free University of West Berlin, has already grown to nearly 1,000,000 volumes, while the University of Frankfurt Library, after being almost destroyed, has come back to nearly 2,000,000 volumes, Many new library buildings and additions have been constructed, including those at Bonn, completed in 1961; at the Free University in Berlin, 1956; and at the University of Mainz in 1964. New technical colleges with their own specialized library systems, have been formed in most of the major cities. All told, the eighteen major university libraries in West Germany and West Berlin have bookstocks of nearly 20,000,000 volumes. Major problems faced by these libraries, besides rebuilding and recouping war losses, have been the acquisition of foreign publications missed during the Hitler years, and the control of the myriad publications currently appearing. The training of new staff members, for the tasks resulting from the large numbers of students and the new subjects being taught, have also been major problems. Some solutions have been found in cooperative purchasing, particularly of foreign materials, and liberal policies and practices in interlibrary lending.

The central libraries of German universities traditionally have been the workshops of scholars rather than study halls or required reading rooms for undergraduates; therefore, a new outlook or philosophy of librarianship was needed for this new era. Moreover, German librarians have generally been scholars rather than administrators or specialists in public service, so here, too, changes have sometimes been in order. The problem of institute libraries connected with the universities still exists. These libraries, usually specialized collections selected by professors, are often uncataloged or poorly cataloged, staffed by untrained personnel, and outside the control of the central library. They contain tens of thousands of useful volumes, but the lack of a union catalog or of centralized selection and acquisition results in much duplication and confusion on most campuses. In East Germany, communist state control has to some extent forced centralization on the university libraries there, but in West Germany the institute and departmental libraries remain a problem. Despite these obstacles, German university libraries continue to make progress and are rapidly regaining their former position in the library world.

In Russia, the Revolution of 1917 brought tremendous changes to university libraries, and new universities were established even before the war was over. The Ural State University at Sverdlovsk was founded by Lenin himself, and others were established in 1918 in Tiflis and Tashkent. By 1925, when the higher education system was centralized under national control, there were universities in virtually every part of the Soviet Union, and their libraries, often enlarged by books taken from religious institutions and private libraries, were seldom smaller than 100,000 volumes. Since that time, the importance of the Soviet university libraries can not be overestimated The communist effort to educate all the people to their highest capacity has brought an emphasis on education and libraries unsurpassed anywhere else in the world. Although the libraries have also served a propaganda purpose and at times have been severely curtailed to keep out non-communist ideas, they have undoubtedly helped bring the people of the Soviet Union from the Middle Ages to the 20th century in little more than a generation.

During World War II, many university libraries in the Ukraine, White Russia, and even in Moscow and Leningrad, were severely damaged if not completely destroyed. The State University of Leningrad, for example, was almost completely razed in the fighting for that city, but most of its book contents had already been moved to Saratov, and after 1945 it was rebuilt even larger than before. All of the libraries at the University of Kiev were destroyed or heavily damaged, and damage was severe at Kharkov, Minsk, and other universities. Since 1945 these institutions have been rebuilt and new ones established, as for example at Daghestan and Yakutsk, along with scores of technical and scientific colleges and institutes. Holdings in the sciences, both Russian and foreign, are often excellent, but the humanities and social sciences sometimes suffer from neglect or regulated purchasing. The Marxist-Leninist philosophy is represented by multiple titles and copies in all institutions, since it represents virtually a curriculum in itself in Russian colleges. The "Regulations for Libraries of Institutes of Higher Learning," issued in 1962, covers all phases of administration of college and university libraries and includes as part of the purpose of those libraries the "Communist training of student youth."

In the early 1970s the Moscow State University library had over 6,000,000 volumes in its combined central and departmental collections, and it received over 2,000 foreign periodicals as well as all major Russian publications. It has a total of forth-five separate reading rooms in its various facilities, with a seating capacity of over 1,900. This is one of the largest of Russian university libraries, but there are many other with over 1,000,000 volumes each, including the Academy of Science at Kiev with over 5,000,000. All university libraries are under the direction of the Ministry of Higher Education which controls the nearly 1,000 universities, colleges, institutes, academies, and conservatories. There are many subsidiary libraries on each university campus, but control is usually in the hands of the central library director and centralized acquisitions and cataloging are more effective than in the universities of western Europe. Library specialization, coupled with good bibliographic controls and easy interlibrary lending, give Soviet Russia a well-organized and efficient educational and research library system.

There are both similarities and differences in the organization and administration of the university libraries of modern Europe. Generally speaking, they differ most from American universities in the large number of more or less autonomous faculty and institute libraries. These specialized collections are valuable to their immediate clientele, but, though many of them are large, they are often poorly cataloged, poorly staffed, and virtually unknown and unavailable to students and faculty of other departments on the same campus. In classification, a variety of individual systems is used, but more are turning in recent years to the Universal Decimal Classification system. Catalogs are usually divided, with an alphabetical author catalog supplemented by a classed or topical catalog. Alphabetical subject indexes to the classed catalog are sometimes found, but completely alphabetical subject catalogs or combined author-subject-title catalogs are rare. Closed stacks are more frequent than open ones, although general reading collections on open shelves are becoming more common. Arrangement within the stacks is usually by accession number or size, a system which aids in keeping the stacks closed but also is useful in crowded conditions and in storage collections. Most libraries lend books for outside use but their non-circulating collections vary considerably in size. Major problems in most European libraries are the low salaries available for professional librarians and the consequent scarcity of competent personnel.

Since 1500 the university libraries of Europe have borne more than their share of the task of preserving and extending the cultural heritage of the western world. National libraries have contributed to this task, and in the past century the public libraries have joined in. On the whole, however, it has been the university libraries that have served as the research centers in all fields--scientific, literary, and historical. In some instances and in some places the university library has curtailed the search for knowledge, limiting the acquisition and use of books according to some preconceived religious belief or political philosophy. But fortunately this has not been the case generally, and the university library has served as a treasure house of old ideas and a fountainhead of new ones. Whether it was the university of 1500--with few books, teachers, and students--or the university of the 1980s, with millions of books, hundreds of teachers, and thousands of students, the basic story has been the same: The university has been a combination of teachers, students, and books that together have preserved, passed on, and increased man's knowledge of himself and his world.

European Public Libraries

Public libraries represent, in aggregate, one of the great cultural resources of modern Europe. And while they vary significantly in size and function from one country to another, they do share one common feature: they are invariably the most "popular" libraries in their respective countries, and as such, serve the people more extensively than any other type of library. As we noted in the discussion of European public libraries in Chapter 9, by the beginning of World War I most European nations had arrived at the point where they agreed that some form of publicly supported library service was desirable. This emerging support for the public library idea was based on a number of assumptions: the value of reading as a harmless form of recreation; the efficacy of the printed word in the control of social and political behavior; and the significance of free access to information to the success of democratic forms of government. Obviously, governments placed varying emphasis on one or another of these justifications for public library support, but the fact remains that public libraries were a reality in most of Europe prior to the outset of World War I. The years following this war were characterized by fifty years of strengthening and expansion, as can be seen in the history of public library development in France, England, East and West Germany, and Russia.

During World War I, there was considerable destruction of public libraries in northeastern France, including those at Rheims, Arras, Lille, and Verdun, and scores of smaller collections. Many rare and valuable books were lost in the ruins of these libraries. After the war, American aid helped in the establishment of model public libraries in Soissons and Paris. Recognition of the public circulating library as distinct from the public research library became more common in France in the 1920s, and several cities made efforts toward reorganizing their libraries in this direction. In 1929-30 a second nationwide library survey was made, with much the same outcome as a generation earlier. This time, however, there were some results. In the 1930s, despite the depression, experiments were made not only with public circulating collections but also with children's libraries, bookmobiles, branch libraries, factory libraries, and even a barge library for families living and working on the network of French rivers and canals. Paris enlarged most of its popular libraries and placed them in larger quarters or separate buildings. An Association for Public Libraries was formed to promote libraries and library services. In 1937 a special appropriation of two million francs was made by the French government for the purchase of public library books. Some 300 libraries throughout the nation shared in this distribution, all of them under the control and supervision of the Ministry of Public Instruction. They were divided into three types: those with large or valuable collections, supervised directly by the national library office; those of smaller size or less important collections, requiring at least one trained librarian to direct; and those smaller libraries without professional staff but visited regularly by supervisors from the national library office. Despite this relative progress, the coming of World War II found France without a modern public library system and still generally under the impression that libraries should be for serious research only.

Because France fell to the German armies early in the conflict, war damage to French libraries was relatively light. In 1944 and 1945, when the Allied invasion took place, there was some damage to libraries, but nothing to compare with that of World War I. However, during the German occupation many libraries were closed, some valuable manuscripts were seized by the Germans, and a few libraries suffered confiscation of materials judged to be anti-Nazi or pro-communist. Some Jewish librarians and others active in the French underground were imprisoned or sent to concentration camps. The librarian of the Bibliothèque Nationale, Julian Cain, was one of these. After the war, the new French government recognized the importance of public libraries by establishing a National Office of Public Libraries and Public Reading. Today France has over 500 municipal libraries and some cities have both central reference libraries and popular circulating library systems. Facilities for children and young people's libraries, phonograph listening rooms, and rooms for public meetings are available in some of the more modern buildings. Some of the French *départements* or regions have established department-wide lending libraries.

For example, the department of Haut-Rhin has a central library at Colmar with over 100,000 volumes for use through its 500 lending stations. In Paris, each of the twenty arrondissements or divisions of the city has its own central library with one or more branch libraries. Generally, however, public library service in France is still poor compared with the best available in other parts of Europe and America. Few trained librarians and low salaries for those employed in libraries are two reasons for relatively poor library service in France. There is also a lack of appreciation of just what efficient public library service is. In the towns where local government has been in the hands of left-wing parties, there is a greater realization of the value of reading matter and public libraries are often strongly supported, possibly more for propaganda purposes than for education. However, the promotion of library service in these towns has stimulated other municipalities to similar action and aroused the general public to the potential value of public libraries.

Despite two world wars and a long period of economic depression in the 20th century, England's public libraries have nevertheless grown and extended their usefulness to all parts of the islands and to all walks of life. In 1919, the County Library Act removed the tax-rate limitations previously imposed on local funds for libraries, thus increasing the financial support of library service considerably. County libraries had been tried in a few places before this date, but the great majority of the rural population had no access to libraries. With permissive legislation and aid from the Carnegie United Kingdom Trust, more county libraries were established, and by 1926, county-wide library service was available in all but five counties in England, Scotland, Wales, and Northern Ireland. The depression years saw increased demands on public libraries but decreased funds at the same time. Nevertheless, the British public libraries have pioneered in branch libraries, bookmobiles, library service by mail, library service to hospitals and institutions, and in general library cooperation, so that they have taken a lead in the library world and set examples of service for all to follow.

One special element of British public library service is that provided by the National Central Library in London. Founded in 1916 as the Central Library for Students, to provide books for the city's adult education classes, it was enlarged in size and purpose in 1927 to provide a source of books for students of all ages throughout the nation. It also serves as a clearing house for interlibrary loans and as a center for cooperative library and bibliographic projects. In 1933 it moved into a new building given by the Carnegie Trust, but this was largely destroyed by bombing raids in World War II. Since 1945 it has been reconstructed, and with its bibliographic tools and union catalogs it aids in making available to all British citizens any book in any British library. Connected with it is the British National Book Centre, which controls exchange and distribution of library duplicates. To supplement and expand the services of the National Central Library, a National Lending Library of Science and Technology was established in the 1960s. This institution, located in the north of England, not only provides the service that its name indicates but is also a national bibliographic and documentation center for the sciences.

Many public libraries suffered great losses during the air raids of the war. The British Museum lost a wing that housed some 150,000 books and 30,000 volumes of bound newspapers, many of them unique. Public libraries in Manchester, Birmingham, Bristol, Liverpool, Sheffield, and Portsmouth were also hard hit by the enemy raids. Numerous smaller libraries and branches suffered partial or complete destruction, and the total book loss of the war in Britain, including libraries, bookstores, and publishers' stocks, has been estimated at over 20,000,000 volumes. In the rebuilding, however, Britain has gained many modern library buildings, and library service has improved in proportion. In the 1980s, public library service is available to one hundred percent of Britain's population. There are some 500 public library administrative units with central libraries, and over 2,000 branches and 20,000 part-time outlets. The public libraries of Manchester and Liverpool, and the county libraries of Lancashire and Essex, each have over 1,000,000 volumes, and under the new British Library System public libraries throughout Great Britain have access to enormous library resources. Nearly thirty percent of the total population are registered library users, making Great Britain one of the most library-conscious nations in the world. No account of the library service of modern Britain should omit the work done by the Library Association, founded in 1877 and now having over 25,000 members. In promoting library education and research, improved library legislation, and the progress of library service in general, the Library Association has played an important part in greatly improving the status of libraries and librarians, not only in Great Britain but throughout the world.

World War I did not seriously affect the physical condition of German public libraries but it slowed down library service in general. After the war, the new Republic of Germany paid more attention to the need for popular library service, and town libraries became more common, particularly in northern and eastern Germany. By 1926 there were 356 Volksbibliotheken, but they were usually small, and since the name implied that they were for the use of the lower classes, they were neither well used nor adequately supported. In the same year there were 273 public research libraries (including state universities and "national" libraries) with holdings of more than 34,000,000 volumes. The gulf between research libraries and popular libraries remained as wide as ever. However, there was now a federal governmental agency to promote library service by assisting the smaller libraries in selecting and acquiring books, and a Society for Library Service in the Frontier States helped provide popular libraries in the eastern area. Among the larger cities, Hamburg and Berlin took the lead in providing popular service, and a few of the smaller towns revised their libraries along western lines with circulating and juvenile collections. Berlin's Municipal Library was given quarters in the former royal stables, and in these quarters it held over 260,000 volumes by 1930. A systematic buildup of all Berlin's library services was begun, with the public, special, and university libraries cooperating to provide the best possible library services, but this progress was slowed in the depression years following 1929.

When the Nazis came into power in 1933, the development of libraries in Germany was seriously curtailed except for a few favored institutions. All public libraries were placed under strict government control, and censorship over their contents was rigidly enforced. Books by Jewish or communist authors were removed from circulation and often publicly burned. Acquisition of books from other countries was virtually stopped. Libraries were made a part of the propaganda system, and all efforts were directed toward the development of a strong German nationalism. In the Slavic areas of eastern Germany, books and libraries were employed to make good "German" citizens out of former Poles and Czechs. Not only was freedom of the press curtailed but the Nazis tried to control the minds of the people as well, and the public library was considered an essential part of this plan.

During World War II, popular and research libraries

suffered from the Allied bombing raids. State libraries in Kassel, Stuttgart, Dresden, and Würtemburg were completely or largely destroyed. Less damage was done at Darmstadt, Kiel, Dortmund, and Düsseldorf. In thirty-one major municipal libraries, with over 14,000,000 volumes between them, more than fifty percent of the bookstock was destroyed. Many smaller public libraries also suffered, and it is estimated that in all of Germany more than one-third of all public library books were destroyed or damaged. Along with popular reading matter, which could eventually be replaced, many irreplaceable manuscripts and unique copies of printed works were lost.

Since 1945 the story of public libraries in West Germany has been one of reconstruction and rapid growth. Particularly on the popular library level, there has been a tremendous increase in service and books available. Some of the larger *Volksbibliotheken* are now adding scholarly collections and reference services to take some of the research load off the reference libraries, while in other cities *Einheitsbibliotheken* or unified reference and popular libraries are being tried. By 1980 there were 10,000 popular libraries together containing over 50,000,000 books. Church libraries for congregational use are also popular in Germany, and although small there are nearly 11,000 of these, including both Catholic and Protestant. In each German state (Land) there are central library agencies to coordinate the work of the public circulating libraries, and in addition they are promoting publicly supported libraries in factories, mines, hospitals, prisons, and even in large department stores. Munich provides a good illustration of the library situation in the larger cities. There one finds a *Stadtsbibliothek* or public reference library of some 500,000 volumes, and a *Stadtbücherei* or public circulating library with 600,000 volumes and twenty-eight branches. Indicative of Bavaria's cultural interests, there is also a public music library with over 100,000 volumes. In West Berlin, the American Memorial Library, opened in 1954, not only serves that isolated city, but is also an example of western-style library service for all of Germany. Elsewhere in Germany, there is still a strong division between the public libraries and the research libraries, even to having separate library associations and separate programs for the training of librarians.

Since the Russian Revolution, the printed word has become a much-used tool and weapon in Soviet Russia.

Books by the million are poured through thousands of libraries to reach an eager public that apparently makes good use of them. This library movement was off to a good start even by 1920. Madame L. Haffkin-Hamburger, who had struggled long before the Revolution for library service for the Russian people, continued to work for libraries under the Soviets, and Madame Lenin (Nedezhda Krupskaya) also encouraged and sponsored libraries. A pamphlet entitled "What Lenin Wrote and Said About Libraries" was printed and widely distributed. By the time Soviet control was firmly established, libraries were growing rapidly, both in numbers and size. State libraries were established in the capitals of the various Soviet Republics, and municipal libraries in the larger towns. For example the state library of Turkmenistan in Ashkabad was organized in 1925, grew to over 150,000 volumes by 1934, and to nearly 500,000 by 1960. Books in Russian public libraries increased from about 10,000,000 before the war to over 125,000,000 in 1934, while the number of readers in the same period jumped from 120,000 to 15,000,000. To encourage and improve libraries--and to control them--library departments were established in each of the Soviet Republics, and library sections in the regional and provincial departments of education. Besides the regular public libraries, there were libraries in factories and collective farms, in construction camps where great projects were being built, and even on the trains of the Trans-Siberian railway. Reading rooms were available in army camps and on naval vessels, in fact wherever large numbers of workers or citizens came together for any purpose. Of libraries of all types--public, school, and special--there were nearly 200,000 in 1934, with some 272,000,000 volumes in them, according to Russian official statistics. This averages out to one library for approximately every 1,200 persons in Russia, and that average library would contain about 1,400 volumes.

World War II caused immense damage to libraries in the areas overrun by the Nazi armies and also in the major cities affected by air raids, not only Moscow and Leningrad, but also large provincial cities such as Minsk, Kiev, Orel, and Kharkov. Dozens of buildings were destroyed or seriously damaged, and losses in books ran into millions of volumes. Since 1945, however, the public libraries of Russia have made a comeback, and new modern library buildings, some of them immense in size, have sprung up in the once-ravaged cities. The post-war era has also brought new types of libraries especially designed to meet the needs of the millions of war veterans--including hospital libraries, veterans'-society libraries, vocational libraries and libraries for the blind. The war also brought a realization of the value of technical and scientific libraries, and the greatest growth since 1945 has been in the spread of scientific literature on the public, academic, and research levels.

All Russian libraries are organized into basic library networks controlled from Moscow. Three of the most important of these networks are the public, or "mass" libraries, the scientific and technical libraries, and the university libraries. The mass libraries are directed by the Ministry of Culture of the U.S.S.R., and at a lower level by the departments of culture in the various Soviet Republics. At the head of the mass libraries stands the Lenin State Library in Moscow. Besides the state or republic libraries, many of which have millions of volumes, there are also large regional libraries, city libraries, district libraries, and rural libraries. In addition to these are the trade union libraries, collective farm libraries, and public children's libraries, as well as others which are semi-public. For Russia's public libraries, the established aims are threefold: to propagate the Marxist-Leninist philosophy, to disseminate the government and communist party news and propaganda, and to improve the material and cultural level of the people so that they can become better Soviet citizens. All public libraries are limited in accessions to books published in Russia or officially approved for Russian use. Some foreign literature, particularly scientific, is available in translation, but only a few of the larger research libraries are permitted to obtain actual books and magazines from foreign countries. Book collections must frequently be "weeded," not for worn-out books, but for books containing undesirable information. In 1950, for example, a government decree ordered the discarding of books including obsolete technical and agricultural titles; political, economic, and communist-party literature published prior to 1938; and legal, war, and defense literature published prior to 1941.

In 1982, there were reported to be about 400,000 libraries of all kinds in the Soviet Union. Of these, some 120,000 were municipal libraries with over 80,000,000 registered readers. Altogether they held two billion volumes, but such magnificent statistics require at least a small amount of interpretation. Many of the "libraries" are little more than a few shelves of books, open a few hours daily with a voluntary worker, in a village community hall or in a factory workers' lounge. Also, the large number of volumes includes multiple copies of the favorite communist writings, and many pamphlets and individual issues of periodicals. Some of the larger public libraries have hundreds of copies of the writings of Lenin and Karl Marx. However, even granting the duplication and some exaggeration, the fact remains that the library picture in Soviet Russia sets an example for serious consideration by the rest of the world.

Public libraries in other countries of Europe have also experienced significant growth since World War II, following the patterns already discussed. To summarize, Europe's publicly owned libraries have long contained treasures of literature and history that cannot be duplicated anywhere else in the world, but these libraries have been poorly housed, supported, and used. On the other hand, public circulating libraries were largely developed by private groups--social, religious, commercial, or benevolent--and eventually taken over in the late 19th or early 20th centuries for public support and control. The concept that the only worthwhile libraries are research libraries, to be used solely by scholars has handicapped the development and use of popular circulating collections. Users of public libraries are often handicapped by fees, short hours of service, poorly cataloged collections, closed stacks, and limited staffs. The result has been that even today the percentage of library users in many parts of Europe is small. Library services available to the public vary considerably between western Europe and eastern Europe, but, despite this variance, the overall picture is one of enlarged interest and continued progress. Many European countries are experimenting with new forms of organization and support, and serious attention is being given to the education of library staffs and the utilization of the latest technologies. Given these trends, public libraries in Europe would appear to be in a position to expand significantly and improve services to their respective clienteles, if the serious financial crises facing these countries, especially those in western Europe, can be successfully met and overcome.

Special Libraries in Modern Europe

So far, three types of libraries in modern Europe have been considered--the national libraries, the university libraries, and the public libraries. Although each of these is, in a way, a special library, holdings are general in subject content and the reading public is broad if not universal. There are other libraries, however, that are limited in subject content or in types of users, or both, and these have come to be designated by the term "special libraries." Although the term is usually used in a more restricted sense, for the purpose of this chapter it will be broadened to include religious and public school libraries.

One way to begin our examination of special library history in Europe is to examine the development of one of the world's most impressive special libraries--the Vatican Library in Rome. After its re-creation in the 15th century, the Vatican Library experienced further growth in the 16th century, and in 1588 moved into magnificent new quarters provided by Pope Sixtus V. He also added to its bookstock with various gifts, and in 1600 it was further enlarged with the library of Fulvio Orsini, a most valuable collection. Pope Paul V (1605-1621) divided the papal library into archives, manuscript, and book collections, and added two large halls to hold the increased number of books. The Palatine Library, a gift of Maximilian I, Duke of Bavaria, was added in 1622, and later came the large and valuable manuscript collection formerly belonging to Queen Christina of Sweden. Important gifts followed each other with regularity in the 17th and 18th centuries, and the Vatican Library became one of the most important storehouses of treasures in Europe. During the French Revolution, however, it was the Vatican Library's turn to suffer, and 500 of its choicest manuscripts were taken by the victorious French to the libraries of Paris. Fortunately, most of these were restored in 1815. By the 1820s the Vatican Library contained over 400,000 books and 50,000 manuscripts. More gifts followed in the 19th century, the major one being the library of Cardinal Angelo Mai, a collection of almost 40,000 volumes amassed over a lifetime and containing histories and records of Christianity from all over the world.

In the late 19th century the Vatican Library experienced a rebirth and renovation, and its great masses of books and manuscripts were arranged and organized; the books at least were made more available to the public. Under Pope Leo XIII a reading room was opened in 1888, and a public reference collection was made available. New collections continued to pour in, and the beautiful halls and rooms soon became crowded. After 1920 another reorganization took place, and American librarians were invited to act as consultants in modernizing the collection. In 1926, the Carnegie Corporation sent Dr. William Warner Bishop to survey the Vatican Library and make recommendations for its future growth and development. Pius XI was then pope and, as a former librarian both at the Ambrosian Library and at the Vatican, he was intensely interested in the suggested reforms. A new cataloging system was adopted, modern bookstacks were installed, new quarters were added, and in general the purpose of the institution was directed toward making its collections available. In 1931 a tragedy occurred when a section of roof over a reference room collapsed, destroying about 1,000 volumes and damaging many others. This, however, was only a temporary setback, and rebuilding and enlarging continued. During World War II, library treasures from other Italian collections were taken into the Vatican for safekeeping. Since the War, the Vatican Library has taken its place as one of the greatest libraries in the world. Scholars from everywhere make use of its treasures, and the services of the library and its staff aid not only other Roman Catholic libraries but libraries in general in virtually every country of the globe. Many of its rarest possessions have been made available in facsimile or photograph, and bibliographies of its collections are available to scholars everywhere. Its modern acquisitions tend to relate more directly to the history and activities of the Church, but its nearly one million volumes still make it one of the world's great bibliographic centers.

Elsewhere in Italy, the special libraries are varied and numerous. Many of the great libraries of the Renaissance survive as either private or public collections, and other endowed libraries of considerable size were added in later centuries. Such libraries as the Ambrosian in Milan, the Biblioteca Estense in Modena, the Casanatense in Rome, and the Medicea-Laurenziana in Florence, with their valuable collections of manuscripts and incunabula, are unequaled anywhere in the world. Many less famous but significant collections are located in other Italian towns and cities. The monastery library at Monte Cassino, with about 20,000 printed books and thousands of manuscripts, some going back to the 7th century, was declared a national monument in 1866. Unfortunately, this famous landmark in western civilization was virtually destroyed in World War II. Another monastic collection to survive into the 20th century is that at La Cava near Salerno, with manuscripts dating from the 11th century.

As in most of Europe, the universities of Italy are surrounded by institute and faculty libraries in many specialized fields. A few of these reach 100,000 volumes in size, but most are much smaller, and there may be fifty or more of them around the larger universities. Though some are well organized and staffed, most are unavailable outside their respective departments. In addition, there are the libraries of the technical institutes not connected with the universities. The library of the Polytechnic Institute in Milan, for example, was founded in 1863 and now has some 95,000 volumes. In Rome there are over 300 special libraries, many of considerable size. The Library of the International Institute of Agriculture (now a part of the United Nations Food and Agriculture Organization's library system) contains over 300,000 volumes, with files of some 3,000 periodicals in agriculture and related fields. Founded in 1905, it went into a new building in 1933. It is organized along the lines of American technical libraries and serves not only its own organization but also agricultural scientists throughout Italy. Its bibliographies and interlibrary loan service are available around the world. A somewhat smaller special library is the Biblioteca Romana, formed in 1930 to be the historical library for the city of Rome, specializing in political, social, and economic history. It also maintains a union catalog of all such materials located anywhere in Italy. Most of the departments of the Italian government have headquarter libraries in Rome, some of considerable size and importance. The Library of the Ministry of Agriculture and Forestry has over 500,000 volumes, while that of the Ministry of Industry and Commerce has about 100,000 volumes. Many other special libraries are found in Rome, ranging from such small collections as the Keats-Shelley Memorial House Library with 7,000 volumes to the library of the Council of National Research with over 250,000 volumes.

School libraries in Italy are largely a 20th-century development, but, although government financial support is available, they still lag behind those of the United States and England. This is due in part to a lack of trained school librarians, and in part to the continued emphasis on textbook teaching rather than individual study and reading. Since World War II the new emphasis on public education has brought an increased interest in school libraries, which are currently improving. Library service to schools through the public libraries is being tried, particularly in the villages and rural areas, and the larger towns and cities are experimenting with centralized school library services for the entire urban area. One interesting phase of Italian library service to children, although not restricted to them, is the park library, available out in the open during the warmer months of the year.

The special libraries of France are similar in many respects to those in Italy, although more numerous. Some of the libraries of Paris, including several now associated with the Bibliothèque Nationale or the University of Paris, have histories going back into the Middle Ages, while others, such as the Savoy Library of the Sciences, are products of the 1960s. The library of the National Civil Engineering College (L'Ecole Nationale des Ponts de Chausées) was founded in 1747 and now has over 160,000 volumes. The Bibliothèque de l'Arsenal, formed in the 18th century, is, despite its name, a remarkable library of French literature, containing over 1,500,000 volumes with thousands of rare literary manuscripts. The Catholic Institute of Paris has a theological library of nearly 500,000 volumes, dating from 1875. The various technical schools and institutes of Paris also have their own libraries, ranging from the general to the very specialized, and from the National Institute of Aeronautics to the National School of Veterinary Science. Many documentation centers supplement the technical libraries of Paris, such as the Documentation Center for Chemistry with its library of 50,000 volumes. The French governmental departments maintain central libraries in Paris, some of them large, important, and semi-public, while others are small working collections for departmental employees. Besides these, there are other special libraries such as those of the Musée et Bibliothèque de la Guerre, which aims at collecting all available printed material on the two World Wars. At the other extreme, there is the Bibliothèque de l'Heure Joyeuse, a children's library founded in the 1830s as a non-circulating model juvenile collection.

In other parts of France, there are technical libraries in the various public institutes and in the technical schools of the universities. Some of the larger municipal libraries are establishing business libraries or special collections, but lack of trained staff members often curtails their value. The larger business firms, particularly banks, the chemical industries, and the metropolitan newspapers, are establishing research and information libraries for their employees. Scattered throughout France are military libraries, both popular ones for the average soldier or sailor and specialized ones for training purposes. The French army has maintained such libraries since the French Revolution, and virtually every military post or naval vessel has its library. The French public schools have had libraries of a sort since the early 19th century, but for many years they were small, out of date, and of little use to students. In Paris, an improved school library system was established in 1862, and by 1880 there were 440 school libraries in the city, but they averaged only about a hundred volumes each. In more recent years, the French schools, particularly the secondary schools, are paying more attention to library service and are providing not only books and periodicals but audio-visual instructional materials as well. Shortages of school librarians or teachers trained in library work continue to limit the number of school libraries that can provide effective service. Rural areas and small towns are still lagging behind the larger urban areas in school libraries, and France, too, must await a change in public school methods and educational philosophy before any great progress can be made.

Some of the most important special libraries in the world are found in England. London alone contains libraries on virtually every possible specialization, and many of them are quite large and filled with rare and valuable works. The British Museum itself is composed of many special collections, such as the Harleian Collection of Manuscripts, the Sloane, and Cottonian libraries. Its newspaper library is probably the largest single collection of newspapers in the world. The various Royal Societies all have notable libraries in their specialties, such as the Royal Society of Medicine, the Royal Geographical Society, and the Royal College of Surgeons, whose library was founded in 1518. There are many specialized libraries connected with the University of London, such as that of the School of Economics, particularly strong in economics and political science relating to all parts of the world. The Public Record Office is the official archives of Britain, and its treasures include Parliamentary records going back for hundreds of years. The Patent Office Library is an outstanding example of the many government departmental libraries, ranging in content from agriculture to foreign affairs. Among the oldest special libraries in London are those of the various law schools known as Gray's Inn, the Inner Temple, and Lincoln's Inn. The latter, founded in 1497, is the largest law library in London and one of the most famous in the world. The Science Museum Library and the Victoria and Albert Art Museum Library are among the best in their fields, and the India Office Library has one of the greatest collections known on the history and culture of India. The Royal College of Music Library specializes in English music and has the original scores of many English and foreign composers. The National Library for the Blind takes a lead in providing talking books and books in braille for blind readers throughout the British Isles.

One of the latest developments in special libraries in England is the formation of the National Lending Library for Science and Technology, now a part of the British Library. This institution provides a national center for technical documentation, and is a clearinghouse for interlibrary loans for all technical and scientific libraries throughout the nation. These include public library technical departments, technical college libraries, research libraries, and industrial collections. The public libraries in particular have created and expanded library service to business and industry since World War I. Leeds established a public technical and commercial library in 1918, and since that time most of the larger municipal and even some of the county libraries have established such collections. In the 1980s attention is being paid to the problems of cooperation between such special libraries, and in one particular area the Liverpool and District Scientific and Industrial Research Libraries Advisory Council has taken a lead in this direction. With union catalogs, teletype service, and liberal photocopying and lending policies, the special libraries of regions or of the entire nation can pool their services. Special research libraries maintained by private firms are also being brought into these cooperative ventures. Above all, the Association of Special Libraries and Information Bureaux (ASLIB), formed in 1924, serves as the professional association and general mentor for the field.

The cathedrals of England and Wales still maintain libraries, although they are largely theological and historical materials, valuable books and manuscripts surviving from medieval collections, for the use of the clergy. The Cathedral at Durham was one of the largest such libraries, numbering well over 40,000 volumes. There are several notable English Catholic libraries, such as those at the Oratory at South Kensington, established in 1849, and at the Catholic Central Library in London. The libraries of the Cathedrals of York and Canterbury are among the richest in rare books and manuscripts, but there are a number of parish churches scattered throughout England that have small but valuable collections in theology and history. A few still keep books chained to desks as they were kept down through the 18th century.

England has been fortunate in the creation of endowed libraries, some specialized, some of rare books, and others for the general public. One of the largest is the John Rylands Library at Manchester, founded in 1899 by Mrs. John Rylands in memory of her husband. Its special holdings include medieval manuscripts, rare Bibles, and some 2,500 incunabula among its total collection of 500,000 volumes. Its scholarly staff issues a regular bulletin relating to the collection and the general field of bibliography. A famous endowed theological library is the Dr. Williams Library, founded by the will of a Presbyterian minister and opened in 1729 in London. It was moved into a new building in 1873, and its 118,000 volumes are strong in Presbyterian history and theology, but also include material on other denominations and religions. Many public libraries in English and Scottish cities stem from endowed collections formed in the 19th century and earlier, but later taken over with public support.

School library history in England is a comparatively recent development, although many of the private schools have had libraries since the 17th century. English public school libraries became a possibility after the passage of the Public School Laws of the 1870s, but for the most part implementation of the laws did not come until the 20th century. Books were sometimes placed in schools by the public library systems, and county libraries used the rural schools as distribution points. Improvement in school library service came in the 1920s, but a group of visiting American librarians in the 1930s cited poor library quarters and unsatisfactory staffing in many localities. They found much to compliment, however, in the quality of the books available and in the interest shown by the children in their school libraries. The Education Act of 1944 recognized the importance of school libraries, along with the modern adjuncts of audio-visual and teaching materials, but noted that progress during the Depression and war years had been slow. Since then, much progress has been made in school libraries, the concept of the library as a teaching materials center is widespread, and standards of library service are approaching the best in the world. Cooperation between school and public libraries remains high, and the use of school libraries per pupil is greater than in most American school libraries.

West Germany is another European country with many special libraries. Berlin alone had over 200 special libraries before 1939. These include government office libraries, special libraries of universities and institutes, and libraries of scientific societies. Governmental libraries were strong, with the library of the Reichstag (Parliament) having over 175,000 volumes; that of the Patent Office, 118,000 volumes; and the Census Office, nearly 200,000. The German Army was supplied with technical libraries, the major one being at the general headquarters in Berlin. These libraries, like the units they served, were disbanded after World War I, but were reformed during the Hitler era. Even in 1924, Germany had some 275 major research libraries with total holdings of over 34,000,000 volumes. Eighty-four of them contained over 100,000 volumes each, thus making Germany one of the most important sources of research information in the western world.

Elsewhere in Germany, the former royal or ducal libraries of the various states that existed before the unification of Germany form a particular type of special library, although they are generally classed as popular reference libraries. Each of them is a special library on the history and culture of its particular area, and most of them contain unique manuscripts and rare books. Each of the great German universities is surrounded by scores of institute and departmental libraries, and in addition there are many _Hochschule_ or colleges and technical institutes that have special libraries. Some of the larger cities have developed commerical or business libraries, and some of them have public music libraries as well. Industrial firms are following their western counterparts and developing research libraries with the latest microcopying facilities and the most modern techniques in storing and retrieving information. Hamburg's commercial library was founded as early as 1735, or at least it is based upon a collection that goes back that far.

Some special libraries that have emerged in Germany since 1945 would include the American Library in Berlin, the International Youth Library in Munich, and a new technical library at Hanover that contains a book collection, a translation center, and a bureau of documentation to give a complete research service. The new national library at Marburg is also a post-war development, and in the sense that it is a bibliographic and reference center, it, too, is a special library. The German research libraries as a group are well organized through their librarians' association and through many public and private cooperative arrangements. There is cooperation not only in union catalogs, union lists of serials, and interlibrary loans, but also in the selection and acquisition of specialized subjects and materials.

For example, some libraries concentrate on acquiring material from specific geographic areas, so there is a complete coverage of literature from all parts of the world. The ultimate aim is that in some German reference library there will be found books or information on almost any subject and from almost any place on earth.

School libraries in West Germany, that is the libraries of the lower schools corresponding to American elementary and high schools, have been very slow in developing. Emphasis on the textbook and lecture have prevented the growth of usable school libraries down to the mid-20th century, and where there have been libraries in the schools, they have usually been small collections of old books rather than living, working libraries. The movement toward popular libraries has often been made with the idea of serving the school children as well as adults, and some of the better public libraries have excellent rooms or collections for children and young people. Central education libraries in the cities and states serve the teachers and school personnel rather than the children. However, since World War II, the influence of American school libraries, particularly the libraries in the schools for children of American military personnel stationed in Germany, has led to an increased interest in the need for improved school libraries and to wide experimentation in the field.

In Russia, the special library is a vital part of the complete library picture of that library-minded nation. Whereas in all of Russia before 1917 there were only 475 libraries that could be classed as special, there were over 6,000 by the 1920s, and over 50,000 by the 1980s. In addition to special collections in the national, public, and university libraries already discussed, Russia and its various federated republics share a widespread system of technical libraries. Many of these are concentrated in the library network of the Academy of Sciences of the U. S. S. R. The Academy library alone has over 7,500,000 cataloged items, and its activities are closely tied to those of the various institutes, academies, museums, and other technical libraries in all parts of the Soviet Union. A series of agricultural libraries is centered in the Central Agricultural Research Library in Moscow, with its 2,500,000 volumes, and a medical library system is headed up by a State Central Research Medical Library in the same city. In most of the constituent republics, there are similar central technical libraries and each of them stocks books in the local languages as well as in Russian. Much foreign technical literature may be found in Russian libraries, but it is usually translated or digested into Russian and the major local languages.

The trade union library is a type of special library that is well developed in Russia, less so in other parts of Europe. This library serves as a technical or sociological library on trade union history and programs, but also on a lower level as a popular library for the workers. The system is headed up by the Gorki Reference Library of the All-Union Central Council of Trade Unions in Moscow. This unit serves labor specialists and advanced students rather than the general public. In addition, it assists in the work of trade union libraries all over the U.S.S.R. by training library workers, providing bibliographies and booklists, and by publishing material in the trade union field.

In Moscow there are technical libraries embracing almost every conceivable field of interest. Some not yet mentioned would include the Geographical Society Library, the Botanical Institute Library, and those of the Institutes of Psychology, Ethnography, Linguistics, History, and Russian Literature. The Fundamental Library of the Social Sciences has over 5,000,000 items, and the All-Union State Library of Foreign Literature contains 3,000,000 volumes in 126 different languages. In the capitals of the other Soviet states, there are similar professional and technical libraries, although usually on a smaller scale. Some of the special libraries in other parts of the country are quite large, as for example the Pushkin Science Library in Yakutsk, which has over 1,000,000 items. Throughout the Soviet Union access to these technical and scientific libraries is free and readily available to any serious student.

The Russian Army libraries form a network all their own and the number of books involved is tremendous. Library service for the Red Army troops began during the Revolution when package libraries by the hundreds were sent to the communist troops in training camps and even on the front lines. The libraries for the troops became permanent after the establishment of the Soviet Union, and they continued to grow in size and usefulness until the mid-thirties, when there were over 16,000,000 volumes in the various military libraries. The military headquarters library in 1941 was a seventeen-story building in Moscow, containing over 1,000,000 volumes. These libraries proved their worth during World War II, both for technical and morale purposes, and since the war they have continued to expand.

Public school libraries in Russia are under the jurisdiction of the National Ministry of Education, which controls libraries in elementary and secondary schools and in teacher-training institutions. Russian school libraries and textbooks are carefully controlled as to content; not only are the books themselves carefully censored and written for full propaganda effect, but the libraries are remarkably alike in all parts of the country and in all schools of the same grade level. Teachers are in charge of libraries in the smaller schools, but the larger ones have one or more trained librarians. Instruction in the use of the library is mandatory, and in some cases the reading of specific books is also required. Close records are kept of each student's reading, both in the school libraries and in the children's sections of the public libraries that are also easily available. In the secondary schools, the libraries are more practical, and the library reading becomes a required part of the school curriculum. At this stage, the student has reached a point where his concentration on mathematics, science, foreign languages, and Communist theory makes it almost impossible for him to have time for leisure reading, so popular literature, available on a small scale in the lower school libraries, tends to disappear on the secondary school level. Whatever the library contents, technical or popular, the library is part of an educational system that is designed to produce the same end product--the well-trained and well-indoctrinated Soviet citizen. Certainly no country on earth makes more use of the printed page in all its forms than the Soviet Union.

In Europe as a whole, the special libraries meet special needs and supplement the services of more general collections. Their progress, size, and effectiveness vary from country to country, and from library to library, but in general, their development in the period since 1945 has been tremendous. In numbers, in size, in variety, and in techniques used, the European special library is a field in itself. The demands of education, industry, and scientific research have led to the use of photographic and electronic means of producing, duplicating, storing, and retrieving information. Documentation centers are appearing where public library service is hardly known, and in some cases, particularly in eastern Europe, it seems that the transition from manuscript to computers was made almost overnight. Progress is uneven, however, and much remains to be done, particularly in school libraries in central and southern Europe.

Conclusion

The impressive growth of European libraries since World War I is clearly obvious to anyone familiar with the history of these libraries. And yet, in many parts of Europe the gains made in the past sixty years appear to be threatened by the tenacious and widespread financial depression besetting the continent. It remains to be seen whether library development in countries like England, France, and Italy will be permanently stunted by lack of nourishment, or whether these nations will recover their economic vitality, and find the resources necessary to continue the development of their extensive library services.

Additional Readings

The literature relating to modern European libraries is extensive and diverse. Furthermore, it exists in a dozen languages. Readers who desire access to this literature might best begin with the ALA World Encyclopedia of Library and Information Services (Chicago: American Library Association, 1980), which contains carefully documented essays on library developments in each of the countries covered in this chapter. More recent work can be located by using the bibliographies in the British journal Library History. Other work of particular interest is listed below.

Danton, J. Periam. Book Selection and Collections: A Comparison of German and American University Libraries (New York: Columbia University Press, 1963).

Dosa, Marta L. Libraries in the Political Scene [the library career of Georg Leyh] (Westport, Conn.: Greenwood Press, 1974).

Ellis, Alec. Library Services for Young People in England and Wales, 1830-1970 (Oxford: Oxford University Press, 1971).

Kelly, Thomas. History of Public Libraries in Great Britain, 1845-1975 (London: The Library Association, 1977).

Metcalfe, John. Information Retrieval, British and American, 1876-1976 (Metuchen, N.J.: Scarecrow Press, 1976).

Metie, A. "Libraries on the Left: Ideology in the Communist Library," PNLA Quarterly 33 (1969): 4-11.

Miller, Edward. _That Noble Cabinet: A History of the British Museum_ (London: Andre Deutsch, 1974).

Mohrhardt, Foster and Carlos Penna, "National Planning for Library and Information Services," _Advances in Librarianship_ 5 (1975): 62-123.

Mumford, W. A. _History of the Library Association, 1877-1977_ (London: the Library Association, 1977).

Rayward, W. Boyd. _The Universe of Information: The Work of Paul Otlet for Documentation and International Organization_ (Moscow: FID, 1975).

Chapter 12

MODERN AMERICAN LIBRARIES

Since about 1850, American libraries have grown significantly in number and scope. The rapid growth of American libraries was due to the happy mingling of a number of positive factors: 1) the enormous natural resources of the country, which offered a continuing stimulus to the economy, thus generating great wealth, part of which was available for the support of cultural institutions like libraries; 2) the rapidly increasing population, which supplied the voracious needs of American industry, and in turn provided an ever larger audience for libraries; 3) the amazing industrialization of the country which required increasingly sophisticated information sources for its continued development and demanded a more sophisticated level of knowledge among its workers; and 4) the democratic cast of American life which encouraged the free flow of information and depended, at least in theory, upon the "informed citizen" as the very foundation of its existence.

Using economic terms, the "take off" in the development of American libraries can be said to have occurred between 1850 and 1900, and by the latter date most of the library forms known to modern librarians were firmly established and their patterns of development clearly visible.

The Rise of the American Public Library

While greatly stimulated by the positive factors influencing American life, the American public library developed as the natural outgrowth of a number of social and political changes sweeping the country in the late antebellum period. One of the most significant developments for public library growth was the slowly changing attitude toward the establishment and support of public services generally. As already pointed out, the social library form was flawed by its dependence on the "voluntary" support of its members and the beneficence of its supporters. In difficult financial times, or times of cultural indifference, the social library was threatened by a loss of financial support and, not infrequently, with extinction. All of the publicly supported institutions so familiar to modern Americans had to await the time when the people, or at least those in control of the government, reached the conclusion that the principle of voluntarism was inadequate to the needs of the Republic, and that some form of government support must be instituted. This change of mind came during the late Jacksonian period, when many Americans became convinced that what was needed was, in Lee Benson's words, "a positive liberal state" where "the state had the responsibility to ... regulate society so as to promote the general welfare."

This change of mind was prompted by the serious, and, in many cases, disturbing changes taking place in antebellum America. To the establishment in America, the increasing industrialization of the country was viewed as a mixed blessing. On the one hand it promised prosperity and continued economic growth; on the other, it was giving rise to large cities with their manifold problems, and it was luring millions of poorly educated immigrants to the country--immigrants, who in the eyes of the "best men" of America, were ill-equipped to function effectively as citizens of a democracy.

The appearance of more and more immigrants in the large urban centers, and the general feeling that older socializing and stabilizing voluntaristic institutions like the church and the family were disintegrating, led the country's leadership to cast about for ways of channeling the restive and potentially disruptive elements in American society into constructive channels. Increasingly, they came to view formal, carefully organized, and publicly funded educational institutions as the best means of securing the Republic against the winds of destructive change.

But while the "best men" had inordinate power in relation to their numbers, they could never have established public schools and libraries without at least the tacit approval of the people. This support began to emerge in the late 1820s as the nascent workingmen's movement in America came to identify publicly supported education as an important bulwark of democracy and an essential ingredient in the workingman's aggressive drive for political power and economic prosperity. And though they soon came to view more immediate concerns such as the ten-hour day, better working conditions, and child labor laws as the most pressing issues, they nevertheless maintained a firm belief in education as the surest shield of the political authority of the people and came to view universal public education in an abstract sense, as the panacea that once achieved, "would eradicate obstacles to democracy and maintain equality and prosperity."

Thus, by 1850, the ground was prepared; the democratic dogma was generally accepted. Few would quarrel with its basic premise: that the success of the Republic was inseparably tied to the enlightenment of its citizenry. Although this faith in the democratic dogma was based on drastically different conceptions of the purpose of education, the general consensus was nevertheless complete.

It only remained for educators and civic leaders to demonstrate the ways in which the public library might contribute to the enlightenment of the people. Some scattered attempts were made at this task before 1852, but in that year the Trustees of the Boston Public Library issued their now famous Report, which articulated, perhaps better than any document before or since, the ideal conception of public library service.

This Report, written jointly by Edward Everett, one of the country's leading political figures, and George Ticknor, the acknowledged social and intellectual arbiter of Boston, traced the history of printing and libraries and then argued forcefully for the establishment of a public library in Boston. To Everett and Ticknor it was clear that:

> Reading ought to be furnished to all, as a matter of public policy and duty, on the same principle that we furnish free education, and in fact, as a part and a most important part, of the education of all. For it has been rightly judged that--under political, social and religious institutions like ours--it is of paramount importance that the means of general information should be so diffused that the largest possible number of persons should be induced to read and understand questions going down to the very foundations of social order, which are constantly

> presenting themselves, and which we, as a people, are constantly required to decide, and do decide, either ignorantly or wisely.

To these men, steeped in enlightenment principles, there was a direct connection between knowledge and virtue, and in their report they stated the very heart of what was to become the public library creed: the future of a democratic republic is directly dependent upon the education of its citizenry, and the library is an important element in the educational process. In 1854, as a result of the efforts of Everett and Ticknor and the city fathers, the Boston Public Library was opened.

Of course, the Boston Public Library was not the first public library established in the country, not if we define a public library as one supported by local taxation and open to all citizens of the community. Using this definition, a few earlier examples of the public library form deserve mention.

In Salisbury, Connecticut, in 1803 a collection of books donated by Caleb Bingham was preserved and made available by the town as the Bingham Library for Youth. It survived to become a part of the modern Scoville Memorial Library. In Lexington, Massachusetts, in 1827, the town meeting voted to purchase a library for the youth of the town and to employ a librarian to manage it. The collection was deposited in the town church, but so small was the public support that it went out of existence in 1839. In Castine, Maine, a social library founded in 1801 became the property of the town about 1827, and continued to operate as a free public library. Other examples of small collections, more or less publicly owned and supported, can be found elsewhere in New England, but the town usually considered to be the pioneer in permanent public library service was Peterborough, New Hampshire. In 1833 it was decided by the town meeting that a part of the State Literary Fund, usually applied to the support of schools, should be used for the purchase of books for a free public library. Other donations added to the size of the book collection, and it was kept for public use in the store that housed the local post office, with the postmaster acting as librarian. By 1837 the collection numbered 465 titles, made up largely of religion, history, and biography. The Peterborough Public Library was followed by several similar ventures in New England towns in the next decade, as for example in Orange, Massachusetts, where in 1846, $100 was voted to establish a free town library.

It was the passage of state laws enabling the local governmental units to levy taxes for the support of public libraries that really began the modern library movement. New Hampshire took the lead in 1849 with a law authorizing towns to appropriate money for the establishment and maintenance of public libraries. In 1851 Massachusetts passed a similar law, to be followed by Maine in 1854, and, after the Civil War, by several other New England and Middle West states.

Despite this early activity, it was the founding of the Boston Public Library that really gave impetus to the public library movement. Boston was the leading social and intellectual center in the country, and other cities watched jealously for new developments in Boston, and quickly followed its lead. The inordinate influence of the Boston Public Library, based partly on the impact of the widely read 1852 Report, partly on the leadership of its first two Superintendents: Charles Coffin Jewett (1858-68) and Justin Winsor (1868-77), and partly on the substantial resources available to develop the collection and innovate in matters of library service, continued unchallenged until the end of the 19th century.

At the outset, the administration of the Boston public library was focused on the collection and organization of books. Charles Coffin Jewett is remembered as one of the greatest bookmen in American library history, and his leadership in cataloging practice has led experts on this subject to label the third quarter of the 19th century the "Age of Jewett" in American cataloging history. His successor, the prominent historian and literary figure Justin Winsor focused his attention on "getting books used" in an attempt to implement Ticknor's concept of the library as a great civilizing and stabilizing force in America. His establishment of branches, utilization of selected reading lists, and provision of popular reading fare attest to his commitment to the popular nature of public library service.

Other municipalities throughout the country followed a pattern similar to that already seen in Boston and New York in their attempts to establish public library service in their respective communities. Tax support became the obvious key to library development and civic leaders quickly pushed for its adoption as the principal means of library support. In the beginning stimulus was frequently provided by public-spirited benefactors who provided substantial sums of money for the construction of buildings and the acquisition of library materials. Also common was the process whereby an existing social or endowed library would be donated or purchased by the city as the nucleus for a new public library. By 1913 the U.S. Office of Education could report that the process had advanced to the stage where the nation boasted some 3,000 public libraries containing over 1,000 volumes each.

In the last quarter of the 19th century three developments occurred which contributed mightily to the rise of public libraries, and indeed, libraries generally. First, the American Library Association was organized in Philadelphia in 1876. The ALA provided librarians with the long-needed organizational structure and public forum required if the library profession was to develop professional cohesiveness and philosophical consistency.

Second, the long-standing and frequently lamented lack of a professional literature designed to provide guidance and inspiration to librarians was met with the publication of the now classic 1876 _Report on Public Libraries in the United States of America_, and the establishment of the _Library Journal_ in that same year. The former, a massive compendium of articles written by the nation's leading library authorities, dealt with every conceivable aspect of library development and management, and represented the standard handbook of library practice for years to come. The latter, founded by the publishers R. R. Bowker and Frederick Leypoldt, and edited by the dynamic and controversial Melvil Dewey, came to represent the library profession's most articulate and influential medium of communication, a position it still holds some 100 years after its founding.

The third, and perhaps most immediately obvious impetus to public library development was the wholesale philanthropy of history's greatest library benefactor, Andrew Carnegie. This immigrant from Scotland had made millions in the steel industry and in his later years turned his interest toward the gifts of funds for the erection of libraries in the United States and the United Kingdom. As early as 1881 he began to encourage the construction of free public libraries with the gift of a library to the Pittsburgh area where many of his steelworkers lived. After this he began to offer library buildings to any municipality that would guarantee to maintain a public library, and by 1920 he had provided some $50,000,000 for the construction of no fewer than 2,500 buildings. In explaining his choice of libraries as an outlet for his philanthropy, Carnegie was reported as saying in 1900:

> I choose free libraries as the best agencies for improving the masses of the people, because they give nothing for nothing. They only help those who help themselves. They never pauperize. They reach the aspiring, and open to these the chief treasures of the world--those stored up in books. A taste for reading drives out lower tastes.

Despite his generous motives, some cities did not want Carnegie's "tainted" money. In 1901 Detroit was offered $750,000 contingent on its raising another $500,000, but opposition was so strong that the offer was not accepted until 1910. It is true that in some cases the libraries begun in substantial buildings never fulfilled their promise, were poorly stocked and staffed, but in most cases the libraries were continued and provided at least a moderate amount of library service for millions of people. Besides Carnegie, other philanthropists turned their attention to aid to public libraries, and various buildings with "memorial" names still dot the nation. The Enoch Pratt Free Library in Baltimore, the Cossitt Library in Memphis, and the Pack Memorial Public Library in Asheville, N.C., are a few examples.

The establishment of the American Library Association, the development of a professional literature, and the widespread philanthropy of Andrew Carnegie and other library benefactors firmly rooted the public library in American life. As public libraries spread across the nation, their staffs worked diligently to expand and strengthen the services offered to users. In the late 19th and early 20th centuries branches were established, women and children were recognized as legitimate clientele for the library, the concept of open stacks was generally accepted, hours of service were greatly increased, and the belief that the library should provide informational or reference service to its patrons was widely endorsed. All of this was done despite the intrusion of financial crises like the great depression of 1929.

The development of public libraries in America was at times a mindless and careless process; at others, it was accompanied by a consistent attempt to systematize and articulate both philosophy and practice. Public library philosophy up through the 19th century was characterized by a decidedly authoritarian and missionary cast. Justin Winsor, who served as President of the American Library Association for the first ten years of its existence, clearly stated this thrust when he noted that the public library could be wielded as a "great engine" for "good or evil" among the "masses of the people." Using a similar analogy in one of his presidential addresses to his colleagues, he said that he thought of the public library as "a derrick, lifting the inert masses and swinging them round to the surer foundations upon which the national character shall rise." Following Winsor's lead, librarians were soon touting the public library as a panacea for most of the country's social ills: crime, disease, illiteracy, prostitution, intemperance, and the reckless and un-American ways of the waves of new immigrants sweeping into the country. In the latter case librarians viewed as one of their most sacred trusts the "Americanization of the immigrant," and led the way in developing programs to contribute to the success of this movement. Similarly, during the recurring financial depressions of the 19th and early 20th centuries, the library was hailed as a stabilizing force in society. As one librarian put it: "if society cannot provide work for all, the idle--chronic or temporary--are much safer with a book in the library than elsewhere."

In the early decades of the 20th century, librarians, faced with the rapid increase in the number and size of libraries and their concomitant complexity as administrative organizations, seemed to turn inward and focus increasingly on internal matters of management, attempting to make public librarianship what Melvil Dewey frequently referred to as a perfect "mechanical art." However, by the 1930s librarians were again deeply concerned with the purpose of the public library, and in light of the Nazi and Fascist advances in Europe the public library's role was being redefined as a "guardian of the people's right to know." This new view of the library's purpose represented an abandonment of the earlier authoritarian and elitist philosophy of service and emphasized the librarian's obligation to provide a balanced and unbiased picture of issues so that the citizen might make an independent decision. This philosophy, gaining increasing acceptance in the forties, is generally subscribed to by all public librarians, at least in theory, and is embodied in all basic policy statements, such as ALA's Library Bill of Rights and Statement on Labeling, both currently in force.

More recently, public librarians, stung by criticisms regarding lack of use of the public library, have taken a more aggressive stance in the area of service and have initiated numerous "outreach" programs designed to increase the availability and use of library facilities by those, especially the lower classes, who formerly made scant or no use of public libraries. This new thrust was greatly facilitated by the widespread funding of library programs by federal and state government in the late fifties and the sixties. Access to such large sums of money contributed to the exuberant nature of American public librarianship and soon led to the development of a system of public libraries unrivaled in the world. It remains to be seen whether this renewed commitment to the aggressive delivery of public library services to all classes of American society can survive the serious financial restraints evident today, or whether public librarians will retreat to the more efficient and less expensive pattern of serving only the intellectual minority in American society.

College and University Libraries

As noted in Chapter 10, college libraries before 1850 were generally small and unimpressive collections of books--poorly housed, little used, and strictly guarded. After 1850 a number of developments conspired to alter radically the nature of American higher education and, concomitantly, to revolutionize the nature and role of the library in the academic setting. These developments can be discussed under three basic headings: financial, educational, and professional.

It is clear that the nation underwent an enormous and momentous commercial and industrial development after 1850. This rapid and unprecedented growth in financial resources influenced American colleges and universities in a number of ways prior to 1900. First, the development of a surplus of wealth, a proportion of which found its way into the coffers of academic institutions, had a significant effect on the development of American higher education. Increasingly, large-scale philanthropy was being directed toward American higher education, and not a small proportion of this money was being devoted to the construction and development of library resources. At the same time, American business, industry, and government were becoming acutely aware of the need to produce the specialized technical experts necessary to staff the burgeoning research and development wings of American industry. Consequently, all these sectors pushed actively for the establishment of institutions of higher education explicitly charged with the responsibility of training such personnel, and perhaps the most significant outgrowth of this movement was the passage of the Morrill Land Grant Act of

1862, which provided federal land grants for the establishment of technical and agricultural colleges. This stimulus led to the establishment in many states of educational institutions that were to become some of America's most prestigious universities in the early 20th century, and as a result of their burgeoning financial support, their libraries soon became some of the finest in the land.

A number of developments in the nature of American higher education also influenced the development of academic libraries. First, the introduction of new courses, especially in the biological and physical sciences, contributed to an increased specialization. Further, the gradual acceptance of the "elective system," as opposed to the prescribed curriculum so common to earlier higher education, provided for the development of a more sophisticated curriculum and a degree of specialization among students and faculty that had previously been unknown. Finally, the influence of the German educational system contributed greatly to the rise of American higher education and the development of academic libraries. Perhaps most important was the growing emphasis on the significance of research as a major component of the academic institution's role in society. This concept, combined with the German idea of the seminar as a principal means of education, especially with graduate students, made library resources a high priority. All of these developments placed increased pressures on the academic library and contributed to the emerging consensus that the library constituted the very "heart" of any self-respecting academic institution. This new awareness of the importance of the library in the academic setting quickly generated increased financial support for library programs, and by 1900 the academic library was firmly established as a central component in the educational process.

A last, but not unimportant, series of professional developments contributed to the rise of the academic library. The establishment of the American Library Association, and the emergence of a number of vigorous and respected library administrators, like Melvil Dewey of Columbia and Justin Winsor of Harvard, heralded the rise of a new class of professional librarians dedicated to the ideal that books in libraries were an essential ingredient in any educational recipe. Librarians like Dewey and Winsor articulated the growing consensus relating to the library's new significance to the educational effort and provided effective professional leadership in the development of library services and collections.

Given these influences the academic library developed with rapidity. Book collections grew with such speed that it was soon accepted as a fact of life that these libraries could be expected to double in size every sixteen years. This growth was at first welcome, but it placed enormous strains on the staffs charged with the responsibility of acquiring and organizing the ever larger collections for use and would eventually create nightmarish strains on library building programs.

For example, in the East, Harvard's University Library plus the other collections on its campus, totaled over 225,000 volumes by 1875 and over 560,000 by 1900. By 1925 it had reached nearly 2,500,000 and by 1940 nearly 4,000,000 volumes were crowded into its varied facilities. In 1900 Harvard's main library was still in Gore Hall, but in 1915 it moved into the new Widener Library, a building that was supposed to meet the university's needs for a half-century at least. By 1930, however, it was filled to overflowing, and the Widener Library has since been supplemented by the Houghton Library for rare books and the Lamont Library for undergraduates. In addition, in the 1930s there were some seventy departmental and associated libraries, many of them almost definitive in their subject coverage, plus hundreds of thousands of books in storage.

Among other university libraries, Yale had nearly 300,000 volumes in its library by 1900, and over 1,000,000 by 1925; Princeton University had moved its library into a new building in 1873, and by 1900 this was crowded with over 150,000 volumes; the University of Pennsylvania had 182,000 volumes at the turn of the century; Columbia had reached 250,000 in all of its collections; Brown University's library was about half as large. In 1897 Columbia had moved to a new campus at Morningside Heights in New York City, and the next year Low Memorial Library, planned to hold 750,000 volumes, was opened. By 1934 the Nicholas Murray Butler Library, with its fifteen-tier bookstack and capacity for 3,000,000 volumes, was added to meet the expanding demand for space. Cornell University Library at Ithaca, New York, nonexistent before 1865, had about 40,000 volumes in 1875 and over 200,000 by 1900. Its rapid growth was aided by a generous endowment and the support of a sympathetic administration. It moved to its own building, Sage Hall, in 1891. By 1900 Dartmouth had only 90,000 volumes; Amherst, 72,000; Rutgers, 41,000; and in Washington, D.C., Georgetown University Library had 88,000. Among the larger state university libraries in the South,

Virginia had about 50,000 volumes, North Carolina about 30,000 and the University of Texas, 34,000. Vanderbilt University in Nashville, founded in 1872, had a library of 32,000 volumes by 1900, but elsewhere in the South college libraries were generally smaller than 20,000 volumes.

In the Middle West, the new University of Chicago, founded in 1892, had taken a commanding lead in bookstock by 1900, with nearly 300,000 volumes, making it one of the leading libraries of the nation. Backed by the philanthropy of John D. Rockefeller, whole libraries were acquired in both Europe and America to build up the University of Chicago Library, and even one entire bookstore, that of S. Calvary & Company of Berlin, was purchased. The University of Michigan library bookstock had reached 145,000 by 1900, but other neighboring collections were smaller, with 65,000 at the University of Minnesota, 42,000 at the University of Illinois, and 34,000 at the University of Missouri.

Total numbers of volumes do not, of course, tell the whole story of library development in the colleges and universities of this era. The approach to library service on the campuses was changing rapidly, with longer hours, better catalogs, and more efficient library service to students and faculty. The development of the Indiana University Library in the latter quarter of the 19th century may be typical of many other university libraries. In 1880 the library of about 10,000 volumes was poorly cataloged and open only a few hours a week. In that year the first full-time librarian was employed and, despite a disastrous fire in 1883, a card catalog was prepared and new books purchased; by 1888 three additional library staff members were needed. In 1891 the library moved into a new building, Maxwell Hall, with a large reading and reference room. In addition to a law library, other departmental collections were started in the 1890s. Additional staff members, student assistants, longer hours of service, and a reserve reading room gave the library a 20th century air by 1900, and the library budget in that year was twenty times what it had been in 1875.

Throughout the country, the university libraries in the early part of the new century continued to grow more and more rapidly, with bookstocks expanding far beyond the capacity of old buildings, and new buildings quickly filled to capacity. New buildings appeared on many campuses, and for the first time they were being planned for library purposes rather than for architectural splendor. On larger campuses, departmental libraries and special collections grew both in size and numbers, although in a few cases there was a tendency to return all books to a centralized collection. Library staffs became more professionalized as library schools developed, although many a small college did not have a trained librarian until the 1920s, and the one-member staff was all too common. But gradually the college library ceased being a museum and became a more active part of the academic program. Newer teaching methods called for more student use of the library, more faculty interest in book selection, and larger expenditures for the library. The seminar method of teaching especially called for greater emphasis on the use and proximity of books. Growing graduate schools demanded rare and expensive books and periodicals for research. Moreover, the increased size of libraries meant that books and other materials had to be better organized and arranged, so that in many cases whole libraries had to be recataloged and new classification systems employed. Fortunately, this was also a period of library philanthropy, when most of the major universities and many of the colleges received substantial gifts in money, buildings, and books. The Carnegie Corporation in particular gave money for buildings on literally hundreds of campuses. Later in the century, the same institution provided funds for library schools, surveys, recataloging projects, and publications. Public interest and support of the state institutions also increased and library budgets grew, although usually not in proportion to the need.

The 1920s saw a number of university libraries in the South and West beginning to compete in size and importance with the older ones in the Northeast. The Universities of Virginia, North Carolina, Florida, and Texas, along with the private universities of Duke, Tulane, Emory, and Vanderbilt, began to attract attention as major area research centers. Of these, the library of the University of Texas was largest, with some 400,000 volumes in 1929, while North Carolina was second and the others contained well over 100,000 volumes each. In the West, the University of California at Berkeley was in a class by itself with over 700,000 volumes, but the university libraries of Colorado, Washington, Oregon, and Nebraska each contained over 200,000 volumes by 1929. The libraries of liberal arts colleges, teachers' colleges, technical and agricultural institutions, although much smaller than those of the universities, increased in size and significance in their own fields. On many campuses, there was a conflict between those who wanted departmental libraries and those who wanted everything in a central collection, and, as new buildings were constructed, the latter often won out. Each type of organization had its own good and bad points, but the departmental systems, by choice or necessity, remained in vogue in most of the larger institutions. As the donations of books and funds for library purposes became smaller in comparison to needs, many libraries turned to the formation of Friends of the Library groups, where many could give small gifts to take the place of the few large ones formerly received.

The economic depression in the 1920s hit hard at college and university libraries. Building programs were shelved, staffs and budgets were curtailed, yet needs and demands for services remained high. Fortunately, federal government assistance in the form of the Works Progress Administration and the National Youth Administration provided much needed assistance, and useful projects in binding, cataloging, indexing, and building repairs were carried out. In a few cases, library buildings were constructed with federal aid, and on almost all campuses federally aided student assistants were plentiful. Moreover, the W.P.A. public records projects gave great aid to libraries in general through their indexing, abstracting, microfilming, and publishing of research materials.

Probably the most important beneficial effect of the Depression on college and university libraries was that it caused them to pause and reflect on their nature and purpose in the general educational scene. Library standards, codes of ethics, and education for librarians received serious study at both general and special library conferences. The need to extend services with strained budgets led to a search for new and more efficient means of providing library service. Various new methods of book charging and circulation control were introduced, some of them being widely adopted and others soon disappearing. As book acquisitions far exceeded stack space, ideas for reducing the size of bookforms were investigated, and from these experiments came a wide variety of microforms as means of storing large quantities of graphic materials in a small space. Microfilms and microcards in particular became widely used, and newspapers, periodicals, and government publications were soon reproduced in these forms. Cooperative acquisition programs, especially for foreign publications, were tried and some of them adopted. Duke University (North Carolina) and Tulane (Louisiana), for example, cooperated in the acquisition of Latin American materials, each specializing in one or more of the countries south of the border. On a larger scale, the Farmington Plan, uniting many of the major research libraries of the nation, assured complete coverage in the acquisition of foreign newspapers and governmental publications. Union catalogs and interlibrary loans furthered this cooperation, and photomechanical means of reproducing printed materials made possible the acquisition of copies of rare materials at a reasonable cost.

Before the college and university libraries had recovered from the effects of the Depression, World War II caused new problems. Colleges and universities were called upon to supply the special training for soldiers and specialists needed in the war, and their libraries felt the strain. Funds were usually plentiful but staff members were scarce, and the demands for books and services for the new programs, the newly organized academic departments, and the war information centers severely taxed the abilities of even the largest libraries. Under pressure, however, new methods were employed, new tools were developed, thousands of new workers were introduced to the library field, and by the end of the war the nation's college and university libraries were stronger than ever. Not only were their bookstocks larger but their position on the campus was stronger. The trite expression that "the library is the heart of the college" became nearer the truth than ever, and from one end of the nation to the other, college and university administrators pressed for more funds, bigger buildings, and larger staffs for their libraries. The thousands of war veterans flooding the campuses after 1945 made these library needs more urgent, and library progress was rapid, if not spectacular. Both graduate and undergraduate enrollments rose to new heights, and the presence of the older veterans on the campus made all students more serious in their work. Capacity use was made of all library facilities, and once again the libraries faced a crisis with more demands for their services than facilities to fill them. By the 1950s most college and university libraries had building programs, either in the form of new buildings or annexes, often accompanied by reorganization of library procedures and reclassification of the book collections. The increasing use of non-book materials in the teaching processes led the academic library to widen its viewpoint and include in its programs a wide variety of audio-visual materials including tapes, discs, films, and filmstrips. Once again departmental libraries flourished even on small campuses, due to lack of space in the main libraries, and storage facilities for little-used materials became a necessity. The new library buildings were constructed with the new services in mind, and most of them adopted the modular arrangement, with open shelving and divisional plans to make books and other library materials as easily available as possible.

In 1980 Harvard University's library still led the nation in bookstock with over 10,000,000 volumes, not counting manuscripts, maps, recordings, and micro-materials. In addition to the Widener, Houghton, Lamont, and Pusey libraries, over ninety other library units served the university, some of them having hundreds of thousands of volumes themselves. Yale's library was probably second largest, with some 5,000,000 volumes, but Columbia University, the University of Illinois, and the University of California at Berkeley were close behind. Tremendous new buildings were completed or under way on many major campuses in the late sixties and early seventies, one of the most ambitious at the University of Chicago. In 1968 alone, there were at least sixty-eight major library building projects in process on American college campuses. Throughout the nation, university libraries with 1,000,000 volumes, budgets of over $1,000,000, and staffs in the hundreds became almost the norm. On the other end of the college scale, dozens of junior colleges became four-year colleges without sufficient regard to adequate library facilities, and as many more four-year colleges began offering graduate work without research libraries. Scores of new junior or "community" colleges were formed throughout the nation, often with inadequate high-school libraries. Some states established entirely new universities, planned from the start to serve thousands of students, and here library facilities were usually adequately planned, often designed with all the newest facilities and theories of library operation in mind. Thanks to microforms and widely reprinted source materials, it was possible to begin these institutions with collections that were reasonably adequate on opening day.

However, there were still many college and smaller university libraries that fell short of meeting the needs of their faculties and students. Among these were some of the newer colleges, small church-supported institutions, Negro colleges, and institutions in the economically poorer areas. Colleges in the South were particularly noted for their inadequate library facilities, but meager collections and small staffs were not restricted to any particular area. Regional accrediting agencies, such as the Southern Association of

Colleges and Secondary Schools, have done much to improve library conditions in colleges and universities through their library standards. As late as 1950, however, it was still true that almost two thirds of the colleges in the Southeastern states failed to meet Southern Association standards on one or more points. Once again, federal aid to education has provided both funds and a new stimulus to college library growth. The Higher Education Act of 1965 provided funds for college library resources, for training librarians, and for research in the field of library science. Over 1,800 institutions received funds during the first year of operation of this act, and its impact on book collections, library schools, and higher education in general has been tremendous.

While most institutions were having trouble getting enough books to meet demands and standards, many of the larger university libraries were having difficulties in finding space to house all the books and other informational materials produced by the "information explosion." When microforms and compact shelving failed to provide the answers, these libraries turned to various forms of storage plans. Some found the necessary space on their own campuses or in rented areas nearby, while others turned to interlibrary storage centers. The first of these was the New England Deposit Library in Boston, maintained by the major libraries of that area, including Harvard and the Massachusetts Institute of Technology. In it are deposited newspaper files, runs of older periodicals, sets of little-used works, state and foreign documents, and miscellaneous ephemeral material. In most cases, this material is not duplicated in any of the member libraries, but is available to any of them. Duplicates usually are not kept in the storage centers either, but are sold or exchanged. Another major storage library, the Midwest Inter-Library Center at Chicago, was the result of cooperation among a dozen or so Middle Western university libraries. It was formed in 1951, with a capacity of over 2,000,000 volumes. This center functioned much the same as the one in New England, but it also has the task of acquiring certain types of little used materials itself, thus relieving its constituent libraries of that task. Since 1965, this Center has broadened its activities under the new title of Center for Research Libraries, but its functions are essentially the same. Cooperation between college libraries in other fields also became more general in the 1960s. Ohio's College Library Center at Columbus was established to provide a computerized regional library facility to serve all academic libraries in Ohio in a cooperative cataloging and union catalog service. In the seventies the OCLC, aided by increasing pressure on library budgets, has vastly expanded its program and influence, and has spawned a number of similar bibliographic networks throughout the nation. Elsewhere in the nation, other cooperative projects are in the planning stage, and the advanced techniques of computers, teletypes, and even closed circuit television have been employed to extend and strengthen library services. Most impressive of the new networks is RLIN (Research Libraries Information Network). Based on the BALLOTS system developed in the late sixties at Stanford University, RLIN officially became a network in 1978. RLIN is designed to serve major research libraries with shared cataloging, interlibrary loan, serials control, and acquisitions assistance. Within libraries themselves, continued efforts have been made to improve library efficiency. The rapid growth of library resources, new educational methods, burgeoning student populations, and the increasing sophistication of faculties have forced academic libraries to explore every new technical development in their search for improved library service.

The recent past has witnessed a return of tight budgets in the wake of the nearly uncontrolled growth of the sixties. Academic libraries, large and small, are entering into a multitude of cooperative agreements designed to stretch the budget dollar. At the same time, the cherished ideal of "local self-sufficiency" is being abandoned by even the largest and most respected academic libraries. How well academic libraries can meet the increased demands of users in the face of stable or decreasing funding will dictate their success in the years to come.

School Libraries

Although some feeble beginnings in the area of school library services were made early in the 19th century, it was not until after 1900 that school libraries in the modern sense of the term became fairly general. Before that, there was a period of confusion and experimentation in the provision of library service to children. The failure of the school-district library idea in many areas resulted in a setback for school library development. Often, school-district books were brought together in an attempt to form township libraries, but this, too, was unsuccessful. As public libraries began to be formed, taxpayers in many areas were reluctant to support two systems of public library service, and many attempts were made to serve the schoolchildren through public libraries. In some towns and villages, the public library or a branch would be located in the vicinity of the school and opened for school use by groups during school hours and by individual children afterward. In others, public libraries simply provided books to the schools in deposits, either by classrooms or in central collections. In a few cases the public library was actually located in the school building, serving both school and public from one point. None of these plans was particularly successful, and by 1900 there was a controversy between those who favored public library service to schools and those who favored independent school libraries. In 1896 the National Education Association formed a Library Section that was interested in bringing library service to all children by the best means possible. In 1898, at its national conference, this group was divided, with strong voices raised in favor of each type of library service. After 1900, however, the majority seemed to favor independent school libraries, particularly classroom libraries selected according to the reading level and interests of each grade. The discussion over the two methods of reaching schoolchildren was lively in both school and library circles for another decade, but by 1910 the concept of the independent school library had become widely adopted. Although in some cities and counties the link between public and school libraries has been successfully maintained, the main trend has been toward separate library systems.

Although public high schools had begun in New England even before the Civil War and were fairly widespread in much of the country before 1900, their libraries, if any, were usually small and little used. The books were often old, poorly selected, unavailable for much of the time, and under the care of teachers or other school personnel with little interest in their condition or use. By 1900 this situation was changing in a few states and in most of the larger cities. Whether the high school library was a unit in itself, a part of a school system library or of a public library, its content became updated, its financial support more regular, and, more important, it became available to the students. Full-time librarians were employed in the larger schools, teacher-librarians in the smaller ones, and the trained school librarian began to appear. Some colleges and normal schools had offered courses in library science as early as the 1870s, but it was not until the 1890s that Melvil Dewey's library school at Albany and the Pratt Institute in Brooklyn began to turn out professionally trained librarians. Erasmus Hall

High School in Brooklyn had a trained librarian in 1900, and Brooklyn Girls High in 1903. Morris High School in New York City obtained its first trained librarian in 1905, and in the same year there were high school librarians in Albany and Rochester, New York, New Jersey, and Washington, D.C., in the East; Michigan and Minnesota in the Middle West. California and Oregon in the Far West took the lead in the establishment of high school libraries and in the employment of full-time librarians for them. Elsewhere in the nation, particularly in the South, the development of independent high school libraries was spotty, but by 1915 most of the larger high schools had some kind of central library, however inadequate.

One reason for the trend toward the independent school library as distinct from the public library school deposit can be found in the newer methods of teaching adopted after 1900. The idea of learning to read for the pleasure of reading was stressed, and the importance of having good books in addition to textbooks in the schools began to be realized. The newer theories of the child-centered school, where the pupil was educated not for a profession but for a well-rounded, meaningful life, called for the availability of books at all times. Such programs of learning as the platoon school, which varied the school day by a work-play-study routine; or the Winnetka plan, which emphasized the individual abilities of each pupil, called for free and frequent use of library materials, and therefore a permanent school library and a trained school librarian. After this idea was adopted, there was still the debate over the single, central library or multiple classroom libraries. The elementary schools that had libraries usually preferred the classroom collections, but most secondary schools preferred the central library. By 1913 the U.S. Office of Education could report that there were approximately 10,000 public school libraries in the nation, but only about 250 of them contained more than 3,000 volumes. Most of the others were characterized as being out of date or too small, poorly housed, unclassified and uncataloged, and sometimes completely unavailable for use. A few cities, including Washington, D.C., Spokane, and Detroit, were commended for having excellent school library systems, but for the rest of the nation there was still a long way to go in school library service.

The idea of the school library as a vital part of the public school was becoming generally accepted by 1915, with one writer calling it "the laboratory of the social sciences and humanities and the laboratory annex for the sciences." In that year, the number of school librarians had increased to the extent that the American Library Association formed its School Librarians Section, and "the new high school library" was widely discussed. This more or less idealized library was described as a large, airy, well-lighted room, cheery and inviting, with books readily available for all grades and all subjects taught in the school. There was to be a "librarian's office and work-room" next to the library room. Something anticipating the audio-visual program of later years was included with the listing of lantern slides, pictures, postcards, and "Victrola records" as suitable adjuncts to the book and magazine contents of the library, and a well-organized clipping file was heartily recommended. This type of library and library service was described as "dynamic," in contrast to the old "static" library that merely preserved collections of unused books in out-of-the-way places. It was admitted that libraries of this type were scarce, but they were held up as goals for all schools to approach.

After 1920 this "ideal" school library became more common, and new developments in the field of school library service came rapidly. In 1920 the N.E.A. Committee on Library Organization and Equipment issued its Standards for Library Organization and Equipment for Secondary Schools, and in 1925 this was followed by Elementary School Library Standards, prepared by a Joint Committee of the N.E.A. and the A.L.A. These standards enabled schools throughout the nation to compare their libraries with adequate school library conditions and provided school administrators and local government officials with the definite goals needed for school library support. Other national organizations interested themselves in school library improvement, as when the National Council of Teachers of English created a permanent committee on the use of school libraries. Regional accrediting associations conducted surveys of school libraries within their areas and prepared standards of library service for accreditation. Surveys of school library conditions by towns, cities, and states brought out the strengths and weaknesses of existing libraries and pointed the way for future improvement. These surveys culminated in a national secondary-school library survey conducted in 1932 for the U.S. Office of Education by Dr. B. Lamar Johnson. This was a selective survey of some 390 schools throughout the nation, and although it did not make specific recommendations it provided a basis from which school administrators could draw their own conclusions. Probably the most important factor in school-library progress, however, was the work done by state and local governments in promoting school libraries. Many states, for example, created the office of school library supervisor to encourage and supervise the development of school libraries throughout the state. Selected book lists, school library handbooks and other valuable library aids were prepared by these state offices. Cities, towns, and counties followed this lead and employed library specialists who advised school librarians in the larger schools and the teachers and teacher-librarians in the smaller ones.

In addition to progress in the general school library scene, there were many changes in the school library itself. In addition to more trained librarians and more cooperation between librarians and teachers, there were also new and better library quarters within the school buildings. Instead of occupying any available room, school libraries were being planned for library services. In 1922, when a large bond issue was passed for the construction of new schools in Los Angeles, library quarters were planned in each building, and a committee of librarians was invited to help plan those quarters. With the growth of school systems in the more populated areas, the necessity for centralizing the purchasing and processing of school library materials became obvious. In 1927 Los Angeles began centralized purchasing and cataloging for its high schools, special schools and a junior college. Centralized cataloging was also tried in Seattle, and other larger cities had adopted the idea by the early 1930s. The advantages were not only the obvious ones in economy; librarians also were given more time to spend in working with students and teachers rather than in processing duties. Probably more important than physical changes was the change in the approach toward school library service. In the better libraries throughout the nation, the emphasis was being placed on service to students and teachers and on making the library an active part of the school program. To this end, the teaching of the use of the library was widely recommended and units on the library were available for English and social science courses at almost all grade levels.

Charitable foundations continued to aid the development of libraries, and school libraries benefited directly in several instances. In 1929 the Julius Rosenwald Fund provided aid for eleven county library systems to demonstrate public library service to rural schools. These demonstration libraries were in the South, and library service was provided on equal terms to both white and Negro schools. This same organization also gave direct financial aid to Negro high and elementary schools for the purchase of library books and materials in the early Depression years. The Carnegie Corporation's aid to library schools also aided school libraries indirectly, as did the work of the General Education Board and the Rockefeller Foundation. Publications to aid the school librarian came from the American Library Association, the National Educational Association, the U.S. Office of Education, and most of the state library and education departments. In some states, state aid for the purchase of school library materials was available, but in most this was left entirely to the local school system.

Unfortunately, school library progress begun in the 1920s was to be seriously hampered after 1929 by the Depression. School budgets were hard hit and the library was often the first to suffer. Funds for new books or current periodicals were often unavailable when even teachers were going unpaid for months. For example, the state of Tennessee reported, as late as 1936, that eighty percent of its high schools had no funds at all for books. But there was still some progress in the 1930s in spite of and partly because of, the Depression. After 1933, federal aid came in the form of workers paid by the W.P.A. and N.Y.A. and schools built by the W.P.A. and P.W.A. With federal aid, the trend in consolidating small schools into larger, more modern, and more efficient ones progressed, and these new buildings provided quarters for school libraries. State aid for school libraries became more general, particularly in the states with large rural populations. In 1938-40, in the South alone, Tennessee, Georgia, Louisiana, and Virginia were providing direct state aid to their school libraries.

The Depression also brought about a reappraisal of the relationship between public and school libraries, and cooperation between the two took several forms. In some cases, there was a single library system, with a public library in the county seat providing rotating book deposits for the schools. This had many advantages in lower operating costs, with need for only one set of books for both school and public library use. In other systems the school libraries were permanent collections but they were bought and processed by the central public library. Each way brought obvious benefits but also some disadvantages, such as the slowness of obtaining new books, lack of participation by the teachers in book selection, and lack of trained librarians to give the necessary library service along with the books. Often centralized purchasing and processing meant that all the available professional staff would be employed at the central library so the schools would be left with good books but no librarians. Where professional libraries for teachers were incorporated into the public library-school library cooperative system, the advantages were even greater, and this feature often proved very popular.

The effect of World War II on school libraries was similar to that on libraries in general. Population shifts brought the building of new schools and the abandonment of old ones. Emphasis on training for special skills, and on the rapid flow of information, was as important to school libraries as it was to college and public libraries. Hence, the school library scene during the war years was hectic, with rapid developments and often increased funds, but with librarians almost impossible to obtain. Out of this period of change, however, came a new appreciation of the value of school libraries and a thorough rethinking of their nature and function in the educational system as a whole. Plans for future library services were made even before the war ended, and their implementation was to come, slowly but surely, in the post-war years.

In 1945 the American Library Association published School Libraries for Today and Tomorrow, which outlined programs and established guidelines for the future development of the nation's school library services, including a statement of objectives, necessary services, and required facilities for that development. Implementation of these standards, however, was slow, although much progress was made in many individual instances. In 1953 it could be pointed out that more than half of the nation's schools still lacked adequate libraries. The combined efforts of state and local governmental units were not enough to assure good libraries in all schools. Fortunately, the mood of the country was changing, and the necessity of federal aid for the improvement of educational facilities was recognized. The National Defense Education Act of 1958 led the way, and although its action was not directly aimed at library service, its funds for the improvement of training in mathematics, science and foreign languages often led to the purchase of additional books and teaching materials for the school libraries. Similarly, the Vocational Education Act of 1963 provided funds for school libraries in some cases. The most important federal legislation for school libraries, however, came with the Elementary and Secondary Education Act of 1965. Title II of ESEA, in particular, provided millions of dollars for the purchase of books, periodicals, tapes, records, and other instructional materials for school libraries, and other parts of the act also had promising implications. Under Title III, for example, demonstration libraries have been established with new facilities and services hitherto untried and unavailable. Finally, the Higher Education Acts of 1965 and 1966 have aided school libraries in provision of aid in the training of school librarians.

To supplement the various federal acts and to help put them into effect, several significant special library projects were inaugurated. The Knapp School Libraries Project, financed by a grant from the Knapp Foundation, provided demonstration libraries in eight schools from 1963 to 1968. In five elementary schools and three high schools, ranging from New York to Oregon, libraries were provided with the best book collections, equipment, and staffs that could be obtained, to demonstrate what ideal school library service could be. Thousands of librarians and educators visited these demonstrations and profited from their experiences. The American Library Association, with funds from the Council of Library Resources, carried out a School Library Development Project to show how its 1960 Standards for School Library Programs could be achieved. Many states and school districts used ESEA Title III funds to carry out their own demonstration library projects. By the late 1960s, it was no longer a question of how to achieve good school libraries, but where the librarians could be found, and when the local school systems would take advantage of the many aids available.

The decade after 1965, aided and stimulated from many directions, may turn out to be one of the greatest in the history of American school libraries. In fact, it may well be remembered as the era when the school library disappeared and the teaching materials center took its place. Changes in this direction had begun as early as 1947, when California established central teaching materials centers in each county. The idea spread to other states in the 1950s, and such centers were established within libraries, or outside of libraries in separate systems, on both district and school levels. The cost of the equipment and materials needed usually resulted in centralized district collections until federal funds made it possible for the larger schools to establish their own teaching materials centers. Today, the expanded school library, or teaching materials center, is a far cry from that of the 1930s. It is equipped to supply all kinds of instructional aids, including books, periodicals pamphlets, pictures, charts, maps, films, filmstrips, microfilms, tape recordings and disc recordings, and even three-dimensional models. It may include a suite of several rooms, with open-shelf reading rooms, offices, conference rooms, a classroom, workrooms, and individual study carrels. It may have special audio-visual rooms with projection equipment, record players, tape players, television, radio, filmstrip and film-loop viewers, and even teletype equipment available.

Another bright aspect of the school library scene in the 1950s and 1960s was the increasing number of elementary school libraries. Long the stepchild of the school library world, depending on small classroom collections or deposits from public libraries, the elementary school library was finally recognized as an important part of elementary education. Increased emphasis on individual effort by the pupil and on learning by doing rather than memorizing textbooks meant that a wider variety of materials entered into the daily elementary school teaching and learning experience. The classroom library, long favored by elementary school teachers, became inadequate and was being replaced by the centralized elementary school library, while the trained elementary school librarian took her place as part of the teaching team. Both elementary and high school librarians have begun to place more emphasis on teaching students to use books and libraries. This wider concept of the use of library materials as a subject in itself has greatly enhanced the value of both the school library and the school librarian.

Statistically, the school library scene at the close of the 1960s was both gratifying and disturbing. Of the 88,000 schools in the United States, two-thirds had centralized libraries, but only about forty percent had full-time librarians and teaching materials collections. Moreover, of the elementary schools, only one third had centralized libraries. A.L.A.'s 1965 National Inventory of Library Needs found that even those 56,000 schools with centralized libraries had less than half (collectively) of the volumes to meet the 1960 standards. To fill this "volume gap," an expenditure of nearly $1,000,000,000 would be necessary. Not only was there a great shortage of volumes, but the "staff gap" was even greater. Instead of the 32,000 "professional" librarians employed in schools in 1964, the standards called for 112,000. A survey conducted in 1974, The Library and General Information Survey (LIBGIS), demonstrated the strides taken over the decade. For instance, some 90% of the schools surveyed had centralized libraries and library services were provided for 50% more school children--nearly 15,000,000 more--than in 1964. Much of the gain was due to the infusion of funds derived from the ESEA Title II program. The decade 1974 to 1984 witnessed some retrenchment as a result of a declining economy and Federal budget cuts, but school library media centers were generally established as essential elements in the elementary and secondary school system.

Libraries Serving Government

Since 1850, libraries serving federal and state government in the United States, like other types of libraries, have undergone rapid and revolutionary growth. By far the most significant of government libraries is the Library of Congress, a library which in terms of size of collection and extent and nature of services may well be the most impressive such institution in the world. The Library of Congress began its remarkable development when Ainsworth Rand Spofford was appointed Librarian of Congress by President Lincoln in 1864, and under his leadership the library soon became one of the most important in the world. It was still housed in the Capitol building, but it was rapidly overflowing its quarters.

As early as 1871, Dr. Spofford suggested the library needed a building specifically designed for the collection, and in 1874, Congress appointed a committee to look into the possibilities of building a national library structure. But the wheels of government grind slowly and it was not until 1887 that construction finally began. The resulting building, not completed until 1897, forms the present main part of the library, capable of holding nearly three million volumes and covering nearly four acres. It had all the latest in library equipment for its day, with everything from well-lighted reading rooms and steel stacks to book conveyers and inter-office speaking tubes. Though Librarian Spofford's staff of 1864 had only five members, the new building required one hundred eighty-five workers in 1900, with an additional crew of forty-five in the copyright office. The old system of classification, an adaptation of Jefferson's original private library scheme, was outmoded by the multitudes of new books of the late 19th century. To meet this need a number of classification schemes were considered, but in the end a system particularly adapted to the needs of the Library of Congress was developed, and the entire library was reclassified and cataloged. As the books were reprocessed, printed catalog cards were produced and made available for purchase to libraries all over the nation. Thus the Library of Congress card-distribution program was begun, one of its most valued and appreciated services to the library world.

Although the Library of Congress was still essentially a collection of books designed to aid the Congress and other government officials in the performance of their duties, by 1900 it had come a long way toward being the national library. After that date it soon became the nation's largest single library, and under the capable leadership of Dr. Herbert Putnam it extended its influence far beyond the needs of Congress or the confines of Washington. Besides the printed catalog cards, its services soon included published bibliographies and other library tools, the maintenance of a national union catalog, the sponsorship of a national and international book exchanges, and many other library innovations. The National library for the blind is centered in the Library of Congress and reaches blind readers throughout the nation with deposit libraries in each state. In 1937, the completion of the new National Archives removed many of the public records and manuscript materials from the Library of Congress, and in 1938 the completion of a new annex relieved the crowded conditions in the forty-year old main building. This new addition more than doubled the available space, but still there was hardly enough room to meet the needs for book preservation and library service that the growing nation demanded. A third major addition, named after President James Madison, was opened in 1983 but it also promises to be filled to overflowing in a few years.

Something of the enormous work done by the Library of Congress can be seen from the statistics related to its operation. Slightly over $200,000,000 was appropriated for the operation of the Library in fiscal 1983. More than half of this sum provides for the employment of over 3,000 people at the Library. This huge staff manages a book collection that numbers over 20,000,000 volumes and provides invaluable services to scholars, members of Congress, the Executive Branch, and citizens. The National Union Catalog, with its records of the location of some 14,000,000 volumes in North American libraries, is a most valuable part of the Library, and the Legislative Reference Service for the congressmen and other government officials provides a most valuable service. Like the British Museum, the Library of Congress is many libraries in one, with, for example, a collection of over 350,000 volumes in Chinese, and an equal number in Russian or about Russia. Its files of newspapers, music scores, motion pictures, and maps are unsurpassed. Its additional services in publications, catalog cards, books and recordings for the blind, cultural programs and exhibitions, and photoduplication make it indeed the cultural center of the nation.

Besides the Library of Congress, the city of Washington and its immediate vicinity contain more than a hundred other government libraries, many of which are notable collections. Two in particular bear the well-deserved titles of "national libraries." The National Library of Medicine, in suburban Bethesda, Maryland, is probably the largest single medical library in the world. Its interesting history began in 1836, with the creation by Congress of the Army Medical Library, but its growth was slow until after the Civil War, when Dr. John Shaw Billings became its librarian. From a miscellaneous group of some 1,800 books in 1865, he developed it into a well-organized library of 50,000 books and 60,000 pamphlets by 1880. He made it one of the major medical libraries of the world, developed a subject card catalog for it, began indexing medical journals, and published a comprehensive bibliography of medical literature. By 1910 the Army Medical Library had over 100,000 volumes, and after moving into its new building in 1962, it reached a position of preeminence among the world's medical libraries, with collections numbering over 2,000,000 volumes in 1983. Serving the nation's physicians and scientists, it has pioneered in the computerized storage and retrieval of medical information as evidenced in MEDLARS, the Medical Literature Analysis and Retrieval System and MEDLINE. From this, it produces the current index of medical literature, Index Medicus, and is able to provide almost instantaneous information on any medical question. The National Agricultural Library has developed out of the Department of Agriculture Library, founded in 1862. It, too, grew slowly at first and had only 7,000 volumes in 1875, but by the early 1980s it had some 1,500,000 volumes and a staff of over 200. Its contents are virtually definitive in subjects relating to agriculture, including botany, chemistry, forestry, and zoology. One of its strongest points is its holdings in agricultural periodicals and the publications of societies, institutes, and government agencies in the field of agriculture from all over the world. It, too, has pioneered in the application of electronics to the storage and dissemination of information and produces indexes and bibliographies of tremendous value to its field.

The rapidly increasing number of government agencies that have come into being in the 20th century have multiplied the number of government libraries in Washington, and they vary widely in subject and size. New departments, such as Commerce and Labor, have libraries in the neighborhood of 500,000 volumes, and even the Department of Housing and Urban Development, created in 1965, has combined earlier housing agency collections with new purchases to build up a 300,000-volume library. Such agencies as the Federal Reserve System, the Federal Aviation Administration, and the Civil Service Commission have libraries of around 100,000 volumes each, while those of the National Archives and the Patent Office are even larger. By contrast, there are dozens of smaller, more specialized agency libraries in the 10,000- to 50,000-volume class, such as those of the Selective Service System, the Naval Intelligence School, and Walter Reed Army Hospital, to mention only a few examples. Possibly one of the most unusual libraries in Washington is that of the Government Printing Office whose nearly 2,000,000 items consist largely of U.S. government publications. These libraries, considered along with older collections, like those serving the Department of State and the Treasury Department, constitute a significant resource for the federal government.

Not all United States government libraries are in Washington. In fact, there are more libraries, and probably more volumes belonging to the government, outside the capital than in it. Some of them are completely independent libraries, others are branches of libraries that have their main collections in Washington. The military services, in particular, have libraries in large numbers, scattered around most of the world. The Military Academy at West Point, New York, has a library that was founded in 1812. The Naval Academy Library at Annapolis was organized in 1845. The Coast Guard Academy has a library at New London, Connecticut, and the new Air Force Academy has a library at Colorado Springs.

From the Civil War onward, the United States military services have attempted to provide libraries for all servicemen, whether in war or peace. In 1861 the U.S. Military Post Library Association was founded to provide reading matter for the soldiers in the field and, although largely voluntary, has been successful. By 1875 nearly every military post and garrison with a permanent staff was supplied with a small library of about 50 to 2,500 volumes, depending upon the number of troops. For example, the first library in the newly acquired territory of Alaska was a garrison collection at Sitka. With benevolent funds, post petty cash, soldiers' reading clubs, and a little official support, these post libraries survived down to the period of World War I. During that war, with the aid of the American Red Cross, the American Library Association, and the YMCA, a renewed effort was made to provide the best library service possible for the men in uniform, and from it developed a system of permanent government-supported libraries for all the military and naval services. After 1920 there were libraries with full-time librarians in all posts, camps, and stations of over 2,500 men, and smaller collections under special service officers at smaller posts. During World War II a wide network of military libraries was developed. Wherever servicemen were stationed--in training camps, at permanent bases, on naval vessels, overseas, or in hospitals--there were books available. At the larger posts, well-stocked and well-staffed libraries of several thousand volumes were maintained, while even the smallest units had package libraries of fifty or a hundred paperbacks, considered expendable and passed from man to man until they were worn out. In 1943 there were over 2,000 post and hospital libraries in the United States alone, requiring more than 600 trained librarians and hundreds of service personnel to staff them. About the same time, the U.S. Navy had over 16,000 library stations serving its various ship and shore units. To meet the need for inexpensive editions of desirable books, the book publishers produced the Armed Services Editions of popular and serious works that were printed and distributed by the hundreds of thousands. Since the war the military library services have continued their important role, providing technical and professional as well as recreational books for all phases of the defense program. The Bureau of Naval Personnel, Library Services Branch, serves over 1,300 libraries for naval units around the world, while hundreds of other base and unit libraries are provided by the Army and Air Force.

Other federal government libraries outside of Washington are operated by a variety of agencies. The Veterans' Administration provides libraries in each of the many Veterans' Hospitals throughout the country. The Department of Agriculture has technical and professional libraries in many places in connection with its experimental stations and research posts. The Atomic Energy Commission has libraries at its research bases, such as Oak Ridge, Tennessee, and the Savannah River Authority in South Carolina. One of the newest research agencies, the National Aeronautics and Space Administration, is rapidly providing library service at its bases in Houston, Texas, Cape Canaveral, Florida, and Hampton, Virginia. The scope and variety of federal agency libraries outside the nation's capital can be exemplified by the state of Washington on the West Coast. In this one state, in the 1960s, there were five Veterans' Hospital Libraries, three U.S. Air Force Base Libraries, five Army installation libraries, five Navy installation libraries, one Fish and Wildlife Service Library, one Department of Commerce Library, and a library at the U.S. Penitentiary on McNeil Island. These were the ones large enough to have professional librarians in charge; they do not include smaller government libraries without full-time librarians.

A new type of government library, or at least one that is under the control of a government agency, the National Archives, is the presidential library, usually located at the birthplace of a former president, and containing books, documents, manuscripts, and momentoes relating to his life and administration. The first of these, possibly the largest and best known, is the Franklin Delano Roosevelt Library at Hyde Park, N.Y., established in 1939. In 1955 the Presidential Libraries Act provided for the government administration of this and other collections honoring former presidents, although most of the funds for the construction of such libraries would have to come from private donations. The Harry S Truman Library at Independence, Missouri, the Dwight D. Eisenhower Library at Abilene, Kansas, and the Lyndon Baines Johnson Library in Austin, Texas, are examples.

All in all, in its hundreds of libraries, the United States government operates the greatest system of organized information in the world today. In fact, its very size and diversity present immense problems, and there was much discussion and study in the 1960s concerning the future of government library services. Various groups, committees, and associations concerned themselves with the problems of space, staff, and availability that trouble all libraries, but also with automation, bibliographic control, cooperation, duplication, photo-reproduction, and the many questions brought on by the astronomical growth of recorded information. Several new agencies were organized to help solve some of these problems. The Clearinghouse for Federal Science and Technical Information was established in 1965, and the

Educational Resources Information Center (ERIC) in 1966. The former attempts to coordinate and disseminate technical bibliographic information, while the latter does the same for educational research. ERIC operates clearinghouses throughout the United States, each specializing in a particular phase of educational information. The Library of Congress has developed a system of Machine-Readable Cataloging (MARC) by which complete catalog cards can be transmitted on electronic tapes and printed out by a receiving library. To coordinate information concerning the use of automation in libraries, LC has set up the Library of Congress Automation Techniques Exchange (LOCATE). In these and many other instances, the government libraries are in the vanguard of library progress in the United States and in the world.

A second major type of library serving government in the United States is the state library. While many state libraries can trace their origins to the early 19th century, they began their most rapid development after 1900. By this date and later, many of the state libraries were taking on other functions designed to serve the state as a whole rather than merely the state officials. In Ohio, a state law of 1882 opened the state library for reference use to all citizens, and in 1896 it began to offer circulation service to the entire state with a few special restrictions. By that time, the services of a typical state library might include a legislative reference division, a library organizing division, and a traveling library service. The latter two functions were added to state library duties in some states, while others created special library commissions for these purposes. The promotion of public library service, with or without financial aid from the state, and the distribution of reading material by mail service, or package libraries to citizens without local libraries became accepted state library functions. The allocation of library extension services varied considerably from state to state, since they could be found under the state library, a library commission, the state department of education, or even a state university.

Development of state library agencies has continued to vary greatly since the 1920s. Some state libraries have grown into major research libraries, such as those of Massachusetts, New York, Illinois, and California. Others have concentrated on public library development and library extension services, and serve as headquarters or coordinating agencies for statewide library networks. The Pennsylvania State Library at Harrisburg heads up a statewide system of four research centers and thirty district library centers. Indiana's State Library at Indianapolis is an example of a central research center connected by teletype with county libraries throughout the state. Hawaii's public libraries are all in one statewide library system, headed up by a central library and processing center in Honolulu. Maryland, on the other hand, has a library extension division under the State Department of Education, which in turn contracts with the Enoch Pratt Free Library of Baltimore to serve as a state library center. The Library Services Act of 1956, and later acts of the Federal Government designed to aid library development, have had tremendous impact on the states' official libraries. The federal funds for library aid have generally been made available through a central state agency, and this has usually been the state library. These federal funds have been wonderful assets, of course, but they have also brought problems. Their allocation and use called for more staff members, often difficult to obtain. Some funds had to be used for surveys, to determine the greatest areas of need and how the federal funds could best be employed. Other funds went for equipment and supplies necessary to handle the great influx of books, particularly where they came into centralized processing centers. Some funds went for demonstration libraries and bookmobiles. Most, however, went for books and materials that went directly into use in the state's public libraries. Increased federal funds often brought increased, matching state funds, and thus library finances expanded rapidly in a few years. By 1962 the states were spending three times as much as the federal government for library service, not including county and municipal library appropriations.

In addition to the central state libraries, the 20th century has seen the growth of many specialized libraries at the state level, generally designed to aid the services of a state governmental agency. A few of these had been established before 1900, such as Massachusetts' Department of Labor and Industries Library in 1869. Most state departmental libraries, however, began in the 1920s and later, but as of the 1980s there were a wide variety of state agency libraries serving public welfare departments, departments of education or public health, state museums, highway commissions, insurance commissions, mineral boards, and even geological surveys. Most of these are small, but a few are in the 20,000- to 30,000-volume class. Even on the local level some government collections, such as county law libraries and county medical libraries, are found. In the larger cities, metropolitan departments of health, police, and welfare sometimes have official libraries for the use of public employees in those fields. Thus, at all levels of government, the necessity of organized collections of information is felt, and specialized libraries are the answer. Whether centralized or decentralized, statewide library systems or local library units, the development of government libraries proceeds at a rapid pace, and as in almost all other fields of library service, demand often exceeds supply. All possibilities of cooperation, automation, and bibliographic control are being studied and considered by the nation's government librarians in their attempts to provide improved service.

One other type of governmental library found in the United States is the international library, serving the United Nations or other multi-nation organizations. The United Nations headquarters library in New York City is the Dag Hammarskjold Library which was founded in 1947. Its contents, in five official languages of the United Nations plus many others, are strongly related to international law and relations, plus history and the social sciences. One of its strongest holdings is in the history and publications of the League of Nations. It also contains the Woodrow Wilson Memorial Library, particularly devoted to the history of peace efforts in the modern world.

Special Libraries in the United States

Although all libraries are specialized to a certain extent, the special library in the United States is in a category of its own and deserves separate attention. Two types of special libraries--schools and government agencies--have already been considered, but there are a large number and a wide variety of libraries that contain some of the most valuable single collections in the country. Where the general collection stops and the specialized collection begins is difficult to delineate exactly, but for the purposes of this chapter the term "special library" can be defined as that library which is restricted in content and, usually, also in clientele served.

On the whole, special libraries tend to be smaller than general ones, and the average special library is usually in the 10,000-volume range rather than the 100,000. Furthermore, the special library usually differs considerably in size and training of staff, in hours of service, general organization, and materials handled. It can often experiment with new ideas, new methods, new machines, and new services more easily than the older, larger, and more standardized libraries. Thus, it is fortunate for the library profession that special libraries exist, not only for the services that they render but also for their leadership in the library world generally.

Special libraries may be divided into two types: those that are independent in themselves and those that are part of, or related to, general public or university libraries. Also, they may be classified into three other groups: professional, business, and government. The more general governmental libraries have already been discussed, but there are many smaller technical libraries in governmental agencies that are special libraries in the fullest meaning of the term. Professional libraries are those that serve professional schools and organizations. Business libraries include a wide variety of libraries, while early medical societies with libraries included the Worcester, Massachusetts, Medical Society, and the Boston Society for Medical Improvement. Each of these had collections of 5,000 volumes or more by 1875, as did the Rhode Island Hospital of Providence, the Cincinnati Hospital, and the Massachusetts General Hospital in Boston. There were also the medical libraries that were part of general collections, such as the 11,000 volumes in the Boston Public Library, or the 5,000 volumes on medicine in the Boston Athenaeum. It should be noted that the preponderance of medical libraries was in the Northeast.

By 1875 there were also a few libraries in public institutions such as prisons, reformatories, and insane asylums. For the most part, they were the result of gifts from charitable individuals and groups, and were cared for by interested inmates. A library in the State Penitentiary at Philadelphia was begun in 1829 with a gift of books, and that at Sing Sing in New York started with a donation from Governor William H. Seward in 1840. One prison library, at Alton, Illinois, began with books donated by the inmates of another prison at Charlestown, Massachusetts, in 1846. By 1867 thirteen prisons reported libraries with an average of about 1,500 volumes each. Sing Sing had the largest at that time with some 4,000 volumes, but thirteen states reported appropriations of small funds for books in their prison libraries. Ten years later the number had risen to forty, and most of them reported their contents as well used. Most of the titles included were classed as "entertaining," although a fair proportion were "instructive," or "religious." The reformatory movement for young criminals began in New York in 1825, although most of the similar institutions in other states came after 1850. In 1875, of fifty-six reformatories in the United States, forty-nine reported libraries ranging from 150 volumes to 4,000, for an average of about 1,000. Again, the largest was in New York, this time in the New York City House of Refuge. Both prisons and reformatories reported heavy use of their books by all the inmates who could read. Besides the small funds received in a few states, the institutional libraries depended almost entirely on gifts for their acquisitions and on inmates for their staffs. There were a few libraries reported in 1875 in hospitals for the insane, but they were apparently for staff use rather than for inmates.

One other 19th-century special library worthy of mention is the newspaper library. This institution tended to take two forms: the "morgue," a specialized file of clippings of past newspaper issues, topically arranged and forming something of an index to the paper as well as an information file, and the regular research library for the use of staff reporters and editors. The *New York Tribune* had a research library before 1850, and by 1874 it contained over 5,000 volumes. Its morgue, which was begun in 1860, was largely biographical and designed to provide quick information on the lives and careers of all important and newsworthy people in New York and the nation. The New York *Herald* had a well-established reference library of some 8,000 volumes in 1870, but its morgue was not begun until later. Two other newspaper libraries, established shortly after the Civil War, were those of the *Boston Herald* and the *New York Times*. Most newspapers in larger cities followed suit in the late 19th and early 20th centuries, and the morgue in particular became standard equipment for the average newspaper office. The research library, on the other hand, was confined to the very largest papers, and for smaller ones a few standard reference works usually sufficed.

The period after 1875 and before World War I was one of slow growth in the special library field, but one in which the special library came into its own and was recognized as an institution in itself. Although in types of libraries and fields of service it varied more than those in any other library group, it was recognized that the special libraries, whether large or small, part of a larger system or not, had something in common, and so in 1909 the Special Libraries Association was founded. The formation of such a group was first proposed at the Bretton Woods Conference of the American Library Association, when some forty-five special library representatives followed the suggestion of John Cotton Dana in joining together. After its formation, the Special Libraries Association took a prominent part in promoting the interests of special libraries and in giving leadership and direction to the profession.

Although there had been a few small "company libraries" in existence before 1910, it was not until after that date that the special library field was enlarged to any great extent by business and industrial libraries. At first, their libraries were largely collections of company records and studies made by firm specialists, but soon they began to include specialized reference materials, technical journals, and general scientific works of value to the particular industry. In the East, some of the early industrial libraries were those of the American Brass Company, the United Gas Improvement Company, and the New York Merchants Association. The National City Bank of New York and Harvey Fisk and Sons were among the earliest banks and financial houses to provide research libraries for their employees and customers. In smaller cities, Chambers of Commerce and other businessmen's associations sometimes provided business libraries for their members, and public libraries also began to provide "business and technical" branches in some instances.

Among all special libraries, one of the most valuable is the endowed reference library, of which the nation is most fortunate in having a reasonably large number. The trend was already beginning in the 19th century, but even more have been added in the 20th. Although these libraries may not be limited in subject content, they are not public in either support or general use, usually limited to a restricted clientele of scholars and special students. Two of these, the Lenox and Astor libraries, proved instrumental in connection with the formation of the New York Public Library, but another most valuable one is the Folger Shakespeare Library in Washington, D. C. Henry Clay Folger began collecting Shakespeare material as a youth at Amherst College in the late 19th century, and by 1909 his collection was noted as the largest in the United States. A few years later it was called the largest Shakespearean collection in the world, and, before his death, he arranged to have it housed in an appropriate building and eventually opened to research by serious scholars. This library was opened in 1933, containing, besides books and pamphlets, many manuscripts, documents, relics, curios, drawings, paintings, prints, medals, coins, tapestries, playbills, prompt-books, and even furniture and costumes relating to Shakespeare and the time in which he lived. Today, the Folger Library contains over 260,000 volumes, not counting its thousands of other prized possessions.

Chicago is fortunate in having two major research libraries, the Crerar and Newberry libraries. The Newberry Reference Library was founded in 1887, by Walter L. Newberry, as a public reference library in the humanities and social sciences. The John Crerar Library was begun by its namesake in 1895, as a scientific library to balance and complete the work begun by the Newberry collection. In New York City, the Pierpont Morgan Library is particularly strong in the history of the book, incunabula, and Americana. On the West Coast, the Henry E. Huntington Library in San Marino, California, is one of the finest rare book collections in the world. Its 425,000 volumes and over 1,000,000 manuscripts make it a scholar's paradise, and much of the research completed in its resources is published in the _Huntington Library Quarterly_. Also in California, on the campus of Stanford University, is the Hoover Library on War, Revolution and Peace, with its hundreds of thousands of books, pamphlets, government documents, newspapers, and periodicals dealing largely with the history of the 20th century. Elsewhere in the nation are such endowed collections as the Linda Hall Library of Science and Technology in Kansas City, and the Lloyd Library and Museum in Cincinnati. The former has some 350,000 volumes while the latter collection contains about 275,000 books and pamphlets. The Robert Browning Collection on the Baylor University campus in Waco, Texas, is an example of a very specialized collection, while the William L. Clements Library of American History at the University of Michigan in Ann Arbor is much broader in content. Its 40,000 volumes and 200,000 manuscripts, together with an appropriate building, were given to the University in 1923. Among more recent libraries of this type is the Marshall Research Library, opened in Lexington, Virginia, in 1964. This collection, in memory of General George C. Marshall, focuses on its subject in particular and the diplomatic and military history of the United States in the 20th century in general.

By 1920 or shortly after, most of the university libraries

had become so large and unwieldy that they had begun to break up into departmental or special college libraries. This trend was noticeable in a few cases in the 19th century with the formation of law, theology, and medical libraries on a few campuses, but in the 20th century it extended to other subject fields. A reverse trend can be noticed after World War II, with some universities returning their departmental collections to a new central library, or at least attempting to do so. The special library on the campus, however, seems to be well established, and with the proliferation of literature in the special fields, there seems to be no end to them. The University of Michigan, for example, has some twenty-eight special or departmental collections on its campus, and it is only about average in this respect among the larger universities. Its special libraries range in subject from architecture to transportation, and from a few thousand in the smaller collections to more than 100,000 in the medical library and over 300,000 in the law library. Besides these special libraries, moreover, there are also many special collections inside the main university library, some of them running into thousands of volumes. This situation is duplicated on a hundred other campuses, and it is obvious that the special library is a definite part of the university library program.

The few industrial research libraries established before World War I have been followed in more recent years by thousands of similar establishments. The technical and scientific revolution that accompanied and followed World War II has particularly emphasized the value of research to the industrial firm, and the company library has become a necessity. The E. I. du Pont de Nemours Company not only has seven technical libraries in its headquarters city of Wilmington, Delaware, but also has branch libraries in Du Pont plants in fifteen other cities. The libraries in Wilmington range in size from a few thousand volumes to over 57,000 in the Central Research Library. Among the specialties in the Du Pont libraries are not only such subjects as chemistry, physics, engineering, business, and manufacturing, but also biology, bacteriology, biochemistry, and even a legal research library. Westinghouse Electric Corporation has four libraries in Pittsburgh, with another in East Pittsburgh. General Electric Company has five libraries in Schenectady, with forty others scattered among its plants elsewhere. These are representative of the larger industrial library systems, and there are hundreds of examples of companies with a single research library. For example, the Corning Glass

Works of Corning, New York, has a library of some 20,000 volumes; General Tire and Rubber Company of Akron, Ohio, has 8,000; and the Allied Chemical Corporation of Morristown, New Jersey, has some 11,000. Although the preponderance of special libraries remains in the East and Middle West, there are others in all parts of the country. The Texas Instruments Company of Dallas has four libraries containing some 20,000 volumes between them, and the Humble Oil and Refining Company of Houston not only has a main library of some 25,000 volumes, but five others including a law library, a geological library, a medical library, and an employee relations library. In central North Carolina, a Research Triangle grew up in the 1960s and there are today almost a score of research agencies, complete with technical library facilities, where only piney woods existed a few years ago. The growth of industry on the West Coast, from San Diego to Seattle, has been accompanied by the development of industrial libraries, and there are at least twenty-five major ones in the Los Angeles area alone.

If industry has come to appreciate the research library, the fields of banking and insurance are not less responsive to the value of books in the conduct of their business. Banking and insurance companies were among the first to develop special libraries, but again their widespread use has come only since the 1940s. New York City is a center of such libraries, and those of Chase Manhattan Bank (40,000 volumes); Dun and Bradstreet (17,000); Bankers' Trust Company (12,000); and the American Bankers' Association (20,000) all bear this out. Among the insurance firms, Equitable Life Assurance Society has a library of nearly 40,000 items and New York Life Insurance Company has over 25,000. However, this type of library is not limited to the Northeast, and such firms as the Prudential Insurance Company of Chicago, the National Bank of Detroit, the Bank of America in San Francisco, and the Southwestern Life Insurance Company of Dallas all have research libraries for their employees and clients. In some cases, insurance firms and agents join together to support libraries, as in the case of the Insurance Society of Boston with its 60,000-volume library and the Insurance Library Association of Atlanta with 3,500.

Newspaper libraries have come far since its early beginnings in the 19th century, and today there are scores of them ranging in size up to many thousands of volumes. The New York Times has a reference library of some 38,000 volumes, plus some 10,000 maps, 3,000,000 prints, and a morgue of over 1,500,000 clippings. In Boston, the Globe has a library of 15,000 volumes, 350,000 pictures, and 3,000,000 clippings, while in Chicago the Tribune has a library of 22,000 volumes besides its morgue of clippings. Elsewhere, the book collections in the newspaper libraries may be smaller but the collections of clippings and pictures are constantly growing. In recent years, the newspaper library has been joined by the magazine headquarters library. For example, Time, Incorporated has a headquarters library of some 85,000 volumes; Newsweek has some 20,000 volumes with nearly 200,000 other additional items of information on file; McGraw-Hill Publishing Company has a library of some 30,000 volumes for its several publications; and the Curtis Publishing Company has libraries in both Philadelphia and New York. Other popular magazines, such as McCall's, Popular Science and Reader's Digest, to name only a few, have libraries at their headquarters offices. This system of research and reference libraries to provide quick and accurate information on persons, places, and events is considered most important in the operation of magazines, particularly for the news weeklies.

Not the least important of modern special libraries are those of national and international organizations. Professional societies, educational associations, labor organizations, and many other types of associations have developed headquarters libraries for the use of their professional staffs, visiting members, and even for the public. Some of these, as for example the Engineering Societies Library of New York with its 190,000 volumes, not only provide a magnificent library, but carry on publishing activities as well. The Engineering Societies Library began the Engineering Index, now compiled and published by its own firm. A few others, among many such libraries in New York City alone, are the Explorers' Club with its 20,000 books and pamphlets; the Family Service Association with 3,000 volumes; the International Ladies' Garment Workers' Union Library with 17,000 volumes; and the National Association of Manufacturers 'Library with about 20,000. Chicago has the National Association of Real Estate Boards Library, the American Library Association headquarters library, and the National Livestock and Meat Board Library, among others. Washington, D.C., has its share of associational and institute libraries, and still others are to be found in almost all of the states in the union.

Hospital libraries and prison libraries have also come

into their own in recent years. Particularly in the hospital field, the number and size of libraries have increased considerably since 1945. Both technical libraries for the use of doctors and nurses and popular libraries for the patients have become standard items in the larger hospitals. Chicago, for example, has at least forty-four medically related libraries, including those in hospitals, medical, and nursing schools, and others in various association headquarters. The Children's Memorial Hospital there not only has a doctors' library and a nurses' library but a children's library as well. Prison libraries, led by those of the federal prison system, have grown in importance and size, with many professional librarians employed. The larger libraries in correctional institutions range from 20,000 to 30,000 volumes. In addition to its value as a recreational and educational aid in the reform program, the library is now being studied for its inspirational and psycho-therapeutic value. Both the American Correctional Association and the Association of Hospital and Institution Libraries are concerned about the quality of prison and reformatory libraries, and the two together have drawn up standards for such institutional libraries. A substantial impetus to correctional library development came in 1977 when the Supreme Court ruled that prisoners have a constitutional right to access to legal resources. This and other court decisions, combined with the library profession's growing concern for prison libraries, has vastly increased the size and scope of most correctional facility libraries.

Special libraries in general, and more particularly those in the technical and scientific fields, were faced in the 1960s with the tremendous task of controlling the vast amounts of information pouring from the presses and processing machines all over the world. Even in the relatively restricted field of an individual industry, the information has increased in geometric proportions in recent years, and the special librarian and information specialist have the task of organizing this material for quick and orderly use by scientists and researchers. Time is money for the industrial concern, and the quicker the information can be retrieved from the books and files, the more valuable it is to the company. Add to the quantity of material available the fact that it comes in many varieties of format, and it is easy to see what a task special librarianship can be. Information in a technical library can be in the usual form of books, periodicals, and films, but it can also be in the form of maps, oilwell logs, meter readings, punched cards, perforated tapes, sound-recorded tapes, and other electronically recorded materials, as well as manuscript, typed, processed, or filmed reports. The tasks of organizing all of this information call for new techniques, and the special librarian has risen to the challenge with a variety of devices for information storage and retrieval. Automated processes in library routines and services were first employed, in most cases, by special libraries, and special libraries in general have taken the lead in exploring new ideas and services.

Closely allied to, or perhaps encompassing, the field of special librarianship is the field of documentation or information science. Documentation has been defined as "the complex of activities required in the communication of specialized information including the preparation, reproduction, collection, analysis, organization and dissemination...." It is generally accepted to mean the storage and retrieval of technical information, but it can also be applied to all recorded or preserved knowledge, in which case it would include all of library service itself. The term "documentation" seems to have been replaced in the late 1960s by "information science" as best describing the multiple connotations to be included. The American Documentation Institute, organized in 1937, concerned itself largely with microreproduction in its early years, but broadened its interests considerably during World War II with the flood of technical and intelligence reports that failed to fit neatly into the librarian's usual processes. Through the journal *American Documentation*, the Institute provided the library world with research and interpretation during documentation's infancy and adolescence. Now with the Institute's new name of American Society for Information Science, the same services are continued and enlarged, and it is joined by the A.L.A.'s new information Science and Automation Division and the *Journal of Library Automation* to provide the extended coverage which the subject deserves.

The Special Libraries Association continues to be one of the most effective and productive groups of its kind, and it has in recent years been joined by several other groups in even more restricted library areas. These include the Music Library Association, the Theater Library Association, the American Association of Law Libraries, the Medical Library Association, the American Theological Library Association, the Association of Jewish Libraries, and the Catholic Library Association, among others.

Canadian Libraries

Significant progress in the development of Canadian libraries came only in the last quarter of the 19th century. New colleges and universities were established, particularly in the western provinces; more attention was paid to school libraries; and legislation by the provinces provided for the formation of municipally supported free public libraries. The Ontario Free Libraries Act of 1882 authorized towns to levy taxes for free libraries, and by 1900 there were some 390 public libraries listed in the province. However, most of these were small holdovers from the mechanics' institutes and association libraries. In 1895 the partially subsidized mechanics' institutes were given the choice of either becoming free public libraries, with support, or joining the subscription-type association libraries. This resulted in more free public libraries, and by 1900 interest in libraries had reached the point where the Ontario Library Association was formed. Portland, New Brunswick, formed a free public library in 1882, and St. John, in the same province, followed the next year. The St. John Free Public Library started in two rooms in the City Market Building, where it remained until a Carnegie building was erected in 1904. In Halifax, Nova Scotia, the Mechanics' Library, formed in 1831, was given to the city in 1864 and combined with an earlier circulating library to form the Halifax Citizens' Library, housed in the City Hall. In the western provinces, British Columbia enacted a public library law in 1891, and the libraries were begun in Vancouver and Victoria. Elsewhere, from Ontario to the Pacific, subscription libraries remained the general rule before 1900, and several of them were quite large and successful. Among new colleges founded during this period were Dalhousie University in Halifax, begun in 1867; Acadia University in Wolfville, Nova Scotia, in 1877; Ontario Agricultural College in 1874; and McMaster University in Toronto in 1887. Each of them had libraries of only a few thousand volumes at the turn of the century. McGill University in Montreal, founded in 1855, with about 100,000 volumes, and Laval University in Quebec with about the same, were Canada's largest university collections at this time.

Public library development was faster in the early 20th century, thanks to Andrew Carnegie's philanthropy, improved transportation, and heightened interest in education. Between 1901 and 1917, 125 Carnegie library buildings were constructed in Canada, the great majority of them public libraries and the remainder on college campuses. A survey of public library facilities in 1909 found Ontario fairly active, with 131 free public libraries and 234 association libraries. Together they made over 1,000,000 volumes available to the people of the province, the Public Library of Toronto being the largest with its 150,000 volumes. In Quebec, a public library was founded in Montreal in 1903, but it was initially limited to technical and scientific works. Quebec City had the Fraser-Hickson Institute, an endowed public library with some 38,000 volumes, of which 13,000 were in French. Elsewhere in the province, there were library associations, usually small, serving the English population, and religion-oriented parish libraries concentrating on French materials. In the Maritime Provinces, there were public libraries in Halifax, Nova Scotia, and Saint John, New Brunswick. The western provinces were beginning or enlarging public libraries, particularly in Winnipeg, Edmonton, Victoria, and Vancouver. An interesting development after 1900 was the formation of the McLennan Traveling Libraries, privately endowed but serviced by McGill University. This service, beginning in 1901, loaned collections of thirty to forty books for a fee of $4 for three months, including transportation costs. It was available anywhere in the Dominion, to almost any responsible group or individual, from small colleges to mining camps, even including some theological collections for ministers and churches. Some of the western provinces offered similar traveling libraries as a free public service, such as the Saskatchewan Traveling Library Service, begun in 1914.

By the 1920s another mild spurt of progress took place in Canadian public libraries. Trained librarians began to appear in the larger libraries, and branches were established. Broader public library acts were passed, with provincial aid and encouragement to a small degree. Toronto still had the largest public library in Canada; it moved into a new central building in 1930, and served some 500,000 people with its sixteen branches, including the first branch exclusively for children in the British Empire. Other large public libraries in Ontario were those at Ottawa, Hamilton, and London, but despite the fact that this one province contained over half the public libraries in Canada, there was still some forty percent of its population not reached by them. Quebec lagged in public libraries in the 1920s and 1930s, although the Montreal Public Library opened branches, and in the English-speaking suburb of Westmount a public library flourished and opened a children's room in 1922. Also in Montreal, the Bibliothèque Saint Sulpice, an old and valuable library formed in 1845, was given to the city in 1931, opening as a public reference library. In Nova Scotia, the Halifax Public Library had 89,000 volumes in 1927, while in New Brunswick the St. John Free Public Library had some 45,000 volumes. Two experiments in regional library service came with Carnegie funds in the early 1930s. One of these, on Prince Edward Island, resulted in the formation of a province-wide library service, centered in the town libraries of Charlottetown and Summerside. The other, in the Fraser River Valley of British Columbia, was also successful, demonstrating the feasibility of regional libraries by serving 40,000 people over several hundred square miles with seven branches and a book-truck. In British Columbia's major city, the Vancouver Public Library had its first public libraries in 1921 and opened its first branch in 1922. Its collection numbered some 40,000 volumes by 1927, and the provincial capital city of Victoria had a library that was slightly larger. The inland provinces of Manitoba, Alberta, and Saskatchewan had good public library services in their major cities of Winnipeg, Calgary, Edmonton, and Regina, but the smaller towns continued to be served by subscription libraries or by traveling libraries from the provincial capitals. In 1930 a survey of Canadian public library services, conducted by John Ridington, librarian of the University of British Columbia, reported a general lack of interest in promoting public libraries except in the provinces of Ontario and British Columbia. The report also noted public apathy on the subject of libraries, but that where services were available, as in the Fraser Valley demonstration, libraries were well used and appreciated. The recommendations of the survey were unfortunately slow in being implemented due to the Depression and World War II.

Since 1945, however, the public library scene in Canada has shown remarkable progress. One of the suggestions of the Ridington Survey had called for the creation of regional libraries for more efficient service to small town and rural areas. This form of library has proven particularly adaptable to the Canadian provinces and has been widely used in almost all of them. Ontario continues to be the most library-minded province, but it was being challenged in the 1960s by several others. New library laws have provided for multiple unit services, and cooperation between large and small libraries have extended public library service to over seventy-five percent of all Canadians. Local taxes continue to provide most of the support for public libraries, and this became more generous in the 1960s in most cases. There is some provincial support, but virtually none from the Dominion government.

The Metropolitan Toronto Library moved into its magnificent new library building in 1977. Hailed world wide as a model of library construction, the system remains Canada's largest. Toronto also cooperates in serving the surrounding areas under the coordination of the Metropolitan Toronto Library Board. One exception to the essentially local funding pattern for public library service in Canada came in Quebec, where in 1960 the whole public library system was reorganized under provincial auspices. The implementation of the new plan completely transformed library service in Quebec and dramatically increased the quality and extent of library services to the Province's citizens.

Other extremely impressive library systems are located in large metropolitan areas throughout Canada, such as those in Winnipeg and Vancouver. In the 1980's most Canadian libraries remain tied to local funding, but there has been increased provincial funding for library support. The Province of Saskatchewan has been particularly agressive in providing direct services such as centralized cataloging and assistance in collection development.

In the early years of the 20th century, Canada's university and college libraries were, like their counterparts in the United States, usually small, poorly organized and staffed, and of doubtful value to their students and faculties. A few of the older institutions had book rarities, often the gifts of private libraries, but these too were hardly usable. In Ontario, Queen's University at Kingston had about 40,000 volumes in 1909, and the University of Toronto Library was slightly larger. McGill University in Montreal and Laval University in Quebec had collections of more than 100,000 volumes, but Dalhousie University in Halifax had only about 20,000 volumes. One of Canada's oldest colleges, King's College at Windsor, Nova Scotia, was destroyed by a fire in 1920, and when it was reestablished in 1924 it moved to Halifax and joined with Dalhousie. Their combined libraries came to only about 30,000 volumes. Even in the late 1920s university libraries were still relatively small, numbering their books in the tens of thousands, with the exception of the University of Toronto with some 210,000 in 1927, and Queen's University with 175,000 volumes. Several new colleges were added during this era, including the University of Western Ontario and most of the provincial universities in the West, but in addition to inadequate collections on the individual campuses, there was too little cooperation between libraries, and many of them depended more on their neighbors in the United States than on each other.

The great growth in university libraries has come since World War II, and this growth has been not only in size but in numbers of institutions, new buildings, and new approaches to library service. Among the new institutions, Ontario alone has four, all founded since 1945: Guelph, Trent, Brock, and Carleton. Each has constructed its library along the latest lines and taken advantage of the best techniques introduced in both British and American universities. Quebec has, among others, the University of Sherbrooke, founded in 1954, with a library of 220,000 volumes in 1968; and Sir George Williams University at Montreal, founded in 1948, had a library of some 100,000 volumes two decades later. A recent study of Canadian university libraries indicates that only one, the University of Toronto with its nearly 2,000,000 volumes, approaches a true research collection, but there are several others that are rapidly developing. Laval University and the University of Montreal each have about 500,000 volumes in their libraries, and the University of Ottawa has about 350,000. In the western provinces, the libraries of the Universities of British Columbia and Alberta have about 500,000 volumes each, while those of Saskatchewan and Manitoba are somewhat smaller. A number of new university libraries were constructed in the 1960s, including Acadia, Dalhousie, University of New Brunswick, Toronto, McGill, and Laval. In addition to the universities, there are also regional and specialized colleges, plus those with religious affiliations, especially in Quebec. Junior and community colleges are not as numerous as in the United States, but there are a few. Cooperation among university libraries has taken the form of interlibrary loans, teletype, and in the metropolitan areas particularly, a few tentative moves have been taken toward selective purchasing to avoid duplication of rare and expensive materials. The Canadian Association of College and University Libraries takes a lead in enabling its member libraries to work together and solve mutual problems. Since one of the most important problems is staff, the work of Canada's two library schools at McGill and Toronto was supplemented by a new one at the University of British Columbia in 1962 and one at Dalhousie University in 1969. By 1983 there were seven accredited Canadian Library Schools.

Canada's school libraries in general also have lagged

until recent years. Ontario's schools have had small libraries throughout the 20th century, but only since 1945 have there been serious efforts to staff and use them properly. In 1916 the western province of Alberta reported that ninety percent of its 2,300 schools had libraries, but the average size was only about 50 volumes. In 1927 Manitoba's 1,800 public schools had libraries ranging from 50 to 400 volumes each. Even in 1965, Quebec's 1,043 school libraries averaged less than 500 volumes each. On the other hand, many schools have been at least partially served by public libraries, either by deposits in the schools or by direct service after school hours. In fact, in several of the provinces the public libraries are administered from the provincial departments of education. In British Columbia, for example, the Public Library Commission is directly under the provincial Minister of Education. Thus, cooperation between public and school libraries is excellent, as it should be. Recent developments in school library service in Canada are similar to those in the United States, with concern for centralized libraries in the elementary schools, multi-media centers in the high schools, and with making school and public library resources interchangeably useful.

Government libraries in Canada consist of those of the Dominion and those of the Provinces. In the early years of the 20th century the nearest thing to a national library was the Library of Parliament, which had some 250,000 volumes. However, this was largely a legal and legislative reference library and served only the Parliament members and their employees, together with a few other government officials. In 1953 the National Library of Canada was created and in 1967 it moved into an entirely new and modern building. It serves as the legal depository for all copyrighted materials appearing in Canada, and as the bibliographic center for the nation. It also coordinates interlibrary activities among Canada's research libraries and maintains a union catalog of the holdings of some 200 major libraries. In 1978 its bookstock had already passed the 1,000,000 mark. There is also a National Science Library of some 700,000 volumes in Ottawa, the outgrowth of a national science research center established after World War II, and the Canadian Supreme Court Library serves as a national law library. There is still a large and active Parliamentary Library of nearly 500,000 volumes as well as many specialized libraries of the various government departments. There are at least fifty-seven government libraries in Ottawa, and about the same number situated elsewhere in the Dominion, mostly small research collections. The Department of Agriculture in particular has research station libraries all over Canada.

Each of the provinces also has one or more provincial libraries. There is usually one major collection known as the Provincial Library, and/or the Legislative Reference Library, a Supreme Court Library, and several departmental collections. The Provincial Libraries range in size from Prince Edward Island's 10,000 volumes to British Columbia's 380,000. Alberta, for example, has a Provincial Library of some 75,000 volumes, an Attorney General's Library, a Department of Mines and Minerals Library, and a Department of Education Library, among others. Provincial Libraries, especially in the western provinces, often provide mail library service, or rotating book collections for citizens outside the reach of public libraries. Reference service by mail or telephone is another valuable Provincial Library service.

After academic libraries, special libraries are probably the most rapidly growing book collections in both size and numbers since World War II. Earlier years had seen a moderate development in theological libraries, historical collections, and governmental research units, but in recent years there have been added many industrial, banking and private research libraries. Law and medical society libraries are among the oldest and most active special libraries, with many of them dating well back into the 19th century. The Advocates Library in Montreal, for example, was founded in 1849, and contained some 70,000 volumes in 1970. In British Columbia, the Law Society has major libraries in Victoria, Vancouver, and New Westminster, with smaller courthouse libraries at fourteen other points in the province. Victoria's Medical Society Library was founded in 1922, and its counterpart in Vancouver dates from 1906. Throughout Canada, hospital libraries have been formed, particularly since 1945, and they often provide separate book collections for doctors, nurses, and patients. Vancouver, to use one major western city as an example, has two major hospital libraries, two nursing libraries, the British Columbia Medical Centre Library, the Department of Health and Welfare Library, and the University of British Columbia Medical Faculty Library among its medical research facilities. Another type of special library is the headquarters collection of a national association. There are several of these in Canada's eastern cities. Montreal contains those of the Canadian Jewish Congress, the Canadian Red Cross

Society, and the National Film Board, and Toronto has libraries of the Royal Astronomical Society of Canada, the Canadian Manufacturers' Association, and the Canadian Association for Adult Education, among others.

Among industrial libraries, those of insurance, mining, and chemical firms are the largest. Sun Insurance Company of Montreal has a library of some 80,000 volumes, and the Aluminum Company of Canada has a library of 70,000 items at Kingston, Ontario. Atomic Energy of Canada, Ltd., in Toronto, has a research collection of over 60,000 volumes, while out in the new petroleum fields of the West, British American Oil Company has a 15,000-volume library at Calgary, Alberta. One of the largest Canadian newspaper libraries is that of the *Toronto Star*. Not the least important of Canada's special libraries are those connected with the universities, either as departmental or institute libraries, or as special collections in main libraries. For example, one of the largest collections in braille is the Charles A. Crane Memorial Library at the University of British Columbia.

Thus, one can see in the history of Canadian libraries a long era of slow growth followed by a few decades of rapid change. There are still millions of Canadians without good public libraries, and hundreds of schools with inadequate supplies of books and teaching materials. College libraries are small, and most university collections have far to go before meeting the needs of modern research. But on the positive side there is the new National Library, the mounting financial support for libraries, the active library associations, and the willingness to break with tradition and try new methods as illustrated in the Toronto materials center. Canada is in the fortunate position of being able to benefit from the library developments of both Europe and the United States; her bilingual status can be a major asset instead of a handicap. Her resources, both economic and human, are relatively limitless, and the future of libraries there can be just as hopeful. Canada will be an interesting nation to watch in the future development of libraries and information control.

Latin American Libraries

Library development in Latin America over the last century is extremely difficult to characterize in a concise manner. For, unlike the history of libraries in Canada and the United States, where development has been rapid and fairly even, the history of Latin American library development is widely varied from country to country; indeed, it is so uneven as to defy generalization. Some countries of Latin America--Brazil for instance--appear to have made the transition from underdeveloped countries to industrialized nations with burgeoning economies and flourishing libraries. The majority of Latin American countries, however, remain in the pre-industrial stage and little money has been available for the development of social institutions like libraries. Then too, the unstable and varied nature of government in the various countries dictates wide variations in the nature and extent of library service available to the people. Given these conditions, the following discussion can only be suggestive of the complex and rapidly changing nature of Latin American libraries.

The greatest library development has taken place in the ABC countries--Argentina, Brazil, and Chile. Argentina in particular has made excellent progress in the 20th century. There were only 49 public libraries in all of Argentina in 1915, but in the 1970s there were some 115 major public libraries, with over 1,700 public library outlets, including the smaller "bibliotecas populares." Altogether these public collections contain some 10,000,000 volumes. Similarly, book collections in 24,000 Argentine public schools place another 7,000,000 volumes at public disposal. Buenos Aires has over 70 major libraries, ranging from the Biblioteca Nacional with its 700,000 volumes, and the National Congressional Library with 300,000 down to many small academic and special collections. Public libraries are under the direction of the Commission for the Protection of Public Libraries, formed in 1870. One interesting feature of Latin American libraries is that banks and newspapers often have libraries open for public use. In Buenos Aires, the Central Bank has a library of 42,000 volumes, and the newspaper La Prensa has a collection of 75,000 volumes, also open to the public. Other interesting and important libraries of Buenos Aires include the Biblioteca Nacional de Maestros, an education and reference library of some 100,000 volumes, and a public art library. Government libraries include the Department of Agriculture Library of some 75,000 volumes; the Ministry of Foreign Affairs Library, almost as large, and such smaller ones as those of the Department of Treasury and of the Bureau of Geology and Mines.

Outside the capital city, there are major libraries at the larger universities, such as those of Córdoba, Santa Fe, and Tucuman, and also some significant public libraries. The university libraries, like those in Europe, have separate departmental and institute libraries outside the main collection, and these constitute both an asset and an administrative problem. The largest of the university libraries is at Santa Fe, with over 1,500,000 volumes in all its collections. The Juan Alvarez Public Library in Rosario is one of the largest provincial public libraries, with some 120,000 volumes, but there are other public libraries in each of the provinces and in most of the larger towns. In 1964 the Argentine National Commission on Education recommended the extension of school libraries to the elementary level, and much progress has been made in this direction. Leadership in the Argentine library world stems from the School of Library Science at the University of Buenos Aires. A center for research in bibliography, information science, and library science has been established there with the aid of Unesco. Today, Argentine libraries are making progress on all levels and the other nations of Latin America are looking to them for leadership.

Brazil's libraries are also progressive, but vast areas to be served and millions of uneducated people make the task much more difficult. Much of Brazil's hinterland in the Amazon valley is still unexplored and inhabited by primitive Indian peoples. Since the early 19th century, however, Brazil has had major libraries in her larger cities, and Rio de Janeiro in particular has been the home of several internationally known collections. Today the capital city has such libraries as the National Library with over 1,000,000 volumes, the municipal library with over 100,000 volumes and ten major branches, and the Library of the Chamber of Deputies with over 100,000 volumes. Rio de Janeiro has two old and respected special libraries in the Biblioteca Britannica, founded in 1826, and the Royal Portuguese Reading Room, founded in 1837. The former, relatively small, is a library of English language works of interest to Brazilians; the latter, with over 200,000 items today, serves as a cultural link between the Portuguese and Brazilian peoples and concentrates on the history and literature of those two nations. Government libraries include those of the Ministry of Finance, with 50,000 volumes; the Ministry of Mines and Power, with 75,000; the Ministry of Labor, Industry and Commerce, with over 250,000. The latter has a valuable cartographical collection of over 30,000 items in its "mapateca." An interesting endowed library was founded by author, lawyer, and philologist Rui Barbarosa, and is now housed in his former home, open to the public with some 45,000 volumes.

São Paulo, Brazil's largest city, also has an interesting variety of libraries. Its municipal library, the finest in Latin America, has over 400,000 volumes, housed in a modern twenty-story building, with branches throughout the city. São Paulo has many specialized libraries, ranging from state government libraries, such as the Department of Agriculture Library with over 50,000 volumes, to private industrial libraries, academic libraries, and religious collections. One interesting feature is the separate library for children, a fortunate development found in a few other Latin American cities.

Although there are other state, college, and religious libraries outside the major cities, the most significant recent development in Brazilian library history has been in the new capital established at Brasilia, several hundred miles in the interior. Here there are not only the libraries of the Brazilian Congress (other government agencies may or may not move their major collections to the new capital) but also exciting new library developments at the University of Brasilia. The new library building, begun in 1968, houses about 2,000,000 volumes, and seats about 4,000 students. It has open shelves, an innovation for Latin American libraries, and serves as a public library also for Brasilia and the surrounding area. The university will have a school of library and information science, and the library will house a union catalog of all major research holdings in the nation. Together with the services stemming from the National Library in Rio de Janeiro, which include a catalog card service, national bibliographical publications, and a national legal depository, the university at Brasilia will provide the nation with the planning and leadership necessary for library progress. A National Federation of Library Associations also promotes library development at all levels in Brazil.

Chile's national library in Santiago has long been considered one of the major collections in Latin America. With nearly 1,000,000 volumes, it heads up a system of over one hundred public libraries throughout the nation. It has several specialized reading rooms, including the Medina Collection of Historical Manuscripts which is one of the most valuable in the western hemisphere. Other significant libraries in Santiago include the forty or more special libraries at the University of Chile, academic libraries at the School of Fine Arts, the Catholic University, and the national military and teacher training institutions. The central library of the University of Chile contains over 200,000 volumes, as does also the Chilean Congressional Library.

Three other nations of the northern and western part of South America present a varied library picture, in general unfavorable. These are Venezuela, Ecuador, and Bolivia. Venezuela has several modern cities, and with its new-found wealth from oil it is rapidly becoming industrialized. But it still has large rural areas that are quite primitive, and its libraries are scattered and generally poor in size and content. Its national library in Caracas has some 400,000 volumes, and there are several other government libraries including those of the National Congress, the Supreme Court, and various ministerial departments. The National Academy of History Library, founded in 1888, serves as something of a second national library, specializing in the history of Latin America. Major Venezuelan university libraries include those at the Central University of Venezuela, Caracas, and Los Andes University at Mérida, but there are also thirty-eight other institutions of higher learning in the nation. Special industrial collections are maintained by several international firms in Caracas, but these are not publicly available. Public and school libraries are small where they exist, and often there are none.

In Ecuador public libraries are largely confined to reference services, and of the twenty-four listed in the nation in 1955, only one had more than 50,000 volumes. University libraries include those at Central University in Quito, and at the Catholic University in the same city. In the 1960s, the latter received considerable aid in books and advice from St. Louis University in the United States. The university library at Cuenca has a modern collection of some 60,000 volumes. Only four percent of Ecuador's secondary schools had working libraries in 1964, and this represented less than one book per student for the nation as a whole. Bolivia was even less adequately supplied with libraries than the other Latin American countries. Only one of its secondary schools reported a workable collection of library materials in 1960, and this one had only about 500 books. Elsewhere in Bolivia, the National library and Archives at Sucre has approximately 30,000 volumes, while the national Congressional Library at La Paz is only half as large. The Ministry of Foreign Affairs has a modern library of 10,000 volumes, and the Municipal Library of La Paz has about 30,000. The seven institutions of higher education in Bolivia have libraries that average fewer than 20,000 volumes each. Bolivia is undoubtedly one of the poorest nations of the western world in library facilities.

Among the Central American countries, Mexico has

the best system of libraries, but even here there is much to be desired in library service. There were private and religious libraries from the 16th century onward in Mexico City and a few scattered points throughout the nation. Before Mexico obtained its independence in 1823, there were no public libraries in the nation, but in 1833 the national library was formed from sequestered religious collections. It had little support, however, and was not publicly available until 1869, receiving only small funds from the government until after 1882. By 1910 it had over 150,000 volumes, and by 1926 over 250,000, but it was still housed in a former church building and poorly organized. By the 1970s, with over 800,000 volumes and housed in a beautiful building on the campus of the national university, it was a modern library in every sense of the word. Some other large libraries in Mexico City include those of the National Anthropological and Historical Society with 250,000 volumes; the National Academy of Science Library with 120,000; and the National Teachers College Library with about 100,000. Various government departments have effective libraries, including the Congressional Library of 50,000 volumes; the library of the Ministry of Economics, 65,000; and a national library of periodicals with with over 100,000.

Public libraries in general made little progress before the 1920s. As late as 1915 there were only ninety-two libraries of all kinds except private in all of Mexico. In 1923 José Vasoncelos, Minister of Public Education, began establishing public libraries and secured the formation of a Bureau of Libraries in his Ministry. By 1926 there were some 1,600 small libraries and reading centers throughout Mexico. The first Congress of Mexican Librarians met in 1925, and a training school for librarians was established in the National Library. By 1965 Mexico reported 263 major public libraries, averaging around 5,000 volumes each. School libraries are being established, but still hardly one in ten of Mexico's secondary schools has a library. Elementary library services are even less satisfactory, but public collections often emphasize books for children. Outside Mexico City the major libraries are those of colleges and universities, although there are a few special libraries in the major cities, such as that of the Technical Institute at Monterey with its 100,000 volumes.

In Central America, the library pattern is much the same as in the smaller countries of South America. This means a national library and one or more university libraries, few or no public libraries, and only a smattering of library service for schools. The national libraries of Costa Rica, Guatemala, and Nicaragua are nearing the 100,000-volume size, and a few of the larger university libraries, with all their departmental collections, approach this number. Panama is an exception because an effort has been made to supply public library service and most of the towns have small public libraries. The Bank of Guatemala provides a public reference library in Managua. In British Honduras, there is a National Library Service which supplies seven branches, and some forty stations throughout that small dependency. In each country, the national library provides a moderate amount of leadership to the profession, and often serves as a bibliographic center as well.

In Latin America as a whole, library service has made slow progress. This is partly due to social and cultural conditions in general, to economic and political problems that must be solved first, and to a lack of appreciation of the value of books and libraries. Unstable governments and lack of economic security have prevented the financial support necessary to library development. But lack of respect for learning, added to a lack of respect for the profession of librarianship, has handicapped the growth of libraries even when economic support might have been available. Fortunately, the scene is gradually changing. Organizations of professional librarians, many trained in other countries, and the growing number of library schools are combining to upgrade the profession in Latin America and provide many new librarians to fill the growing number of positions. Support and encouragement from the outside, such as that from the United Nations, the Pan-American Union, and the various United States agencies, have done much to encourage library development "south of the border." Finally, cooperation between libraries, between nations, and between interested groups is beginning to solve some of the numerous problems. The provision of adequate library service for all Latin Americans is not likely in the immediate future, but in the long run, the prospects are bright.

Additional Readings

There is no single-volume history of American libraries. However, a number of collections of essays do offer fairly even and systematic coverage. A number of the best would include _Reader in American Library History_, Michael H.

Harris, ed. (Washington, D.C.: NCR, 1971); "American Library History, 1876-1976," Howard Winger, ed., Library Trends 25 (1976): whole issue; A Century of Service: Librarianship in the United States and Canada, Sidney Jackson, ed. (Chicago: American Library Association, 1976); Milestones to the Present, Harold Goldstein, ed. (Syracuse, N.Y.: Gaylord Professional Publications, 1978). Readers should also see the bibliographical works cited at the end of Chapter 10.

The items cited below represent a selective list of recent work in American library history.

Adkinson, Burton W. Two Centuries of Federal Information (Stroudsburg, Pa.: Dowden, Hutchinson, and Ross, 1978).

Braverman, Miriam. Youth, Society and the Public Library (Chicago: American Library Association, 1979).

Casey, Marion. Charles McCarthy: Librarianship and Reform (Chicago: American Library Association, 1981).

Cole, John. For Congress and the Nation: A Chronological History of the Library of Congress (Washington, D.C.: the Library of Congress, 1979).

Cutler, Wayne and Michael H. Harris. Justin Winsor: Scholar-Librarian (Littleton, Colo.: Libraries Unlimited, 1980).

Dumont, Rosemary Ruhig. Reform and Reaction: The Big Public Library in American Life (Westport, Conn.: Greenwood Press, 1977).

Fain, Elaine. "The Library and American Education: Through Secondary School," Library Trends 22 (1979): 327-52.

Garrison, Dee. Apostles of Culture: The Public Librarian and American Society, 1876-1920 (New York: Free Press, 1979).

Hamlin, Arthur T. The University Library in the United States: Its Origins and Development (Philadelphia: University of Pennsylvania Press, 1981).

Harris, Michael H. The Role of the Public Library in

American Life: A Speculative Essay. University of Illinois, Graduate School of Library Science, Occasional Paper, no. 117, 1975.

Miksa, Francis. The Subject in the Dictionary Catalog from Cutter to the Present (Chicago: American Library Association, 1983).

Ring, Daniel F. Studies in Creative Partnership: Federal to Public Libraries During the New Deal (Metuchen, N.J.: Scarecrow Press, 1980).

Shifflet, Orvin L. Origins of American Academic Librarianship (Norwood, N.J.: Ablex, 1981).

Sullivan, Peggy. Carl H. Milam and the American Library Association (Chicago: American Library Association, 1976).

Thomison, Dennis. The History of the American Library Association, 1876-1972 (Chicago: American Library Association, 1977).

Weibel, Kathleen and Kathleen M. Heim. The Role of Women in Librarianship, 1876-1976 (Phoenix: Oryx Press, 1979).

Young, Arthur P. Books for Sammies: The American Library Association and World War I (Beta Phi Mu, 1981).

INDEX